Culture,
Mind and
Therapy

AN INTRODUCTION TO
CULTURAL PSYCHIATRY

Culture, Mind and Therapy

AN INTRODUCTION TO CULTURAL PSYCHIATRY

Wen-Shing Tseng, M. D.
and
John F. McDermott, Jr., M.D.

Department of Psychiatry
John A. Burns School of Medicine
University of Hawaii

BRUNNER/MAZEL, *Publishers* • **New York**

Library of Congress Cataloging in Publication Data

Tseng, Wen-Shing, 1935–
Culture, mind, and therapy.

Includes bibliographies and index.
1. Psychiatry, Transcultural. 2. Social psychiatry. I. McDermott, John F., 1929– II. Title. [DNLM: 1. Cross-Cultural comparison. 2. Culture. 3. Ethnopsychology. 4. Psychotherapy. WM 31 T882c]
RC455.4.E8T76 616.89 81-12290
ISBN 0-87630-283-5 AACR2

Published by

BRUNNER/MAZEL, INC.
19 Union Square
New York, New York, 10003

MANUFACTURED IN THE UNITED STATES OF AMERICA

CONTENTS

PREFACE

In a sense, this book on cultural psychiatry began with a two-person cultural interchange. We come from very different backgrounds: one from the American-Irish-Yankee tradition; one from the cultural roots of China. Working together, we were able to compare, understand, and make use of each other's experiences, observations, and opinions. Our work in both clinical research and teaching is at the University of Hawaii. The multi-ethnic population of Hawaii further stimulated our interest in how cultural beliefs and practices can color mental disorders and influence the choice of therapy for them. We then began developing courses and seminars on cultural elements in psychiatry. As we went through the many writings in the field (we have more than 3,000 in our department alone), it became obvious we must screen them and integrate the subject matter. This volume reflects our efforts. We have attempted to place many isolated works within the broader perspective and to synthesize our findings into a current context. We have also tried to go beyond descriptions of cultural phenomena to consider their implications, whether pathological or healthful, for these implications are vital in the cultural assessments made in clinical practice. We have, in some chapters, focused on the therapies of other cultures and how they influence the expectations of therapy for the patient removed to a new setting. In the field of cultural psychiatry much remains yet unknown. We do not pretend to provide definitive answers. If our efforts raise questions, stimulate thought, and perhaps clarify some issues, we shall be pleased, if not content.

As we worked on this book, we became aware that the history of cultural psychiatry is fascinating but little known. A review of its roots and origins seems in order. One might say that interest in the field began when missionaries and explorers reported on the strange behaviors they encountered in "primitive societies." Interest soon led to theories. Some observers held that mental illness was rare in "savage tribes" because such illness was a by-product of civilization. Others, while postulating that primitive societies were no strangers to mental illness, said they probably experienced this less because the harsh living conditions which promoted the "survival of the fittest" would limit the propagation of the mentally ill. So much for early speculations.

Actual psychiatric work in other cultures was a product of colonialism in the 19th century. Many officials sent from European countries to administer the "colonies" in Africa and Southeast Asia suffered from "nervous breakdowns" as much as they did from tropical diseases. Psychiatrists then were sent out to treat them or send them home, and to study the stresses which produced such a disproportionate incidence. As the century neared its end, European psychiatrists were practicing in these areas of the world and were reporting unusual psychiatric conditions particular to certain cultures, such as *amok* and *latah* (Chapter 4).

The 20th century began the next stage in the development of cultural psychiatry. Most of our readers know Emil Kraepelin as the "Father of Descriptive Psychiatry." However, not everyone realizes that he was also the "Father of Cultural Psychiatry." Kraepelin became intrigued by regional differences in mental illness in Germany and other European countries. As a result, he went to Java (Indonesia) to study cultural influences on the frequency and symptomatology of mental disorders. There, he noted that manic-depressive disorders were uncommon and that depressive reactions, if they occurred, seldom contained elements of guilt.

Sigmund Freud, who also revolutionized the field of psychiatry, wrote about cultural differences in mental illness, but he did not go abroad to study them. His onetime colleague, Carl Jung, is also known for his interest in cultural psychiatry. His concept of the "collective unconscious," the universal nature of some symbols, particularly in dreams, evolved from comparative studies of different cultures in different parts of the world. He held that, because the natives of East Africa and the Eskimos of Alaska used the same symbols in their dreams and expressed common themes in mythologies, these symbols and themes must derive from some common layer of the mind that crossed cultural boundaries.

Freud's and Jung's psychoanalytic theoretical framework soon crystallized into a movement and was quickly absorbed into the social sciences, particularly sociology, anthropology, and social psychology. Roheim, an anthropologist and a student of Freud, was one of the pioneers who tried to determine whether the psychoanalytic model could be applied to other cultures. He found that the classic neuroses were rare in the Australian tribes he studied and speculated that this was because repression was less intense in primitive groups. Benedict and Malinowski were also anthropologists who tested analytic theory in other cultures, e.g., the universality of the Oedipus complex and its variations.

Cultural psychiatry had become a special field. Psychiatry's curiosity about mental illness in other societies had merged with anthropology's concern with cultural aspects of personality, behavior disorder, and healing practices. Systematic explorations of culture and psychopathology continued into the 1940s and '50s as psychiatrists became active in cultural investigations. Many studies focused on cultural aspects of the symptomatic expression of certain psychiatric conditions, particularly schizophrenia. Opler's analysis of the contrast in schizophrenic symptoms of Italians and Irish, and the large-scale epidemiological studies relating social class factors and mental illness by Leighton, as well as those of Hollingshead and Redlich, are good examples of the explosion of interest in the field. The Hutterite Study (see Chapter 2) provides an interesting commentary on cultural background in a community and the frequency and kind of mental illness found there.

The next stage of investigation focused on various practices. Psychotherapy had been considered a Western scientific approach to mental illness; folk healing and, in some parts of the world, primitive or magical rituals had been termed superstitions. But, asked psychiatrist Jerome Frank, what does the shaman have in common with the psychoanalyst? If successful interventions from culture to culture all have a similar degree of success, what do they all have in common? These new efforts to understand the psychotherapeutic process from a broader point of view blended into the concerns of the '60s and '70s, which focused on America's minority groups and the variations of psychological and psychiatric problems and cures for them.

Most important, perhaps, was the controversy over the therapist. Can a majority psychiatrist treat a minority group member and vice versa? As important as these questions were, they also limited the development of cultural psychiatry in the United States. Cultural psychiatry has sometimes been perceived as a subspecialty that concentrates on the mental disorders of minority groups. Its purpose has too often been seen as a limited one: to identify and provide care for the mental and emotional illness of such groups as American Indians, blacks, Chicanos, and Orientals. The truth is that cultural psychiatry must be viewed on a wider screen—one large enough to include an entire population. The last several decades have brought subtle but significant cultural changes to all groups, *including* the WASP. Altered family and marital systems, the feminist movement, sexual liberation, and changes in religious affiliation have all occurred. These affect behavior, behavioral disorders, and treatment approaches.

Attention also needs to be given to the majority groups, in fact the total populations, of other countries. There is a need to investigate how sweeping political-social change affects the mental health of great numbers of people. How has China's changed political ideology influenced the mental health of its people? What effect has the use of "barefoot" mental health workers had? What is the state of mental health in Russia where a vast population lives in an oppressive political climate? What are the stresses and conflicts in India where the people experience efforts to modernize the country?

Cultural psychiatry must not focus unduly on small groups or unique and curious cultural practices; to learn more about humanity and its ills and coping mechanisms we also need to learn about majority groups and mass populations. A new goal of cultural psychiatry might well be to investigate large groups undergoing the rapid changes of today.

If we look to the future, a pertinent question seems to be: Is there a way to plan for culture as we now plan for health? Are there ways to decide on and provide styles of living that promote, rather than impair, mental health? Can cultural psychiatrists, along with architects, city planners, educators, and industry, for example, work together to reduce the stresses of tomorrow's existence?

Whatever the future may be, today's psychiatrists have certainly become more aware of the enormous need for culturally relevant evaluation and treatment as a part of all mental health diagnosis and treatment. Cultural psychiatry has gained recognition not just as a special field, but as an integral part of the everyday practice of general psychiatry.

We will long remain grateful to all those who helped make this book possible: to students, residents, and colleagues who so liberally shared with us their own experiences, put up with our trial runs of readings, and contributed their evaluations and comments. Our special thanks to Catherine A. Lee whose contributions and editorial pen were invaluable, to Theresa Bryant for editorial help with early drafts, to Joy Ashton who collected and organized the literature in cultural psychiatry, and to Kathleen Awakuni, Gail Kuroiwa, and Julie-Ann Takane who gave us their invaluable assistance in the preparation of this manuscript.

WEN-SHING TSENG, M.D.
JOHN F. McDERMOTT, Jr., M.D.

Culture, Mind and Therapy

AN INTRODUCTION TO
CULTURAL PSYCHIATRY

PART I

Orientation

CHAPTER 1

Culture and Human Behavior

THE NATURE OF CULTURE

Each of us lives within an invisible sheath we call our culture. The sheath has many layers: Some were fashioned by neighborhood, religion, race, and country; others owe their origin to climate and geography. These layers touch each of us, leaving their imprints, sometimes lightly, often indelibly. When a layer becomes too confining, we attempt to cast it off, not always with success, for culture is a pervasive and clinging entity.

Because culture influences behavior, it becomes yet another subject therapists now study. The ultimate focus is on the individual patient, his or her culture, and how it affects him or her. Yet it is also pertinent to consider culture in general, for all cultures, no matter how they differ in details, share much in common. This is inevitable, since persons share the same feelings of joy, sadness, anger, and grief. Yet what is common to humans does not stop at basic emotions. As they evolved from primates, humans developed certain shared ways of behavior. Some of these, notably the use of tools, the mother-child bond, and a communication system, existed among our primate ancestors. Certainly before they had stood erect very long, persons shared certain elements of behavior:

- A social system with the family as the basic unit.
- A prolonged period of infantile dependency that was made possible by the family system with the bonding of mother and child.

- A system of sex-role assignment between male and female (a system now undergoing challenge and change).
- Sexual behavior in which the female is receptive at any time.
- Incest taboos.
- The use of tools.
- A sense of territoriality (which is also evidenced in animal life).
- Collective rules and taboos to define and regulate behavior.

Humans also developed concepts, many of them strikingly similar. These similarities are found in the use and interpretations of symbolism in dreams and art and ritual. (Jung [1959] wrote of the mythological associations and images of the collective unconscious.) Virtually all people equate right with maleness and left with female qualities. Dreaming of feces is interpreted to mean wealth by the Ashanti, Tikopia, Western Europeans, Thai, Naga, Chinese, and Sinhalese. Loss of a tooth in a dream means death to the Lolo, Araucanians, Chuckchee, Achelenese, Japanese, Chinese, Western Europeans, and Diegueno people (D'Andrade, 1961). The snake is a phallic symbol (together with other meanings), not only in Freudian thought, but in the symbolism of Africa, Egypt, India, in certain Japanese legends, and among some American Indian tribes (LaBarre, 1962).

Though humans throughout the world share similar elements of behavior and thought and feeling (perhaps even on an unconscious level), they by no means share a culture. Culture varies, sometimes a little, sometimes greatly, from group to group. The very nature of culture is that it establishes and defines certain patterns of behavior that exist in, and are unique to, one group, but are different between groups. These customs are shared and sanctioned by the group. Each culture provides a model, a measuring stick, by which individual behaviors may be prescribed or restricted. But the models do not all look alike; the specifications on each measuring stick will be different.

Yet culture is far more than behavior or custom. It is also made up of ways of feeling that shape (and are shaped by) ways of doing. Culture is the collective expression of the group's personality—its wishes, values, and ideology. It is the sum total of knowledge and attitudes, a vast accumulation of ways of thought, of action, and of emotional expression. Culture is based on behavior and values transmitted through generations. It is traditional and fairly well fixed. Yet it is not cast in mental-emotional-behavioral cement. Culture can also change, slowly in ordinary circumstances, rapidly in stresses, such as invasion by a conquering culture. The behaviors within a culture may change more readily than the thoughts and emotions that underlie them; these are long-lasting. When a second culture is acquired, the original culture may seem lost and forgotten until an individual is in crisis. Sickness, birth, death—these are apt to sweep away the topsoil of an acquired pattern of living to reveal the earlier culture beneath. Cultural roots are planted in childhood and grow deep. For example, when Hawaii's last monarch, Queen Lili'uokalani, died in 1917, almost the entire native Hawaiian population, westernized for nearly a century, spontaneously began loud wailing, their traditional expression of grief. Even as the body was taken to a Christian church, the populace continued to wail.

CONTRASTS OF CULTURES

If we studied only one group, we would have little idea whether a practice was culturally shaped. Comparison is needed. The unique quality of a cultural trait stands out sharp and clear when it is contrasted across cultures. The contrast may be one of presence versus absence of a custom: Most people in one group follow a certain practice; people in comparison groups do not follow this practice at all; therefore, the practice is culturally formed. The Padaung tribeswomen of Burma wear 12 inches of coiled brass wire around their necks, pushing clavicles and ribs downward; other women in Burma do not. Therefore, this practice to display status and wealth is unique to the Padaung tribe.

Comparing cultures also reveals similar traits of behavior and thought. If, theoretically, a Samoan resident compared his culture's characteristic of giving high prestige to oratory with that of the United States, where oratory is largely confined to politicians, he might conclude that this characteristic is unique only to Samoa. But if he extended his comparisons, he would find that the practice and love of oratory exist in many Pacific Island cultures, and that fluent, compelling, and imaginative speech is a characteristic of Ireland. He would then encounter the next aspect of comparing cultures: that this comparison throws a light on what is unique, but what is unique to a culture is not necessarily exclusive to that culture.

When similar traits are revealed, differences in the significance of these traits may exist. For example, both French and Jewish groups drink wine. So far, the information is of little use, except perhaps to wine merchants. What is of value is to know (along with frequency and volume of consumption) the meaning of this wine drinking. For the French, wine is a part of sociability; it is linked with good food and the good life. For Jews, wine is—or at least traditionally was—part of religious ritual and means the affirmation of ethnic identity and family ties.

A practice need not be followed by most of a group to be identified as being culture-connected. Rare behavior may also qualify as being culturally unique to a group if it meets two requirements: 1) Even though it is limited to a small segment of the group, the behavior recurs (we are not considering the once-in-a-century phenomenon), and 2) the behavior must pass the test of contrast (it does not exist in comparison groups). Comparatively few Japanese commit suicide by *seppuku* (ritualized self-disembowelment). But over the years, *seppuku* has recurred. This same ritualized suicide is not observed in other cultures. Therefore, it is uniquely Japanese.

A working definition of a culture might well include the phrase, "The majority do or think or feel in a certain way, but some, and possibly many, do not." With this unmeasured, but certainly existing, range of exceptions kept well in mind, the chances of using an accurate working definition increase. "Japanese eat rice" is a reliable observation, as long as we also remember "but some eat potatoes instead."

A working knowledge of cultural ways becomes more useful when inquiries are stimulated. We must ask why some Japanese eat potatoes instead of rice. We must look for inconsistencies within behavioral profiles. If, for example, a society openly expresses grief and anger, and allows crying and screaming during physical injury, but shames a woman who cries out in childbirth, the apparent inconsistency in itself may carry meaning. Childbirth pain, for some reason, is placed in a different category. But why? The importance of asking "Why?" cannot be overestimated. Why does a behavior exist in one group and not in the other? What purpose does the existing practice serve in one group? Why is it not needed in the other?

Francis Hsu (1961) provides a fascinating example based on Nadel's observations of two neighboring people in the Nuba Mountains of Sudan. There, the Mesakin have an obsessive fear and suspicion of witchcraft; their neighbors, the Korongo, do not even believe in it. What causes this vast difference? It is a complicated chain of beliefs and behaviors. Both groups so value youthful male vigor that, when a young man reaches puberty, his mother's brother gives him a gift. In Korongo custom, the gift is given freely. The Mesakin go through a process in which the mother's brother refuses to give the gift; it is taken from him by force. Quarrels between the young man and his uncle often result. If the young man should be ill, the uncle is suspected of witchcraft. But beneath the ritual refusal and forced giving of the Mesakin, and the freely given gift of the Korongo, are contrasting systems of age and states.

In the Korongo, vigorous masculine activity is relinquished in *six* gradual stages; the Mesakin, with *three* birth-to-death stages, must give up the recognized stage of male vigor early and abruptly. The older Mesakin envies and resents the young man; his decline is emphasized when he must give a gift to a youth. Antagonism in this culture is expressed in witchcraft beliefs and fears. The enviable young man is most frequently seen as the victim; the jealous, older man as the perpetrator of hurtful arts.

If, however, a Mesakin freely and generously offered a gift, and a Korongo refused to give the customary present, we would have examples of individual deviation from cultural practice. Both deviations would inspire the question "Why?" The ways and the reasons for straying outside cultural boundaries are very much the concern of cultural psychiatry.

CULTURE, INDIVIDUAL BEHAVIORS, AND DIVERGING TEMPERAMENTS

Groups, like individuals, exhibit culture-caused stresses. Inadequacies in the existing culture may result in group and individual deviations from it. The People's Temple tragedy at Guyana represented a withdrawal from a culture that seemed unwelcoming and unrewarding. Necessity may force efforts to conform to a new culture, with resulting conflicts: Missionaries of the past put clothing on naked bodies; conquerers have insisted their own language and customs be used. Cultures have felt superior to other cultures; minorities have been made to feel inferior, as have our American blacks. Cultures, exposed to another culture, eventually have lost some of their original values. America's Chinese, who a generation ago had virtually no divorces, now have an increasing number of broken marriages.

Groups, like individuals, may falsely perceive their nature. The idealized culture, not the reality, may be seen. For example, in the United States, middle- and upper-class whites have long held that wife and child abuse was limited to the lower classes. Now, case findings and better reporting have disclosed gaps between the idealized view and the realistic situation. We know now that the battered wife and child syndrome transcends social-economic-educational lines. We now recognize that a wide range of deviation from the ideal of no-abuse exists; that abuse, in the form of mental cruelty, emotional deprivation, or physical neglect, is not ordained or characterized by class.

These cultural stresses, conflicts, and influences of the group may form part of the personal burdens that send individuals to a therapist. (Or they may even keep the troubled one away from help. For example, as long as the misconception prevailed that middle- and upper-class whites never abused wives or children, the problem was concealed; the respected businessman could not admit he had a problem that needed treatment.)

Why Individuals Conform to Their Culture

Everyone conforms to and deviates from his/her culture in varying aspects and degrees. Conforming is not necessarily desirable behavior. Deviating is not necessarily undesirable. Though cultural practices serve to regulate behavior in acceptable ways, they may become outmoded or useless. The nonconformer may simply be ahead of his time. The conformer may be snagged on the shoals of the past. Conversely, the one who conforms may uphold a valid, tested, and appropriate way of life; the one who does not may be exhibiting aberrant, rather than merely atypical, behavior.

Consider some of the reasons people conform to cultural norms.

Conforming to cultural mores may have little to do with personality or psychological factors. An individual may conform merely from social or religious pressure. As LeVine (1973) points out, Hindus are forbidden to eat beef; most conform. But if a Hindu, away from other Hindus, is horrified at the idea of killing and eating cattle, if he even dreams about this and relates his ideas about sacred cows to himself, then personality factors in his non-beef-eating behavior might well be involved. If similar emotion-charged reactions were found in a large proportion of other Hindus, then a psychological function of the prohibition itself would be evident.

If we wanted to evaluate the psychological implications of conforming behavior in an individual, how would we proceed? LeVine suggests we ask the following questions: Is the behavior followed in private, where group judgment does not threaten? Is it followed by migrants who live, not in the midst of fellow migrants, but in a new cultural setting? Is the individual intensely absorbed by this behavior? Does he think of it as a part of his total makeup?

If the answers tend to be "Yes," the chances are that a certain behavior is ingrained into the personality, What is so ingrained often comes out in moments of stress and danger. "There are no atheists in foxholes." Childhood prayers, forgotten for years, emerge when bombs fall. Deeply incorporated behaviors may also emerge at times free from stress or trauma. A Hawaiian, alone in a friend's bedroom, will not sit on the bed. The cultural *kapu* against sitting on sleeping mats or Hawaiian quilts has been incorporated into her total system of values. Inward, rather than outward, directions shape behavior.

When a certain cultural practice weakens, then following the old norm may convey psychological information, for when pressure is removed, choice is possible. Catholics formerly were not allowed to eat meat on Friday; later the restriction was removed. Yet today, many older Catholics observe meatless Fridays or feel guilty if they do eat meat.

When people conform to cultural ways that are outmoded or not to their advantage, any number of reasons, simple and complex, may be involved. This is true among younger American blacks who continue to speak "Black English," though they realize employment and economic advancement often depend on speaking standard English. (We are not discussing older blacks removed from the competition for jobs and higher education.) Why do they conform to an old way and standard of speaking? Many conform without really thinking about it; everybody around them so speaks. For some, it is probably simple discomfort: the same embarrassment the Texan would feel trying to acquire a Boston accent, or the Bostonian would feel trying to speak like the traditional Southern belle. Some are uneasy with any change from traditional ways. Others feel the pressures of peers or family; speaking standard English would be snobbish and affected; it would "put down" family and friends. Some fear failure and believe "I can't learn to speak a new way."

Less obvious psychological factors may be operating. There may be a feeling that black English is a part of the ethnic and personal identity; that with this speech changed or lost, some part of the identity is lost. This has been reinforced by the movement to accept and teach black English as a separate language. Clinging to traditional speech may be a way to emphasize ethnic identity and cope with insecurities; the message is "My speech is good; I and my culture are good." Scorn for white ways may find expression in using non-white speech.

Reasons for Deviating from Culture

Pioneering men and women have cast off the heavy grasp of tradition and found new, often better, ways of living. These persons have deviated from their culture. In our prisons are individuals who have flouted society's laws. These, too, have deviated. In between these two extremes fall the many persons who, in varied ways and for varied reasons, behave, think, and feel somewhat apart from their cultural mainstream.

One factor is merely temperament. Some persons are simply attracted to new ways of living and thinking. The happiest and mentally healthiest of these persons usually add new layers of culture; they do not totally discard previous values and behaviors. When they do discard old ways, it is because they are no longer useful or appropriate. Rejection and rebellion are not the motives. These individuals are quite different from those who adopt what is new and different because they feel any new way of life is better than their present one.

Youthful rebellion is a frequent cause of cultural breakaways. The young person may believe he is separating himself from a society or established religion, or protesting against a political or economic system—and often he is. Yet rebellion against parents is often a fundamental motivation. The social group or religion or socioeconomic class may be rebelled against because it is part of the parents' and the parental generation's culture. Personal relationships and cultural factors are closely intertwined.

Exposure to a new culture sometimes reinforces adherence to the original culture; "culture shock" makes the old and familiar newly precious. Probably more often, acquaintance with another way of life results in some deviation from original behaviors and attitudes and some acquisition of new ones. On a mass scale, migration makes this necessary, though not devoid of trauma. On the more individual level, many other motivations exert their force. Again, youthful separation from parents may be worked out in cultural context. Feelings of ethnic inferiority may be involved: the individual who leaves the ghetto may want to leave ghetto values and behaviors far behind. More personal inferiority feelings may operate; the individual may feel his cultural group is very good indeed, but the group does not accept him; he simply does not fit in.

Psychiatry has long viewed the patient against his backdrop of family, peer group, and social-educational-occupational-economic environment. More recently, that setting has been enlarged to include his culture. Yet even this wider milieu does not have fixed boundaries. Today, we live in a world of travel, migrations, and increasing intercultural marriage. The individual's culture impinges on, and is affected by, other racial, ethnic, and social groups. The mergings, conflicts, and acceptance or rejections of cultural values may increasingly influence both the stresses an individual feels and how he copes with them.

REFERENCES

D'Andrade, R. G.: Anthropological studies of dreams. In: *Psychological Anthropology Approaches to Culture and Personality,* Francis L. K. Hsu (Ed.). Homewood, Illinois: The Dorsey Press, Inc., 1961.

Hsu, F. L. K. (Ed.): *Psychological Anthropology Approaches to Culture and Personality.* Homewood, Illinois: The Dorsey Press, Inc., 1961.

Jung, C. G. *The Basic Writings of C. G. Jung.* Violet S. De Laszlo (Ed.). New York: The Modern Library, Random House, 1959.

LaBarre, W.: *They Shall Take Up Serpents: Psychology of the Southern Snake-Handling Cult.* Minneapolis: University of Minnesota Press, 1962.

LeVine, R.: *Culture, Behavior and Personality.* Chicago: Aldine Publishing, 1973.

CHAPTER 2

Culture, Stress, and Psychopathology

Visit with us an imaginary tribe—let's call it Everyman—that lives surrounded by other tribes. These other tribes are unfriendly. Open attack may come some time in the future. To prepare for this day, the Everyman increase their birthrate. They advocate frequent intercourse, encourage each man to have many mates, and allow no female to remain virgin. Within ten years, they have hundreds of children old enough to shoot bows and arrows. The surrounding tribes witness and do not attack. Their culture, which said "Let's be prolific," has adapted to an environmental need. We call this an adaptive cultural trait, or, more generally, an adaptive culture.

However, as the Everyman tribe continues to have big families, the larger population steadily consumes the food supply; starvation threatens. The culturally prescribed high birthrate is now maladaptive. It does not adapt to life's needs.

This small parable of our times points out the dual nature of the traits, behaviors, beliefs, and attitudes that are integrated into the total system of a culture. Culturally formed nations and beliefs make a certain way of life possible; at the same time, they may produce stresses, problems, and vulnerabilities. A culture which values and creates a high-speed, high-achievement way of life also produces traffic accidents, peptic ulcers, mental and physical exhaustion, workaholics, the overuse of alcohol, and dependence on tranquilizers. The same technology that makes it possible for an ambulance to reach a heart attack victim in minutes also may be partly responsible for the coronary condition.

CULTURE-PRODUCED STRESS

Not all culturally induced or influenced causes of stress are as visible as the speeding car or as audible as the electronic amplifier. Concepts, beliefs, and attitudes and regulations to uphold them can also produce stress. Culturally formed anxiety and culturally demanded performance both produce mental and emotional stresses.

Stress Created by Culturally Formed Anxiety

Societies have a rather grim and joyless tendency to define certain situations as being threatening. The village elder or tribal leader sends down the edict, "If you break this taboo, you will sicken and die." The makers of religious creeds decree, "Obey, or hellfire awaits you." The advertisers proclaim, "Unless you use this deodorant, you will be a social outcast." Anxiety attaches itself to the broken taboo, the disregarded commandment, the neglected rite of hygiene. The taboo, the rule, or the warning may create anxieties or provide a focus for previously existing ones. Anxieties that exist within a certain belief system are projected or displaced within that system. The individual who lives in a culture that believes spells can cause death may readily believe he is under a spell and become ill or even die.

Culture-produced stress can set in motion a cycle in which anxiety produces problems which produce renewed anxiety. For example, Christians once were convinced that "original sin" resulted from the sexual encounter of Adam and Eve. Some retain this literal belief. Others, through generations, absorbed more diffused feelings that sex was sinful; eternal punishment for sex outside marriage or masturbation was dreaded. Even sex within marriage was vaguely "wrong" and justified only as a means of procreation. These beliefs often resulted in inhibiting normal sexual desires; problems of frigidity or impotence arose or were aggravated, producing anxieties about sexual performance which further inhibited sexual fulfillment. Today, premature ejaculation is perhaps the most common symptom of sexual dysfunction related to culture. This compromise between sexual expression and repression is common in some parts of the world, uncommon in others.

Cultural attitudes, based to some extent on realistic circumstance, produce stress. In the United States today, youth is admired and being old carries low status. Small homes and apartments have no place for resident grandparents; retirement from work is arbitrarily decreed; inflation eats up fixed income; retirement homes are too often ghettos; the world of advertising preaches the gospel that only in youth lie beauty and esteem. The culture has produced intense anxiety about growing old. By contrast, in cultures which still maintain a deep regard for elders (Japanese and Chinese are conspicuous examples), anxieties centered on advancing years are minimal.

Stress Produced by Culturally Demanding Performance

In one way or another, every culture values achievement. Admiration goes to the person who weaves a flawless grass mat, plays a Chopin mazurka brilliantly, raises a prize-winning hog, earns a graduate degree with honors, or wins a Nobel Prize. This is all to the good. It is when a culture demands a certain achievement too strongly (and personal vulnerabilities are too weak) that stresses result. To the young piano student, "culture" may be as narrow as the teacher, family, and recital hall audience. However, if he has talent and a wise teacher, and if he himself chooses to work towards concert status, the youthful pianist will probably handle the stresses of musical education and striving without psychic damage. The cultural demands of a society are somewhat different; they are imposed, openly or subtly, on an individual. When the society says, "compete, achieve, be successful," and says this too emphatically, impairment of mental health may result.

A few examples: Many cultures demanded that a woman produce a male child. Some still do. Until the role of chromosomes in sex determination was known, the woman was usually believed responsible for having a boy or girl. The society blamed her, and the woman herself felt guilty if she continued to produce only girls. A culturally demanded performance thus produced fear, anxiety, and shame. It also produced such external penalties as loss of status or replacement by another woman.

A similar culturally caused stress comes in the many societies that demand a woman produce children of either sex. Queens must produce heirs. Among the Shangana-Tsonga people in Southern Africa, when a woman fails to conceive, the cattle paid as "brideprice" by her husband's father must be returned. In this culture, plagued by high infertility, elaborate rituals further stress the society's demand that women give birth. When the woman cannot satisfactorily report seeing expected fertility symbols in visions or receiving certain knowledge when she is given hallucinogens, a further penalty threatens. The officiant of the rites may give her an overdose of the drug, with fatal results (Johnston, 1973). Whether the women learn what they should see (snakes, water, river banks, for example, all colored blue-green) and fake non-existent visions, we do not know. We hope they do.

In the meet-and-mate customs of many societies are stress potentials. When the young compete for mates (in contrast to arranged marriages), each must demonstrate masculinity or femininity as the culture sees it. The demand to perform does not necessarily cease with marriage; the divorce court looms when attraction diminishes. And in much of today's world, both men and women feel their sexual performance must meet the ecstatic standards described in popular magazines and best-selling books.

If we survey the immigrants who have come to the United States, we find that Jewish men have been disproportionately successful. Culture-related attitudes favoring achievement have helped bring this about. There is a traditional love for, and emphasis on, learning; the idealized life for most Jewish men was, for centuries, the life of the scholar. In addition, Jews found that education was a way to establish themselves in a new setting, that education enabled them to deal more effectively with persecutors and prejudice. A handed-down value within Jewish families is that each generation should be better than the preceding one (Smith, Kline, and French, 1978a). This cultural determination to succeed has, in fact, brought success. At the same time, it creates stress for those who cannot meet family and cultural expectations. The demand for intellectual achievement is not exclusively a Jewish characteristic. Japanese so demand educational achievement from young people that suicides after failing a school examination are not uncommon. We sit writing this surrounded by a cultural enclave noted for high performance demand and resulting stress: the medical school.

Once a performance has been achieved, the need to repeat the performance can bring about new stress. Goodman (1973) tells of the Apostolics (a Pentecostal sect in Yucatan) who emphasize the state of altered consciousness as the core of religious service. Nearly all the adults learned to achieve trance and "speak in tongues." Having once achieved this, some of the faithful became extremely anxious when they could not repeat the experience and made "frantic attempts" to regain their previous level of dissociation. In many cultures, the man who must prove he can "drink like a man and hold his liquor" will need to demonstrate this ability over and over again.

Without cultural demands to perform—and to perform well—life would be dull, devoid of challenge, and often lacking in personal progress and improvement. The demand, like stress itself, is not necessarily harmful. What is needed, by therapist and layman alike, is to look at the demands a culture makes and ask, "Is this performance necessary?"

CULTURE-RELATED PROBLEMS

Problems Created by a Culturally Determined, Limited Behavior Range

Consider, please, three examples of cultures which severely limit the range of allowed behavior: a religious sect, a backwoods village, and an army post.

On communal farms in Canada live some 25,000 members of the religious sect called Hutterites. Their dress is prescribed; their duties as farmer, sheepherder, cook, tailor or shoemaker are assigned. Their children are not allowed even to ice skate. Their choice of husband or wife must be approved by the brethren; the request for marriage permission is ritualized. The preparation and eating of food follow the sex-segregation etiquette of tradition. Contacts with nearby towns are limited to necessary business trips.

Not too long ago, a young woman just out of college went to teach school in a tiny hamlet deep in America's Ozark hill region. There, the community forced the young woman to live by its rules: She must not drink, smoke, wear shorts, tight jeans or too-short skirts, be a Catholic, stay out late, or date a divorced man. She must attend the Baptist church, the school basketball games, and the pie suppers. She must not dance; she may only square dance.

In almost any military setting, men, especially enlisted men in barracks, live within a rigid set of rules. They get up, eat, and go to bed on schedule. They work and drill by direction. They leave the post for a definite number of hours by definite permission. If they are wise, they do not question their sergeant.

All—Hutterites, teacher, and soldiers—demonstrate living within a tightly constricted range of behaviors. Yet they do not all react equally. Young Hutterite men sometimes run away, but, writes Holzach (1979), "sooner or later, almost all the runaways come back." Lin (1959) cites the Eaton-Weil study of United States Hutterites that found the overall frequency of psychoses among the sect was about the same as in other populations studied. In contrast, the teacher broke her contract and left the small town. Some of the soldiers developed emotional disorders; others did not. Why these differences? The varying responses serve to illustrate certain points.

When rules are excessive, when the behavior range allowed is too limited, problems are created. This does not mean the problems are always recognized. In the military example and that of the young teacher, the many restrictions certainly created problems. The teacher left; some servicemen broke down. Yet, what else operated where the teacher and the emotionally troubled soldiers were concerned? Why were they disturbed, when the restricted, limited Hutterites are not?

For one thing, the soldiers and the teacher were plunged into a new set of restrictions for which they were not prepared. The Hutterites live within regulations known since birth. What we call arbitrary and confining limits, they may well see as a habit, familiar and comforting.

Perhaps another factor is present. The Hutterites as a group formed their own restrictions; the limited behavior range itself expresses the group's own wishes and personality. The soldiers and the teacher had no part in formulating the rules they were expected to obey; the confining restrictions did not stem from the desires or temperaments of the teacher or of most—not all—of the soldiers. (Some men who thrive on barracks existence want or need directed, structured ways of life.)

In addition, the Hutterites see a reason for their limited style of life. Each rule is clearly rooted in Hutterite interpretation of the Bible; obeying each rule is seen as the way to eternal salvation. On the other hand, though soldiers can see good reasons for weapon practice—especially when war threatens—they may see no connection between tightly-made bunks and the battlefield.

Problems (and Benefits) of Cultural Change

Cultures and the behavior ranges of cultures change. What is too restricting is often modified, sometimes by internal pressure, sometimes by contact with another culture. Today the teacher's small town has developed more tolerant standards; a broader culture has been glimpsed, if only by television. Military discipline has become more relaxed; the need to recruit is in part responsible. The Hutterites change when legal requirements and practical considerations demand. Their children now have some standard schooling; it is the law. Tractors now plow their fields; this is practical. But their basic beliefs and behaviors do not change.

In a society with some degree of cultural elasticity, change is apt to have favorable effects. It is usually a part of progress. But if change is radical, rapid, and without obvious goals, it results in a confused value system. With few existing guides or models for change, it usually produces stress (Zaidi, 1969; Hippler, 1968).

When one culture is exposed to a new and different culture, changes are inevitable. They are also fraught with stress. Berry and Annis (1974) point out that stress is greater when cross-cultural differences are marked. An almost classic example is New Guinea, where, within a few decades, men of a stone age culture have confronted 20th century Western civilization. Many tribesmen can fit neither into the white man's world nor into the rapidly changing native culture. Some have attempted to solve their dilemma by trying to live within a third milieu—that of the mental hospital. The mental hospital, dreaded in so many societies, has become the wanted home, refuge, and "culture."

The impact of change is apt to be especially painful for a highly stable and traditional culture. Many developing countries are suffering a conflict of values between the old, rural way of life and recent shifts to industrialization and urbanization. Often these value conflicts affect family relationships.

Loyalty to the land clashes with the advantages of urban life and employment. Challenges come to established patterns of authority, leadership, and the status of women (Zaidi, 1969).

At first thought, it would seem old persons with their pattern of life long set would be most adversely affected by cultural change. The fact is, the young are. They are in the process of forming their own identities; they are more vulnerable to the ambiguity and confusion of an altered social-cultural system. Distler (1970) saw a shift in contemporary Western society from a culture geared to goals, achievement, personal independence and responsibility, the delay of gratification, and the use and high regard for rationality to one that values feelings, sensory experiences, intimacy, and self-exploration. He characterized this as a shift from a society of *doing* to a society of *being* and *feeling*. Though this shift affected the dominant adult culture, Distler found that the young felt its impact most. The "dropouts" are an example.

Problems Produced by Changing Roles and/or Loss of Source of Support

Today's women's liberation or feminist movement has brought about equal pay for equal work in some professions; it may have improved women's social status and tried to protect their rights—but it has also created new problems. The protection and support women previously obtained from husbands and families have diminished. Women are now more fully confronted with the world of competition and the necessity of self-support. With this "climate of independence," divorces have increased, and more women have become vulnerable to loneliness and depression.

Changing roles, with accompanying problems, occur in other cultures when the extended family system is supplanted by the nuclear family. For the younger generation, this often means freedom. When young people marry, they can establish their own homes; they need not live with their parents. However, the parents face a future of problems. The older generation too often becomes the lost generation, subject to isolation, sadness, and emotional, and occasionally financial, insecurity.

In Hawaii, Harvey and Chung (1980) found that among post-1965 Korean immigrants, the married male felt the full force of a changed role. In Korea, the husband and senior male is the dominant family member. Parts of the house are designated for men or women only. The man would not enter the kitchen. But entertaining in the bedroom is perfectly acceptable. Men eat first; women eat only after men, children, and senior women have eaten. Men have a close circle of male friends who provide emotional support. In Hawaii, the immigrant husband lives in a small apartment. There is no space for any men-only areas. Usually, the only dining space is the kitchen. Crowded housing and financial hardship make it difficult to meet very often with men friends. All this is bad enough, but the proof positive of a diminished male role comes when a wife goes to work. With a job and paycheck, she begins to challenge male supremacy. As the women gain ascendancy, the men feel their loss of status even more keenly. To some extent, this lessening of male dominance also occurs among Japanese and Chinese migrants to Hawaii; yet, the Korean man suffers a more difficult role adjustment. His culture has given the man such exceptionally superior status that his loss is more profound. He feels greater stress. As a result, depression is common and the suicide rate is high among these men, but not among the Korean women.

Problems That Arise From Sociocultural Discrimination

Societies have a dismaying habit of dividing themselves into the accepted and the not-accepted, the chosen and the outcast, the favored and the merely tolerated. The majority group looks down on the minority group. The long established may snub the newcomers. The economically secure may dislike, and even fear, the poor. The educated may disdain the unschooled. Tensions, hidden antagonism or fear, and open conflicts create problems. The Vietnamese "boat people" and Cuban refugees, first given sympathy and help, soon began to be seen as financial burdens and threats to job-seekers; discrimination against these victims of tragedy grew rapidly. America's blacks have been politically liberated, but they still suffer from less education and employment, poor housing, and long-existing racial discrimination. Jews are still subject to social slights. In Hawaii, where many ethnic groups live without outward discord, disdain still finds expression. Earlier immigrant groups, the Chinese and Japanese, may look down on the Johnny-come-lately groups, such as Filipinos. Some Japanese look down on Okinawans. A few Mandarin-class Chinese find the Hakka Chinese inferior. Discrimination may be between ethnic-social groups or within a group.

Discrimination lives on, even after its origin is obscured by time. For example, the Burakumin—the word means "ghetto"—are still considered Japan's outcasts. They were originally called Eta, meaning "excessively dirty," or Hining, with its literal meaning of "not a person." Prejudice came from their occupations; the earliest Eta were butchers, tanners, saddlemakers, caretakers of the dead, or gravediggers. They touched dead bodies or flesh. In Shinto belief, death was the worst form of pollution; therefore, the Eta or Hining were polluted. Later, the prejudicial occupations were expanded and the "no person" status became hereditary. In 1870, the classification was abolished by law, but the discrimination continued. Even today, many Japanese parents check the ancestry of a child's prospective spouse for Burakumin taint. The young people, and occasionally even their parents, do not know how the Burakumin became known as outcasts, yet many believe that Burakumin are mentally inferior, immoral, and aggressive. Some believe they can identify a Burakumin merely by looking at him. The sad outcome of centuries of external scorn, isolation, and discrimination is that the victims believe what others think of them. They incorporate the judgment of others and see themselves as meriting scorn, discrimination, and social punishments. DeVos and Wagatsuma (1969) found that the Burakumin in Japan limit their own educational and occupational opportunities and that they have a high incidence of delinquent and criminal behavior.

CULTURE-INHERITED VULNERABILITY

Culture-inherited Personality Vulnerability

Parents—unless they are rugged individualists—usually bring up their children along culturally prescribed, or more accurately, culturally "absorbed" lines. These child-rearing practices and attitudes influence the child's personality; they contribute to special traits and positive attributes; they also contribute to culturally formed vulnerabilities. Let us consider two contrasting vulnerabilities. American, particularly white Anglo-Saxon Protestant (as opposed to Italian Catholic), parents emphasize independence in their child-rearing. They encourage children to "stand on their own two feet" and make their own decisions. Educated to the dangers of the "silver cord," they encourage their young people to leave home and be independent. This works very well for most young adults, but it puts undue pressure on the young person who "grows up slowly" and needs a longer period of dependency (Smith, Kline, and French, 1978b).

In contrast, Japanese let a baby feel a close, intimate dependency on his mother for a much longer time. This fulfills the need for *amae*. The concept is one of a wish to receive love passively or, as the verb form *amaeru* suggests, "to depend upon another's benevolence." According to Doi (1962), *amaeru* also connotes a feeling of sweetness. It describes not just a child's relationship to his parents, but adult relationships as well. Kasahara (1974) finds that this long-extended dependency leads to later problems in socialization. A child tends to shy away from strangers. Adults suffer anxiety and fears concerning relationships with others, and a special kind of neurosis develops.

Vulnerabilities Within the Culture System Itself

The effects of culture are not limited to psychological vulnerabilities. Beliefs and behaviors may make a society physically vulnerable to certain events and experiences. A classic example came from the Sandwich Islands (Hawaii) of the late 1700s. For generations, Hawaiians had cherished two great beliefs. One was the fundamental belief in the spiritual power called *mana*. All men had some of this force, but the gods had infinitely greater *mana*. The other was that the god Lono, who had left his people in the dim past, would some day return. Lono, some legends said, was fair of face. He would return, said some wise elders, on a "floating island." He would, of course, display the white *lepa* (flags) of sacred status.

Thus, when Captain Cook, white sails fluttering on his floating island of a ship, came to Hawaiian shores, the Sandwich Islanders thought Lono had indeed returned. And since Lono had high and sacred *mana*, so, too, must every man of his crew. Young women swam out to the ship; fathers sent their daughters to spend the night with a sailor. "They wanted to have high *mana* babies," explains Hawaiian translator-scholar Pukui and her colleagues (1979). Instead they acquired syphilis and gonorrhea.

CULTURE CONTRIBUTES TO CHOICE OF PSYCHOPATHOLOGY

Culture not only builds its own vulnerabilities (and strengths), but also plays a part in how these vulnerabilities find expression. Consider, for example, that excessive self-depreciation, which results from compliance to strong external control, can become a cause of depression. In this cause-and-effect chain are cultural factors. Chance (1964) showed that strongly cohesive groups, either highly traditional and culturally stable, or of middle and upper socioeconomic status, tend to have more frequent self-depreciation symptoms that result in depression. Low-cohesion groups, marked by extremely flexible social relations, rapid cultural change, low socioeconomic status, social disorganization, and extensive migration, have less frequent feelings of guilt and depression. The frequency of depression in a community is speculatively related to the level of cohesion.

The form psychopathology takes tends to be linked with the kind of stresses within a society. If a society is excessively one of action, efficiency, and achievement, certain symptoms or diseases may occur as reactions to the high tension situation. In the view of Appels (1973), "the coronary patient seems to mirror the characteristics of a fast moving, competitive, and aggressive society."

The damaging results of certain culturally formed stresses have been predicted quite accurately by studying children's stories. These stories express in simple form a society's values. In 1925, McClelland (Rudin, 1968) analyzed stories from 16 Western or Westernized countries and scored them on motivations expressed. He scored specifically on the need to achieve and the need for power. About 25 years later, he analyzed death rates of the countries for causes of death that seemed to have psychological causes as primary or underlying cause. He found that achievement motivation scores of the children's stories correlated with death rates due to ulcers and hypertension. Power motivation scores had forecast death rates due to murder, suicide, and cirrhosis of the liver.

Sometimes general knowledge of a certain psychopathology continues its existence. The morbid rage reaction of *amok* occurs in the societies which recognize this particular violence as a means of escape from an unbearable situation (Burton-Bradley, 1968).

The disappearance of certain disorders also may be traced to the culture and its changes. This is evident in the hysterical reaction that takes the form of either dissociation or conversion. This hysteria, in the 19th century cases in Vienna described by Freud, formed the cornerstone of modern psychiatry. Today, clinicians are fairly well agreed that both forms are gradually disappearing from some societies, mostly in developed countries where people are better educated, communicate their opinions directly, and express their feelings verbally. However, both hysterical dissociation and conversion are still common in many developing or underdeveloped countries where people are conservative, communicate their ideas indirectly, and act out problems and express emotions through body reactions.

Cultural Influences Model Solutions to Problems

Stresses, vulnerabilities, and, to some extent, pathologies owe their existence to the complex entity we call culture. All call out for easement, treatment, coping or curing. Yet even ways of dealing with problems are shaped by the values, traditions, and experiences of a society. In traditional Chinese thought, somatic illness is a respected and effective way to obtain rest and care; psychological strain is not. A Chinese who feels lonely or anxious does not try to solve his problem by talking about these feelings or asking for understanding and sympathy; instead he complains of a headache or palpitation or a stomach disorder, and becomes the object of care and concern. Therefore, in Chinese society, somatic complaints are relatively common, even among psychiatric patients.

In fact, the sick role is, in part, a cultural role. In the South American tradition, the appeal for help often finds expression in Susto, the illness believed to be caused by the wandering soul that must be brought back. The Maori culture allows for "time out"; the anxious or tense or exhausted one simply stays in bed as long as he wants, without criticism. Nervousness, depression, frustration, or apprehension may be voiced as "I am bewitched" or "I'm under a curse" or "I'm coming apart at the seams" or "Please give me some tranquilizers."

The universally observed father-mother-child triangular conflict is resolved in culturally influenced patterns. This, too, is reflected in children's stories. In Western stories, the child-hero usually wins, and parental authority is sacrificed. In Oriental stories, the child becomes the victim of the conflict (Tseng and Hsu, 1972).

Traditional custom has even resolved some degree of sex-identity conflict. The classic example is that of Couvade, in which a man whose wife has just delivered takes on the postpartum role himself. Munroe et al. (1973) doubt the reporting on many of these cases. However, we believe that the phenomenon, described in Spain, Albania, Brazil, Holland, China and French Guiana over many centuries, must have existed. In the typical Couvade, the husband goes to bed, is fed and cared for, and even complains of an aching stomach. Meanwhile, he is nursed and comforted by his wife. His society allows him, for a time, the feminine role.

The Solution Itself May Be Pathological

Not all efforts to solve problems solve anything at all. The solution itself may be negative or pathological; yet it also may bear the imprint of the society's ways and views. Mass hysteria is often a less-than-conscious effort to solve an intolerable situation. The attempt to lend excitement to a socially restricted existence was one of the reasons behind the Salem witch hunts of the 1700s. The grueling, health-threatening dance marathons of America's Depression were a means of escape from a national sadness as well as a chance to win needed prize money. The ultimate "no-solution solution" is suicide. On this topic, we now challenge the hypothesis that the incidence of suicide is low among pre-literate people because they are protected by extended family support, elaborate mourning rituals, and culturally patterned outlets for hostility (Stainbrook, 1954). The Kandrian district of southwest New Britain has a high incidence of suicide. The very familiarity with suicide as a way out of life's problems contributes to, and maintains, suicide as a "solution" (Hoskin, Friedman, and Cawte, 1969).

SUMMARY

Very probably no clinician reading this will ever treat a practitioner of Couvade or a New Britain potential suicide. Yet these dramatic examples emphasize a point. Each time a patient walks into your office or mine, he brings with him the personal baggage we call background. In it are psychological traumas, childhood experiences, family structure, organic conditions, genetic influences, strengths, weaknesses, personality traits, and potentials. This baggage will not be left with your receptionist. He brings with him, as well, his culture. This, too, he will not check outside your office door.

REFERENCES

Appels, A.: Coronary heart disease as a cultural disease: *Psychother. Psychosom.,* 22:320–324, 1973.

Berry, J. W. and Annis, R. C.: Acculturative stress: The role of ecology, culture, and differentiation. *Journal of Cross-Cultural Psychology,* 5:382–406, 1974.

Burton-Bradley, B. G.: The amok syndrome in Papua and New Guinea. *Med. J. Australia,* 1:252–256, 1968.

Chance, N. A.: A cross-cultural study of social cohesion and depression. *Transcultural Psychiatric Research Review,* 1:19–21, 1964.

DeVos, G. A. and Wagatsuma, H.: Minority status and deviancy in Japan. In: *Mental Health Research in Asia and the Pacific.* W. Caudill and T-Y. Lin (Eds.), Honolulu, Hawaii: East-West Center Press, 1969.

Distler, L. S.: The adolescent "hippie" and the emergence of a matristic culture. *Psychiatry,* 33: 362–371, 1970.

Doi, L. T.: Amae: A key concept for understanding Japanese personality structure. In: *Japanese Culture.* R. J. Smith and R. K. Beardsley (Eds.), Chicago: Aldine Publishing Company, 1962.

Goodman, F. D.: Apostolics of Yucatan: A case study of a religious movement. In: *Religion, Altered States of Consciousness and Social Change.* E. Bourguignon (Ed.), Columbus, Ohio: Ohio State University Press, 1973.

Harvey, Y. S. K. and Chung, S-H.: The Koreans. In: *People and Cultures of Hawaii: A Psychocultural Profile.* J. F. McDermott, Jr., W-S. Tseng, and T. W. Maretzki (Eds.), Honolulu, Hawaii: University Press of Hawaii, 1980.

Hippler, A. E.: Some unplanned consequences of planned culture change. Reprint from: *Higher Latitudes of North America: Socio-Economic Studies in Regional Development.* Boreal Institute, University of Alberta, Occasional Publication, #6:11–21, 1968.

Holzach, M.: The Christian Communists of Canada. *GEO A New View of Our World,* 1:126–154, 1979.

Hoskin, J. O., Friedman, M. I., and Cawte, J. E.: A high incidence of suicide in a preliterate-primitive society. *Psychiatry,* 32:200–210, 1969.

Johnston, T. F.: Believed fertility through altered states of consciousness among the Shangana-Tsonga of Southern Africa. *Transcultural Psychiatric Research Review,* 10:152–159, 1973.

Kasahara, Y.: Fear of eye-to-eye confrontation among neurotic patients in Japan. In: *Japanese Culture and Behavior.* T. S. Lebra and W. P. Lebra (Eds.), Honolulu, Hawaii: University Press of Hawaii, 1974.

Lin, T. Y.: The effects of urbanization on mental health. *International Social Science Journal,* 11:24–33, 1959.

Munroe, R. L., Munroe, R. H., and Whiting, J. W. M.: The Couvade: A psychological analysis. *Ethos,* 1:30–74, 1973.

Pukui, M. K., Haertig, E. W., and Lee, C. A.: *Nana I Ke Kumu (Look to the Source), Volume 2.* Honolulu, Hawaii: Hui Hanai (Queen Lili'uokalani Children's Center), 1979.
Rudin, S. A.: National motives predict psychogenic death rates 25 years later. *Science,* 160:901–903, 1968.
Smith, Kline and French: The American Jew. In: *Cultural Issues in Contemporary Psychiatry, Vol. 1.* Philadelphia, Pa: Smith, Kline and French Laboratories, 1978a.
Smith, Kline and French: The Wasp. In: *Cultural Issues in Contemporary Psychiatry, Vol. 1.* Philadelphia, Pa: Smith, Kline and French Laboratories, 1978b.
Stainbrook, E.: A cross-cultural evaluation of depressive reactions. In: *Depression.* V. P. H. Hoch and J. Zubin (Eds.), New York: Grune & Stratton, 1954.
Tseng, W-S. and Hsu, J.: The Chinese attitude toward parental authority as expressed in Chinese children's stories. *Arch. Gen. Psychiat.* 26:28–34, 1972.
Zaidi, S. M. H.: Sociocultural change and value conflict in developing countries: A case study of Pakistan. In: *Mental Health Research in Asia and the Pacific.* W. Caudill and T-Y. Lin (Eds.), Honolulu, Hawaii: East-West Center Press, 1969.

CHAPTER 3

Culture and Concepts of Mental Illness

The human being whose behavior perplexes, alarms, endangers, awes, or arouses pity has always been labeled by his fellow men. Depending on culture, era, and individual bias, he may be perceived as being physically sick, mentally sick, or not sick at all, but touched by gods or entrapped by demons. With its labels, the society expresses its concepts of mental illness. The labels may be quite specific descriptions of observed behavior; they may also express causes and provide explanations. They may convey social acceptance or rejection of the patient and his illness. The labels may be enduring or they may change with the times, so what is illness in one era may be normal in another. The information on concepts of mental illness throughout the world is fragmentary but fascinating. This chapter presents some of these fragments.

DEGREES AND DISTINCTIONS OF MENTAL DISORDER

Even primitive peoples have recognized and named various types and degrees of mental illness. One example comes from the Bemba of Zimbabwe, where tribal beliefs have not disappeared with Western influences. These people differentiate degrees of mental aberration that range from total incapacity to mere eccentricity. Their terms include: *icipuba* (idiot), a person lacking the mental ability to feed or clothe himself; *ukupena* (madness), crazy and violent conduct; and *icipumputu* (fits), a person suffering from violent seizures who may froth at the mouth or fall into the fire. These obviously observant people also recognized the quiet depression of the person sick in spirit *(alwalo mutima)* and one who was not mad, but merely an eccentric *(uapuntuka)* (Brelsford, 1950).

The Serer of Senegal on Africa's west coast perceive psychiatric illnesses as "illness of the spirit." Within this broad concept are many specifically recognized sufferers and manifestations: *o bodah,* a man who has "no ideas in his head," who cannot understand, talks to himself, and thinks like a child; *o dof,* one who becomes mad with hostility, is overly excited, and displays destructive behavior; *mbefedin,* one who has periodic fits; *o yome,* impotence; and *pobough lang,* one who eats earth (Beiser et al., 1973). It is interesting that eating earth is considered normal behavior for pregnant women and children who have not been weaned.

In the mountains of central Borneo, the Murut distinguish varying types of *ruden* (madness). Their diagnostic vocabulary includes: *ruden rupan,* madness first characterized by hallucinations and flight into the jungle—later, the victim becomes quiet, retarded, and withdrawn; *ruden talai,* with initial manifestations of fatigue, muscle pain, headache, and insomnia, followed by reactive aggressiveness, visual hallucinations, and running amok; *ruden meruai,* fits; and *ruden mebuyai,* "stupid madness," in which one becomes aimless and unable to answer questions clearly (Schmidt, 1967-68).

These and other reports (Gelfand, 1964; Schmidt, 1964; Edgerton, 1966) indicate that mental disorders of primitive peoples can be grouped as disturbances with a cluster of manifestations that include "craziness," talking to self and wandering around, aggressive-destructive catatonic behavior, and convulsions.

These descriptions of mental disturbances by primitive groups are comparable to listings of mental illness in the early medical histories of literate societies. The Chinese text, *Nei Ching* (Classic of Internal Medicine), possibly begun as early as 2000 B.C., recognized excited insanity, delirium, and falling sickness (Tseng, 1973). Caraka, a physician of India between the first and second centuries A.D., distinguished three types of mental disorders: *vata* (wind), with wandering, incoherent talk, and laughing; *pitta* (bile), marked by irritability, anger, and excitement; and *kapha* (phlegm), in which the victim is silent and rooted to one spot (Rao, 1975). In Greece, between the fifth and fourth centuries B.C., Hippocrates described epilepsy, delirium, melancholia, and hysteria; and, early in the second century, A.D., Soranus noted delirium, mania, and melancholy. In the Ming Period (1368–1644) of China, Chin-Yue's *Medical Book* classified depression as anger depression, caused by excessive anger; apprehension depression, caused by excessive brooding; and melancholy depression, caused by excessive worry over a tragic event or life's practical hardships (Tseng, 1973). The first book of psychiatry written in English (rather than Latin) was Timothy Bright's 1568 *A Treatise of Mel-*

ancholy. This recognized a type of melancholy caused by apprehension and treatable by psychological means (Howells, 1975).

Several factors may influence a society's recognition of different kinds of mental disorders. Obviously, the disorder must be sufficiently frequent or noisy or alarming or antisocial to demand attention. Disorders with socially disruptive behavior—being negatively aggressive or destructive, breaking social taboos, or going naked in clothed societies except for ritual or socially defined purposes—were, and are, easily recognized. (In the pre-missionary period, Hawaii allowed nudity for ceremonial reasons and excused it when it accompanied extreme grief.) Conditions with severe socially disruptive behavior (psychoses) were recognized quite early. Mental disorder associated with fever (delirium), senility, or trauma were easily conceptualized as illness. However, as Beiser et al. (1973) noted, society may not recognize as mental illness subjective distresses such as anxiety or depression, which do not noticeably interfere with the social system. This does not mean subjective distress has not existed, perhaps always. Yet until very recently, society did not view anxiety, depression, phobia, or personality disorders as "psychiatric conditions." Until psychological explanations for, and intervention in, such disorders became popular, they seem to have been considered just a part of life's daily problems.

How observers perceive behavior may also influence their recognition of mental disorders. A 1970 study by Lubchansky et al. illustrates this. The authors presented case vignettes to three groups in New York City: Puerto Rican spiritualists (who function as folk healers), Spanish-speaking community leaders, and a cross-section of Puerto Ricans (heads of household and wives) from the Puerto Rican community. The same disorders were described by the spiritualists as impaired judgment and thought disorder; by the community leaders as impaired judgment and bizarre behavior; and by the cross-section of Puerto Ricans as bizarre behavior.

EXPLANATIONS FOR MENTAL DISORDERS

As soon as people recognize mentally disturbed behavior, they try to explain its nature and cause. Explanations are very much influenced by a people's basic orientation to the world, how sophisticated their thinking is, their medical knowledge, and the nature of the disturbed behavior. Thus, reasons for disorders are different among different cultural areas and different times. Various attributions of cause fall into four categories: the supernatural explanation, natural explanations, physical-medical explanations, and sociopsychological explanations.

The Supernatural Explanation

This explanation finds the cause in a supernatural power (Clements, 1932). The supernatural is involved when a disorder results from:

A. Spirit Intrusion/Possession. A spirit, god, demon, or ghost of man or animal enters into the body of the patient.
B. Soul Loss. The soul is somehow lost and illness results. The soul may wander away or be stolen by spirits during sleep, sneezing, or fright.
C. Divine Wrath. Illness is caused, in non-Christian contexts, by gods who become angry after they are treated irreverently. In many Christian beliefs, illness, mental or physical, was thought to be punishment for moral transgression. The cause-effect association has by no means been forgotten.
D. Sorcery/Black Magic. Sickness is caused by way of a sorcerer's (or witch's or magician's) spell.
E. Violation of Taboo. A supernatural power inflicts the disorder as punishment for breaking a taboo or cultural rule. Incest, stealing, or eating forbidden foods are all taboo violations apt to cause illness.

Natural Explanations

These explanations stem from the basic assumption that underlying principles of the universe govern all nature, including man's life, behavior, and health. When illness, mental or physical, misfortune, or great unhappiness occurs, the cause is thought to be:

A. Disharmony of the natural elements. It is believed that the human body contains several basic elements. Harmony of these elements is essential for health; disharmony causes sickness, physical or mental.

This line of reasoning is found, for example, in the hot-cold theory held by some Latin-Americans. Harwood (1971) noted it among Puerto Ricans in New York City. To some extent, the theory is yet under the long shadow of the medical past. Hippocrates taught that the body has four humors (blood, phlegm, black bile, and yellow bile) and that these varied in temperature and moisture. With the humors nicely balanced, man—with a moist, warm body—was in good health; let them go out of balance, and illness, manifested by an excessively hot, cold, wet, or dry body, prevailed. The Arab world enlarged on the theory. With Spanish and Portuguese conquests in the New World, the humoral beliefs entered lives in Mexico and Latin America. Concepts of the humors and wet-dry importance were eventually discarded; belief in the hot-cold theory continued. Diseases were classified as *caliente* (hot) or *frio* (cold); food, drink, and medicine as hot, cold, or cool *(fresco)*. A "cold" disease called for a "hot" remedy; a "hot" condition needed "cold" medication. New foods and medicines have continued to enter the classification system. Penicillin, because it can cause a rash, is "hot," yet it is acceptable in cases of rheumatic fever because the disease involves joint pains and is therefore "cold."

According to Harwood, the elderly and recent immigrants are more likely to observe hot-cold restrictions. For a physician or psychiatrist who prescribes drugs to Puerto Rican patients, the *caliente-frio-fresco* matter can cause difficulties. However, a solution exists within the cultural belief. It is the theory and practice of neutralizing the incompatible medicine. Some mothers who give their children aspirin ("hot") neutralize the effect by giving fruit juice, which is "cool." Tactful questioning can disclose the patient's own convictions about a medicine and how it may be "neutralized."

B. Incompatibility with natural principles. It is believed that the physical environment man creates should be in harmony with natural principles or forces. When the environment is incompatible with such forces, sickness, mental distress, or misfortune results.

The improper location or construction of a dwelling is, in a number of cultures, thought the cause of illness, unhappiness, and failure. Among Chinese, particularly in rural areas, the concept is held even today. It is called, in Cantonese, *fung-shui.* Potter (1970) describes the Cantonese peasants' view of the concept.

Though *fung-shui* is closely linked with belief in the supernatural, in practice it is concerned with natural phenomena and cosmic forces. Specifically concerned are *fung* (wind) and *shui* (water). Wind and water are vastly important, for they can influence the flow of *dey mat,* that great primordial energy, the "pulse of the earth," and at the same time become a part of that force. From this trinity of wind, water, and vitalizing power comes all fortune. A successful man has good *fung-shui;* and a failure has bad *fung-shui.* And because wind and water carry this flow-of-fortune, man must build his house, or even an entire village, with wind and water in mind. A river must never flow away from home, village, or grave; it will carry *fung-shui* powers away. A wall must often be built to keep *fung-shui* from blowing away. Houses must be located and constructed to retain or balance *fung-shui;* a mountain behind a dwelling must be balanced with standing water (or water moving toward the dwelling) in front. The careful man builds nothing until he consults the *fung-shui* specialist.

Should trouble, notably lack of success with its accompanying anxiety, come, misdirected *fung-shui* is believed the cause. Renovating or moving the house can then become the remedy for past errors and provide a second chance to attain health, wealth, or happiness.

C. Noxious factors in the environment. Any natural element, such as wind (even without such power as in *fung-shui*) and water, is thought cause for mental illness. Factors that could be attributed to natural forces or subject to human influence, such as poison, starvation, and gluttony, are included.

One example comes from a community in the highlands of Chiapas, Mexico. (The people involved are of mixed racial stock who speak Spanish and are culturally more Western than Mayan.) There, Fabrega and Metzger (1968) found that the villagers believe cold air or drafts and too little or too much food are among the many causes of mental disorders. A "case history" description of a paranoid woman given by her neighbor makes it clear that manifestation may be mistaken for cause. The neighbor describes a 60-year-old single woman, left—by death and desertion of family members—alone. She became sleepless, talked, sang, and shouted to herself, and then "began losing weight since she didn't cook her meals." When villagers brought her food or medicine, she refused it because it might be "poisoned." She also believed "bandits" would murder her. After she locked herself in the house, with knives and machetes by her bed, the Catholic priest forced his way in and blessed the house. The woman began to calm down. Then one of her sisters began sending her food. In about three months, she "regained her reason."

Disregarding the loneliness and depression that may have begun the loss of appetite, the neighbor summed up her opinion that "her madness comes because of the lack of nourishing meals—what is called weakness of the brain."

Physical-Medical Explanations

Here the focus shifts to the patient himself. Though precipitating causes may be external ones, such as injury or bacteria, the disorder is viewed as originating from the individual. In folk therapy, within this reasoning, no search is made for a supernatural agent or for a natural force, such as heat or cold. The reasons for illness are considered physical or physiological; the illness is thought of as a disease entity in itself. A particular disorder may be thought to result from:

A. Physical-physiognomy problems. The anatomical/physical characteristics of the face, skull, palm, or body build are believed cause of the disorder. This belief is found among Chinese fortune-teller-healers who "read" facial features.

B. Physiological imbalance or insufficiency. A badly balanced diet, exhaustion, or inappropriate activity, especially in sexual life, is said to cause physiological disturbances which result in mental disorders. In the Mexican highlands, excess salt is listed among the causes of mental illness (Fabrega et al., 1967). Loss of energy through sexual activity has been held responsible for psychiatric conditions in both the Orient and the Western world.

C. Disease. Inborn or acquired pathologies cause mental ills. Folk-belief in Korea holds that "obstruction of the heart cavity by sputum" brings about mental disorder (Rhi, 1973). In Africa, Sebi and Pokot tribesmen believe worms moving in the brain cause psychosis. However, they also describe this as a "disease you catch" (Edgerton, 1966). In the Sinhala medical practice of India, mental illness is said to result when the head or brain "goes bad." The "humors" affecting channels and ducts to the brain have been "affected." Consequently, nasal draining is a therapy for many kinds of mental disorders (Obeyesekere, 1978).

Sociopsychological Explanations

In the sociopsychological view, mental disorder is a psychological reaction to the stress of internal or external maladjustment. The American housewife may credit her "nervousness" to crying children, inadequate living space, or personal anxieties. Alcoholism is widely—though not conclusively—thought to be a stress-induced condition. Internal stress was recognized in concepts of ancient India which held that frustration and unexpressed emotion led to mental tensions (Vahia et al., 1966).

CONCEPTS OFTEN COEXIST

Concepts and explanations for mental disorders refuse to be rigidly confined in these classifications. Often they overlap and coexist. For example, many cultures believe that an object intruding into the body causes insanity. Within this concept, some individuals may think only the object itself caused the disturbance. Others may consider the resulting disorder as supernaturally caused and believe that the object was merely the vehicle which transported magic or godly power within the body. The Australian aborigine who believed "holy animals" put "bones" in him (Cawte, 1965) might attribute his illness to both supernatural powers and the intrusion of natural, though noxious, objects. (Either way, removing the bones was the ritual remedy.) Mental disturbance following a sudden fright may be considered a stress-reaction phenomenon; it may be the *susto* (soul loss) of Latin America in which sudden fright is thought to cause the soul to leave the body, thus producing illness, or the somewhat different *haak-ts'an* (injury by fright) of Chinese belief. In *susto,* it is the immortal soul that leaves the body. In the Chinese concept, as Topley (1970) described it, it is the *wan,* the animating force or energy, that, in sudden fright, becomes unbalanced or leaves the body. Only after death does *wan* become a soul. Some Hong Kong mothers with fright-injured children also believe some god or demon caused the precipitating fright.

Mental illness caused by masturbation has been conceptualized in many ways. Christianity has believed it punishment for a grievous sin; less religious Westerners have seen a less supernatural link between "self-abuse" and physical or mental disorders. The Chinese trace a physical chain of occurrences: masturbation causes loss of sperm, lost sperm weakens the body, the weakened body brings about mental ills. Freud wrote of psychological cause-or-consequence. He believed that, "In typical cases of neurasthenia, a history of regular masturbation or persistent emissions was found" (Freud, 1966).

Yet even though concepts coexist within the same society, one certain frame of reference or explanation for illness is usually prevalent. For example, harmony or balance has always been prominent in the Hindu view of health and sickness (Opler, 1963). Balance of *yin* and *yang* (male and female, heat and cold, positive and negative principles) permeates traditional Chinese and Korean ideas of well-being. Denko (1966) formed an interesting hypothesis on how societies regard misfortune. She suggested that when a society has high standards of personal conduct and responsibility, misfortune might be attributed to punishment for not living up to these standards. In a society which believes that external influences shape personal action, misfortune is apt to be blamed on spirits or external causes.

MENTAL HEALING PRACTICES

How a culture sees the cause of mental illness is apt to dictate how healing is sought. If the soul has taken flight, it must be returned. If a spirit has invaded body or mind, it must be removed. When illness is thought to be inflicted by supernatural forces, then exorcism, ritual extraction of an intruding object, counter-sorcery, confession, sacrifice, and purification are prescribed healing practices. When natural influences are believed the causes, rearrangement of living conditions to meet natural principles and balancing one's diet may be ordered. When the physical-medical view is held, treatments may include sexual abstinence to restore physical vitality, rest therapy for nervous exhaustion, and herb teas to dissolve the "heart-obstructing" sputum.

A people's orientation and attitude toward mental illness may influence the choice of treatment. Edgerton (1966), who studied four East African societies, noted that the Sebei of Southeast Uganda and the Pokot of Northwest Kenya think psychosis is incurable and try to manage the patient by restraining, starving, or beating him. However, the Kamba of South Central Kenya and the Hebe of Southwest Tanganyika believe psychosis can sometimes be cured; they use drugs, sacrifice, and incantation to combat the witchcraft that caused the illness.

Kiev (1960) suggested that an association exists between personality patterns and folk therapeutic techniques. He reviewed 75 primitive societies and found that self-punitive practices, such as blood-letting to remove harmful agents, were significantly linked with severe childhood prohibition on expressing negative aggression. Externally-directed punitive measures, such as witch-hunting, showed a relationship to few such prohibitions during childhood.

ATTITUDES TOWARD MENTAL ILLNESS

A people's attitude toward mental illness usually reflects their orientation to such disorders. This is subject to cultural differences. For example, Arab countries encouraged a humanistic attitude toward the mentally ill. Before the 10th century, Arabs had built asylums with fountains and gardens and a generally relaxing atmosphere; their therapeutic regimen included diet, baths, and drugs. At the root of this humanitarian attitude was the Moslem belief that an insane person is loved by God and particularly chosen by Him to tell the truth (Mora, 1967). This is quite a contrast to the European situation in the Middle Ages when the mentally ill were frequently thought of as witches and tortured.

Terashima and Nareta (1964) compared public attitudes toward mental illness among rural Japanese and rural Canadians. The authors found that 67% of the Japanese would be reluctant to have a former mental patient as a neighbor; only 30% of the Canadians expressed reluctance. A high 87% of the Japanese would discourage their children from marrying even a relative of a mentally ill person; only 27% of the Canadians would. Clearly, the Japanese have a stronger belief that mental disorder is inherited; 71% thought the mentally ill should be sterilized.

CONCEPTS OF MODERN PSYCHIATRY

No discussion of how mankind views mental illness would be complete without considering how today's orthodox practitioners—the psychiatrists—

view the conditions they treat. What is noticeable is the broader vision of the present time. Contemporary psychiatry has enlarged its concept of mental disorder to include minor emotional disturbances with psychiatric conditions. The boundary between normality and disorder is also blurred. Because of recently improved results gained especially with psychotropic medication, the attitude toward mental disorders has become more positive. Increased knowledge of medicine and of sociocultural situations necessitates a continuing revision of concepts of mental disorders. (The recently changed view on homosexuality is an example.) Every psychiatrist faces a challenge. We need to continue to examine ourselves to see on what grounds, and for what purposes, we recognize, label, and conceptualize certain emotional behavior disturbances as mental disorders and what are the sociocultural implications of our conclusions.

REFERENCES

Beiser, M., Burr, W. A., Ravel, J. L., and Collonb, H.: Illness of the spirit among the Serer of Senegal. *Am. J. Psychiatry,* 130:881–886, 1973.

Brelsford, W. V.: Insanity among the Bemba of Northern Rhodesia. *Africa,* 20:46–54, 1950.

Cawte, J. E.: Ethnopsychiatry in Central Australia I. Traditional illnesses in the Eastern Aranda people. *Br. J. Psychiatry,* 111:1069–1077, 1965.

Clements, F. E.: Primitive concepts of disease. *University of California Publications in American Archaeology and Ethnology.* 32:2, Berkeley: University of California Press, 1932.

Denko, J. D.: How preliterate peoples explain disturbed behavior. *Archives of General Psychiatry,* 15:398–409, 1966.

Edgerton, R. B.: Conceptions of psychosis in four East African societies. *American Anthropologist,* 68:408–425, 1966.

Fabrega, H. Jr., Rubel, A. J., and Wallace, C. A.: Working class Mexican psychiatric outpatients. *Archives of General Psychiatry,* 16:704–712, 1967.

Fabrega, H. and Metzger, D.: Psychiatric illness in a small Ladino community. *Psychiatry,* 31:339–351, 1968.

Freud, S.: The etiology of the neuroses. In: *The Standard Edition of the Complete Psychological Works of Sigmund Freud, Vol. I.* J. Strachey (Ed.), London: Hogarth, 1966.

Gelfand, M.: Psychiatric disorders as recognized by the Shona. In: *Magic, Faith and Healing.* A. Kiev (Ed.), Glencoe, Ill.: Free Press, 1964.

Harwood, A.: The hot-cold theory of disease: Implications for treatment of Puerto Rican patients. *Journal of the American Medical Association,* 216:1153–1158, 1971.

Howells, J. G. (Ed.): *World History of Psychiatry.* New York: Brunner/Mazel, 1975.

Kiev, A.: Primitive therapy: A cross-cultural study of the relationships between child training and therapeutic practices related to illness. In: *The Psychoanalytic Study of Society, Vol I.* W. Muensterberger and S. Axelrad (Eds.), New York: International Universities Press, 1960.

Lubchansky, I., Egri, G., and Stokes, J.: Puerto Rican spiritualists view mental illness: The faith healer as a paraprofessional. *Am. J. Psychiatry,* 127:312–321, 1970.

Mora, G.: History of psychiatry. In: *Comprehensive Textbook of Psychiatry.* A. M. Freedman and H. I. Kaplan (Eds.), Baltimore: Williams and Wilkins Company, 1967.

Obeyesekere, G.: Illness, culture, and meaning: Some comments on the nature of traditional medicine. In: *Culture and Healing in Asian Societies: Anthropological, Psychiatric and Public Health Studies.* A. Kleinman, P. Kunstadter, E. R. Alexander, and J. L. Gale (Eds.), Cambridge, Massachusetts: Schenkman Publishing Co., 1978.

Opler, M. E.: The cultural definition of illness in village India. *Human Organization,* 22:32–35, 1963.
Potter, J.: Wind, water, bones and souls: The religious world of the Cantonese peasant. *Journal of Oriental Studies,* 8:139–153, 1970.
Rao, A. V.: India. In: *World History of Psychiatry.* J. G. Howells (Ed.), New York: Brunner/Mazel, 1975.
Rhi, B. Y.: A preliminary study on the medical acculturation problems in Korea. *Korean Neuropsychiatric Association Journal,* 12:15–27, 1973.
Schmidt, K. E.: Folk psychiatry in Sarawak: A tentative system of psychiatry of the Iban. In: *Magic, Faith, and Healing.* A. Kiev (Ed.), New York: The Free Press, 1964.
Schmidt, K. E.: Some concepts of mental illness in the Murut. *International Journal of Social Psychiatry,* 14:24–31, 1967–68.
Terashima, S. and Nareta, T.: A rural community's opinion and knowledge about mental illness in Japan. *Transcultural Psychiatry Research Review,* 1:97–100, 1964.
Topley, M.: Chinese traditional ideas and the treatment of disease. *Man,* 5:421–437, 1970.
Tseng, W-S.: The development of psychiatric concepts in traditional Chinese medicine. *Archives of General Psychiatry,* 29:569–575, 1973.
Vahia, N. S., Vinekar, S. L., and Doongaji, D. R.: Some ancient Indian concepts in the treatment of psychiatric disorders. *Br. J. Psychiatry,* 112:1089–1096, 1966.

PART II

Culture and Psychopathology

CHAPTER 4

Culture-related Specific Psychiatric Conditions

Among the number of mental disorders that plague mankind are many that, so far, do not fit neatly into a standard Western psychiatric classification system. Their clinical descriptions, contributed by investigators around the world, seem to be dumped figuratively into some giant, miscellaneous file marked "atypical" and "unclassifiable."

Open that file and study the labels therein. They read: "Exotic Conditions," "Mental Illnesses Peculiar to Certain Cultures," "Folk Illnesses," and "Culture-bound Syndromes." They bear the adjectives "regional," "uncommon," and "rare." Within this file are also specific terms for conditions: *amok, latah, koro, imu, susto, windigo* or *wiitiko,* arctic hysteria, magical death or voodoo, frigophobia, anthrophobia, and malignant anxiety.

The very fact that certain conditions are "unclassifiable" suggests a lack in the scope of present classification systems. It rests on the false assumption that human beings follow standardized behavior patterns, even in mental disorders. It denies the possibility of cultural variations in mental illness. It indicates a need to modify and expand presently used psychiatric classification systems to make them universally applicable. Until that is done, let us take a critical look at the terms that lodge so uncomfortably in our "unclassifiable" catchall.

To us, "exotic" connotes an ethnocentric attitude, a short-sighted view. "Folk" and "regional" merely indicate that local variations of mental illness do exist. "Uncommon" and "rare" are misleading. If the terms mean that a condition is rarely found in a locality (even though it may be closely related to the culture), there is no need to emphasize such a rare case. If it is relatively "rare" and "uncommon" in comparison to other places, but common or frequent enough in a particular setting to be familiar there, then it is worth studying from a cultural, psychiatric point of view.

"Culture-bound syndrome" also calls for scrutiny. Admittedly, the term conveys the close relationship of culture to mental illness; it also implies that this illness is psychogenic and reactive. However the question persists: How much of the disorder is tied or confined to a particular cultural system? So far, there has been no systematic investigation, no cross-cultural epidemiological study, to prove that a certain syndrome is so inextricably "bound" to a particular culture. On the contrary, it is suspected (but not proved) that many so-called culture-bound syndromes exist in different, but basically similar, forms in various places and cultural systems. Until investigative work supports the contention that a "culture-bound syndrome" is confined to one certain culture, the term should be used with reservation.

Which brings us to our credo as cultural psychiatrists. We share the belief that the world holds a great diversity of cultural systems and human behaviors, that cultural, as well as biological and psychological, factors influence the manifestation of mental illness to such an extent that the clinical picture is modified; thus, appropriate nosological consideration is necessary. We also believe that culture, as a way of life, changes over a long time span; thus, the clinical picture of mental illness accordingly changes. Our concern is to identify and study groups of specific psychiatric conditions seen around the world which:

a) manifest certain specific characteristics not usually seen in other kinds of mental illness;
b) are fairly commonly *observed* in *some cultural areas,* but *not* in *others;* and
c) are manifested in a manner *closely related* to the *culture.*

We therefore suggest that these types of psychopathology be referred to as *culture-related specific psychiatric conditions.*

Cultural psychiatry also recognizes that culture can affect: concepts of what is normal or pathological; interpretation of, and attitude toward, mental illness; predisposition to be vulnerable to certain stresses; and ways of coping with these stresses. Thus, culture-related specific psychiatric conditions can be subgrouped in categories that suggest how a culture factor contributes to the condition.

SUBGROUPING OF SPECIFIC PSYCHIATRIC CONDITIONS

Group A: Conditions Given a Cultural Interpretation and Remedy

When a psychiatric condition occurs, it is interpreted in certain ways, and a certain remedy, based on this interpretation, is tried. Both interpretation and remedy are based on a culturally formed belief. For example, in much of Latin America, *susto* (described more fully later) is a condition the people believe happens when a sudden fright results in the loss of the soul or spirit. Remedial rituals to recapture the lost soul are then held. Both the soul-loss interpretation and the soul-regained remedy rest on cultural concepts of the spirit or soul. In Chinese culture, *hsieh-pin* (evil sickness) is a trance state in which the patient identifies with the dead. It is believed that the spirit or ghost of a dead ancestor possesses the patient; therefore, exorcism is the necessary remedy (Lin, 1953).

Group B: Conditions Resulting from Stress Which Stems from Culturally Formed Beliefs

This is perhaps best illustrated by beliefs held in many cultures: that a taboo exists and that breaking this taboo brings illness; and that spells can be cast which cause misfortune, illness, or death. In each case, the person who has broken a taboo, or feels he is under a curse or spell, is then subject to stress. The psychiatric (and often physical) manifestations resulting from this stress are then ascribed to the broken taboo or to the sorcerer's spell. Stress and its manifestations are felt because the individual believes in the taboo system or the power of spell-and-sorcerer. Treatment is also within the cultural belief system: The spell may be nullified with a stronger spell; the gods who are angered at the broken taboo may be pacified. Voodoo death is, of course, a well-known illustration of stress induced by the spell. *Malgri* is an interesting example of stress from the broken taboo. In the Wellesley Islands, off the coast of Australia, it is taboo to carry food from the land into the sea, and vice versa. The unfortunate one who does this (without specified cleansing rituals) suffers from *malgri*—abdominal pain, anxiety and other discomforts (Cawte, 1976). *Malgri* also will be discussed later.

Group C: Conditions Marked by a Well-Defined Psychiatric Syndrome Complex Known to the Society

Here, the psychodynamics are speculative. Even the influence of cultural factors is not clear, though they may contribute to symptom formation. What is definite is that the society—and usually the patient—both recognize the condition in all of its manifestations.

Included in this group are "startle disorders" which exhibit such hysterical features as automatic obedience, echolalia and echopraxia. *Latah* in Malaysia and Indonesia and *imu* among the Ainu in northern Japan are well-known examples. In some instances, the attack may take the form of frenzied dissociation, rather than an imitative state. Also in this group are: *amok,* with its sudden, non-discriminatory, massive homicidal acts; malignant anxiety, marked by chronic anxiety, tension, hostility, restlessness, confusion, and even homicide; the so-called frigophobia, showing excessive preoccupation with, and fearful reaction to, catching cold (Yap, 1951); and anthrophobia, the fear of interpersonal relations described by Kasahara (1974).

Group D: Conditions Influenced on Multiple Levels by Cultural Factors

One illustration: Culturally patterned child-rearing practices lead to a certain personality formation which creates vulnerability to certain stresses. The social and cultural environment which predisposes individuals to these stresses also provides a model for reaction to the stresses. The impotence panic called *koro* and the cannibalistic *wiitiko* psychosis are classic examples.

Group E: Conditions Possibly Culture-related

Open to question as a culture-related condition is the so-called Puerto Rican Syndrome. This is so named because it has been observed in Puerto Ricans, both in their native country and in the United States. It is characterized, according to Maldonado-Sierra and Trent (1960), by great anxiety, regression, transient depersonalization, and bizarre seizure patterns. Other descriptions note mutism, extreme fright, personal violence, and a "full range of psychotic behavior" (Mehlman, 1961). Mehlman strongly believes that "Puerto Rican Syndrome" is a mistaken labeling of a collection of conditions that appear superficially to be similar within a culture, but really represent many diverse disorders. Though "Puerto Rican Syndrome" appears in the language and literature of cultural psychiatry, in our view it is yet to be proved a specifically culture-related condition.

DESCRIPTION OF CULTURE-RELATED SPECIFIC PSYCHIATRIC CONDITIONS

Susto (or Espanto)

In Guatemala, a frustrated and unhappy Indian women quarrels with her husband. Infuriated, he suddenly hits her with a rock. Terribly frightened, though not really injured, she eventually becomes a victim of *susto*.

In the United States, Antonio, a young man who speaks only Spanish, is hospitalized with pneumonia. During the night, his wardmate dies. Antonio is alarmed, but cannot communicate with ward attendants. Soon he develops symptoms (restlessness, loss of appetite, muscle spasm). When Antonio goes home, his mother diagnoses his new ailment: "Est el susto!" In Mexico, a small child is perched on a stone wall. He falls to the ground. The child is uninjured, but his mother is terribly frightened. Eventually, she suffers from *susto* (Gillin, 1948; Rubel, 1964).

The Indian wife, the young man, and the Mexican mother all shared a common experience—that of fright; in Spanish, *susto* or *espanto*. The three are among the many Spanish-speaking persons in certain parts of Latin America, Mexico, and the United States who attribute a wide range of symptoms to a frightening experience, and thus name their resulting discomforts after the *susto* they believe is the cause. The fright may be caused by an unexpected loud noise, a fall, or witnessing an alarming sight or shocking incident. With that fright, so goes the folk belief, the soul leaves the body. Thus *susto,* as the culture's diagnostic term, takes on the connotation (almost the attached definition) of "soul loss." It rests on the basic belief that man has one or more souls or spirits, and that these can separate from the body, wander, and become lost.

El susto tends to be recognized in retrospect, after symptoms bring about the recollection of a traumatic experience. Tousignant (1974) surveyed *susto* victims and found that 90% suffered from weakness, sadness, fatigue, loss of appetite, and headache; 80% of the patients also experienced chills, fever, a feeling of physical heaviness, shortness of breath, and fearfulness. Other complaints (Gillin, 1948) may be diarrhea, various pains, hand tremor, and alternating anxiety and tension. *Susto* really includes many heterogeneous manifestations which may be clinically classified either as depression, anxiety, or fear (Gobeil, 1973) or, in the case of the children, diagnosed as physical illness caused by infection or malnutrition (Meth, 1974). Kiev (1968) calls it a "culturally meaningful anxiety hysteria syndrome."

In some cases, several months may go by before the previously terror-stricken person experiences symptoms and credits them to *susto.* Soul loss through fright thus becomes more the explanation than the illness. The diagnostic explanation may be helpful or harmful. In the Latin American belief, untreated *susto* can be fatal—for who can live long without a soul? With treatment available, knowing the condition is *susto* can be reassuring, for *susto* is socially accepted; it provides a valid excuse for not working and it points the way to a cure. Basically, the cure is the ritual recapture of the soul and its reentry into the body. Yet when healing is conducted by a skilled *curandero* or *parchero* (curer), much more than ritual is involved. Gillin's study of an Indian *susto* patient in Guatemala and her treatment makes this clear. The woman was allowed to ventilate fears and hostilities, experienced some transference to her healer, and received reassurance, both in words and in the administration of medicines. In addition, her attention was diverted from symptoms and she was assigned specific tasks that brought her into social contact, established personal self-worth, and gave purpose to her days. The very rituals of recapturing the soul, preparing medicines, and conducting associated ceremonies brought relatives and community members together in mutual support of the patient. *El susto,* in this case at least, was a condition with a built-in remedial system.

Malgri (Territorial Anxiety Syndrome)

Malgri, as it came to the attention of John Cawte (1976), demonstrated itself in the following ways: Two children ate bread and tinned meat, and then went swimming in an ocean channel. Soon they began screaming with bellyaches; their adult companion said the stomachs were "tight and bulging." When a nurse examined the youngsters, she found the stomachs soft. The children, so their companion explained, had been stricken with *malgri.* In another instance, a middle-aged man ate sea turtle and then waded in a fresh water hole. "His stomach was all blown up," said a friend. The unfortunate man suffered from *malgri.*

The place is the Wellesley Islands in the Gulf of Carpentaria near Australia. The *malgri* sufferers belong to the Lardil group of Australian aborigines. In their view, illness (distended and painful belly, fatigue, drowsiness, sometimes vomiting) had come because they had violated a taboo. The children had eaten "land food" and then gone into the sea without cleansing hands and mouth. The man had eaten food from the sea and then entered fresh water. In doing so, each had offended the totemic spirit of that particular part of the sea or land. The spirit then rushed into the belly "like a bullet." With ritual and song and symbolism, the spirit must then be exorcised and induced to return home. A long cord of grass or hair from an unraveled belt is tied to the sufferer's foot and the other end is taken down to the water. When the string is broken (perhaps after all-night rituals), the invading spirit has then traveled via the cord back to his home territory.

Cawte sees *malgri* as sometimes—but not always—psychopathological, and notes individual susceptibility to the condition. He points out that *malgri,* like its underlying totemic system, also has served a social purpose: that of preserving territorial rights of local groups. These Islanders are hunters and fisherman; there is a basic concern about territory and trespassing on another's food-supply domain.

Later, Hippler and Cawte (1978) described a more far-reaching territorial anxiety among Yolngu aborigines on Elcho Island, Arnhem Land, North Australia. Here, moving from one place to another (and sometimes undertaking any new venture) may result in great fear and dread, loss of appetite, sleeplessness, and an almost paralytic inertia. The Yolngu believe that when one leaves his birthplace or greatly disrupts his way of life, he disturbs the relationship between himself and his ancestors. The traveler also presents a sexual threat to the new territory; he might take someone else's wife. Preventive measures traditionally included asking permission from someone in the territory to be visited. The "host" of this territory would then rub the sweat of his armpit on the stranger; this made the traveler smell right to the clan ancestors of the visited area. These attitudes, customs, and beliefs, plus concern over food availability on land and in the sea, all operate consciously or unconsciously in this still-existing primitive form of agoraphobia.

Latah (Startle Reaction)

Startle almost any woman in Chicago or London, and she will probably blink, jump slightly, or utter some small, surprised exclamation.

Surprise, or just mildly frighten, a women in Malaysia, Indonesia, Burma, Thailand, or the Philippines and you may see only this similar, slight reaction. But if you startle certain women (and sometimes men) in these countries, you may witness a far different response. The startled one may repeat your (or someone else's) words (echolalia); or mimic your actions (echopraxia); or, more commonly, burst forth with obscene or profane words (coprolalia). There may be abrupt body movement, the dropping of what was being held, the immediate taking of a defensive stance, or even striking out. (In 1897, Ellis witnessed a perhaps exceptional case in which the *latah* victim habitually urinated and passed flatus.) These individuals demonstrate the startle reaction called *latah* in Indonesia, *mali-mali* in the Philippines, *yaun* or *young-dah-hte* in Burma, *bah-tsche* in Thailand, *imu* among aborigines in Japan, and *mryiachit* in Siberia.

Latah and its symptomatic kin have had a place in medical-psychiatric literature for a hundred years. Most accounts describe startled or frightened women; yet one tells of Siberian Cossacks, who, in 1868, suddenly began repeating the orders—and later threats and curses—of their commanding officer. What startled the Cossacks, we do not know; we have a somewhat better idea of what precipitates *latah* reactions in other cultural settings. The immediate stimulus may be a sudden noise, a poke in the ribs, or a slap on the back. For the Ainu women in northern Japan, an *imu* attack follows a snake bite, seeing a snake or what looks like a snake, dreaming of a snake, hearing a word that means snake, and sometimes a loud or sharp and unexpected sound

(Winiarz and Wielawski, 1936). Teasing sometimes brings about this startle reaction in Java (Geertz, 1968). Tickling may result in *latah* and similar syndromes in many cultures. Murphy (1976) and Still (1940) remind us that some of the terms for the reaction *(latah, bah-tsche* and *young-dah-hte)* mean "tickling," "tickling madness," and "to be ticklish and nervous." Murphy particularly notes the sexual character of many *latah* manifestations and the common and often erotically stimulating tickling of children.

Yet not all women of these cultures respond to a startling stimulus with *latah*. Both special vulnerabilities and predisposing factors exist. Heredity does not seem to dictate vulnerability. Though *imu* does not otherwise occur among Japanese, Japanese children adopted by Ainus are subject to it (Winiarz and Wielawski, 1936). Among Malays in Borneo, in the Philippines, and in Java, women are now most apt to exhibit *latah* (though in 1897, Malaya had many male cases). Whether women are most vulnerable, or merely most often startled, may be open to question. As one informant explained, it is safe to startle a woman without fear of reprisal; it is wiser to leave a man alone. *Latah*-prone women are predominantly middle-aged and come from lower to barely middle social and economic classes (Chiu et al., 1972; Geertz, 1959; Simons, 1980).

The initial attack of *latah* is most often preceded by some traumatic or anxiety-provoking event, such as a death in the family. Sexual dreams often occur shortly before the actual startle reaction. Once an initial *latah* episode has taken place, other attacks often follow—often for a lifetime. One reason for this is that onlookers many times deliberately startle the known *latah* victim to bring on an attack.

Speculations on the *latah* phenomenon include: that in a male-dominated culture, *latah* is a socially accepted, female, attention-seeking response that allows overtly excited, aggressive and/or sexual demonstrations (Chiu et al., 1972; Winiarz and Wielawski, 1936); that *latah* behavior allows a penalty-free departure from cultural standards, as in Java where elaborately polished speech, formal etiquette and sexual prudery are culturally ordained; and that, because it frequently occurs in front of a higher status person, it further overrides cultural status values (Geertz, 1968).

In the opinion of Simons (1980), *latah* (which has been observed in many, sometimes quite different, cultures) is the culture-specific exploitation of a neurophysiological potential shared by humans and other mammals.

Amok (Massive Homicide)

If you had visited a police station in Malaya not too long ago, you might have seen a curious instrument of law-and-order called *sanggamara*. It looked a little like a six-foot-high trident, with the top or "head" a bit rounded, and the middle prong missing. It had one specific use—to pin a certain type of violent and homicidal man against a wall so he could be subdued. Without this instrument and a convenient wall, this man had to be disabled or killed; he did not give himself up.

Such men's behavior has entered the psychiatric vocabulary as *amok*. The term comes from the Malay *mengamok,* which means something like "to charge furiously because of a desperate nature." The furious charge and the desperation are indeed in evidence. Tan (1965), Teoh (1972) and Yap (1951) have described this morbid rage reaction as an acute outburst of unrestrained violence associated with homicidal attacks. It is preceded by a period of brooding, and ends (if the desperate one lives) with exhaustion and amnesia. *Amok* is most frequent among young men.

Loss, grief, shame, or a public insult raises the curtain on the tragic drama. The afflicted person initially becomes quiet and subdued; he then abruptly "goes bush." He seizes a sword, axe, spear, gun, or hand grenade, chooses a crowded public place, and slaughters everyone he encounters until he is killed, injured, or captured (Burton-Bradley, 1968). *Amok* homicides are distinct from other murders: The killer chooses an extremely destructive weapon, a crowded location, and insanely kills a large number of persons (Westermeyer, 1972). *Amok* has a long history. In 1770, Captain Cook wrote from Batavia that "running *amok* has prevailed in the people from time immemorial" (Teoh, 1972). In the 19th century, it was commonly found among the Javanese and Malays. In the early 1900s, incidents were noted among other ethnic groups in Malaya. After World War II, Teoh (1972) writes, both Malays and Chinese in Malaya ran *amok* with almost the same frequency. In Laos, men afficted with *amok* once used bladed weapons, but began to switch to grenades in 1959 (Westermeyer, 1973). *Amok* has also been observed in Papua and New Guinea (Burton-Bradley, 1968) and in the Philippines (Zaguirre, 1957). In a lesser frequency, it may actually take place anywhere in the world. It was Westermeyer (1973) who pointed out that *amok* homicide tends to increase during times of political, economic, and social upheaval. He emphasized that the susceptibility of an individual living in rapid sociocultural change, plus a social awareness of *amok* violence as a behavioral alternative under appropriate circumstances, may contribute to its occurrence.

Burton-Bradley (1968) calls attention to Wulfften-Palthe's explanation that *amok* is a standardized form of emotional release, recognized by the community, and even expected of someone who is terribly embarrassed or shamed. Wulfften-Palthe notes that, while *amok* occurs among Malays living in their own social structure, no case has been recorded among Malays in Europe. Murphy (1972) and Teoh (1972) both described the changing psychopathology of the condition in this way: *Amok* was once a conscious form of violent behavior accepted or considered heroic. Because of negative reactions by society, it has now become unconsciously motivated and occurs as a dissociated or psychotic condition.

Wiitiko (Cannibalistic Possession Psychosis)

Perhaps the ultimate in pathological possession belief has been experienced by the unfortunate Ojibwa Indian in northern Canada who suffered from *wiitiko* (or *windigo*) psychosis. This unhappy man believed the cannibalistic *wiitiko* monster had taken possession—or that he had totally become a *wiitiko*. As such, he craved human flesh. If no one stopped him, he killed and fed on a relative.

The psychotic transformation to murderer and cannibal did not happen overnight. It was prefaced by a long and lonely time, hunting in isolation and without success in an ice-encrusted forest. Returned home, the hunter began to be morbidly depressed. Ordinary food tasted bad; he felt nauseated. Sometimes he lapsed into periods of semi-stupor. He was sure the *wiitiko* giant was taking possession, and he felt a strange food craving. This was not recognized as wanting human flesh. He saw surrounding family members as "fat, luscious animals" (Parker, 1960).

In another tribe, the Cree Indians of northern Canada, a somewhat similar psychosis has been reported (Cooper, 1933). Here the victim who thinks he has become a *wiitiko* also craves human flesh, but, in addition, he believes that, as a *wiitiko* he has a heart of ice and vomits ice. Actual cannibalism seems to have been limited to periods of famine. The psychosis most often came only after famine-induced cannibalism; occasionally, women as well as men have experienced it.

Whether *wiitiko* psychosis, including cannibalism, actually exists today is debatable. The point of this discussion comes in the background that seems specifically linked to this condition. Both tribes have in common the knowledge and experience of famine and starvation, with its inevitable emphasis on the importance of food. Both know the particular cruelty of intense, long-continued cold. Yet, as Parker (1960) makes clear, environment alone cannot account for *wiitiko*; neighboring Eskimo tribes neither demonstrate this psychosis nor believe in a cannibalistic monster. With both the Cree and Ojibwas, long-established belief in the *wiitiko* giant, or monster, or god, is perpetuated in myths and legends told and retold to the young (Teicher, 1960). Cree children are told, "Do not eat ice; you will turn into a *wiitiko*"

(Cooper, 1933). Ojibwa children grow up hearing myths of hunger, eating, cannibalism, and young boys being starved and neglected by their mothers (Parker, 1960; Landes, 1938).

Parker (1960) examined these myths and found close links between food and fantasies of aggression and death, as well as clear intimations of dependency needs frustrated; of "pushing" boys into maturity and manly behavior; of the loved object turned into the unloving (mother becomes a cannibalistic monster). The myths illustrate, in exaggerated and imaginative form, actual child-rearing practices. Boys as young as four are deliberately deprived of food, both as preparation for food shortages and as discipline. They are trained and expected to become good hunters. They are also expected and urged to see visions. All this reaches a climax at puberty. Then a boy is left alone and without food in a forest. He is expected to stay there until he has a vision and communicates with the supernatural. All through his childhood, the importance and manliness of hunting are stressed. If, as pubescent youth or grown man, he fails to secure food, he is in every sense a failure. The state is set for depression, anxiety, and psychological transformation into the monster. *Wiitiko* is a pathological adjustment of the modal Ojibwa personality to severe pressures. Parker (1960) terms it a probable cultural variation of schizophrenia.

Koro (Impotence Panic)

We invite your attention and sympathy to the plight of the following young man in Kuala Lumpur, as Tan (1972) knew it.

Let us call him Cheng. He is 20, single, Chinese. He is in an emergency hospital. He is short of breath, wet with perspiration. His heart is palpitating. Cheng is terrified; he is afraid he is going to die.

What brings him to this state of anxiety?

To Cheng, it is obvious. His penis, he gasps, is receding into his abdomen. It happened the first time after he masturbated, he explains. That night he grabbed hold of his penis, called for help, and was taken to the emergency room at the hospital. This time, he has not masturbated. The whole panicky situation, the conviction his penis is retracting, has simply swept over him. This time, he has tied some cloth around the glans to try to keep his penis from what he fears might be total disappearance.

His is not an isolated case. Other Chinese men and boys in Taiwan, Singapore, and Hong Kong have been brought to emergency clinics in the same extremities of fright. Their penises have been clutched, held tightly by relatives, tied with string, or clamped with chopsticks, sometimes even bruised in frantic efforts to keep them from retracting.

Cheng and his fellow suffers have been overwhelmed by the syndrome sometimes experienced by Chinese (usually southern) men. In Malay, it is called *koro* ("the head of the turtle"). In Mandarin Chinese, it is *suo-yang*, and in Cantonese, *shook-yang* ("shrinking of the penis"). Whatever the name—*koro* is most often used—the condition is not a new one. Chinese medical literature many centuries ago described shrinking of the penis as a forerunner of death. Underlying the specific conviction that the penis can shrink and retract within the abdomen and thus cause death is a more basic belief: that loss of semen weakens; that excessive sexual activity can be fatal (Tan, 1970; Gwee, 1963, 1968). In normal intercourse a kind of safety-balance occurs, for then, the belief goes, there is an exchange of *yang* (male) and *yin* (female) humors. With masturbation and nocturnal emmission, *yang* is simply lost, the *yang-yin* balance is destroyed, and *koro* may well result (Yap, 1965; Rin, 1965).

The old fear of semen loss is evident in the 20th century. *Koro* sufferers often say that their troubles have been caused by masturbation, "wet dreams," promiscuous or excessive intercourse. The attack itself may follow urination, defecation, or come on spontaneously. As Gwee (1963) points out, a slight and subjective sensation in the genitalia may stimulate *koro* anxiety. This builds to panic when relatives excitedly confirm the victim's fears. In fact, one eight-year-old whose penis was bitten by an insect developed several *koro* attacks after adults made efforts to "anchor" his penis outside the abdomen.

Yap (1965) reviewed 19 *koro* cases in Hong Kong and found that the patients were basically passive-dependent, shy, nervous, and greatly dependent on and attached to their mothers. Their sexual history indicated conflict and maladjustment. They had usually resorted to masturbation for sexual outlet because of lack of confidence in themselves and their sexual capacities. Rin (1965), who reported two cases from Taiwan, found that the background for the pathology was marked by a characteristic childhood experience and premorbid personality, i.e., the lack of paternal identification, overprotection by the mother, and anxiety about achieving masculinity.

Though *koro* has been found predominantly among the southern Chinese, it is by no means limited to them. The Thai epidemic and the 1967 Singapore outbreak (described in Chapter 5) indicate this. Though the Singapore epidemic primarily affected southern Chinese, it also included a few Malays, Indians, and one Eurasian. This epidemic also showed an unusual characteristic. Most of the patients denied having had sexual activity before the symptoms appeared.

COMMENTS AND THEORETICAL RECONSIDERATION

A review of reported culture-related or culturally specific psychiatric conditions makes it obvious that all these syndromes vary in the degree of cultural factors involved.

Some of the syndromes are superficially and secondarily influenced by cultural factors; they are merely colored by the folk interpretation of sick behavior, as in *susto* or *hsieh-pin*. Other syndromes are more heavily and directly influenced by cultural elements; they may be pre-cast by certain personality models or precipitated by culture-related stress Psychopathology may be shaped according to culturally ordained coping patterns, as in the case of *koro* or *wiitiko* psychosis.

From a methodological point of view, the investigation of culture-related special psychiatric conditions is hampered by several factors. First, in most cases there is a lack of comprehensive and dynamic case descriptions of these illnesses, and few personal life histories of the patients are available. Thus, meaningful case analysis is impossible. This is particularly true in the case of voodoo, in which the victim is dead, and usually in *amok*, in which the berserk sufferer is so often killed. Second, most investigations fail to provide data on the frequency of occurrence, so that epidemiological insight is difficult. And, third, uneven quality in investigation exists because investigators lack experience in sophisticated analysis of cultural backgrounds and their influence on the formation of psychopathology.

To deal with the nature of certain specific psychiatric conditions, we must raise several basic questions and consider various approaches. Initially, we ask: To what extent are those reported conditions actually confined to certain geographical and cultural areas? Are they ever observed in other places?

Some investigators suspect that if the term and description of such a psychiatric manifestation were known to clinicians and investigators of other places, they might identify, report and link the condition to their areas as well. For example, the Latin-American concept of *susto* (emotionally disturbed behavior which results from "soul loss") is also found in Oriental countries and Africa; such phenomena are not necessarily confined to Latin America (Gobeil, 1973). The phenomenon of *latah* ("startle reaction") observed among Malays has also been reported as "Jumping Frenchmen" among people of French-Canadian descent in Maine (Stevens, 1965) and, in a milder version, as "startle neurosis" among U.S. Army inductees in Vermont (Thorne, 1944). *Pibloktoq,* an hysterical attack with a wide variety of bizarre behaviors, is found among Eskimo women and, less frequently, men. It has been compared to arctic hysteria among the Paleo-Siberian Indians in Alaska and to behavior during initiation rites of Korean sorcerers (Gussow,

1960). If we broadly define the phenomenon of "running *amok*" (rampant, indiscriminate mass murder by one man) as savage, homicidal behavior and carefully examine it around the world, then we may find such phenomena not only in Malaya, but also in Papua and New Guinea (Burton-Bradley, 1968) and in Laos (Westermeyer, 1973). This same type of behavior has happened in Africa under such names as frenzied anxiety (Carothers, 1948) and malignant anxiety (Lambo, 1962), and may be related to this subgroup of disorder. Certainly, we in North America are not unfamiliar with the phenomenon of a person under emotional pressure who seizes a machine gun and, without warning or provocation, kills a group of people.

If there is sufficient information to support the belief that a specific psychiatric condition is relatively more common in certain areas or cultural groups, even if only at a particular time or era, then it is worthwhile to investigate the distribution of any outbreak or epidemic in terms of its biological, psychological and sociocultural factors. For example, 18.6% of the Japanese university students at a student health service facility complained of fear of eye-to-eye contact or confrontation—the so-called anthrophobia (Kasahara, 1974). This certainly merits further investigation and alerting of attention to its possible existence elsewhere. If any phenomena are suddenly noted in other cultural areas besides their place of origin, it becomes important to study them in the place and people of predominance, as well as in the locations of recent occurrences.

A third question merits serious thought: Are reported specific psychiatric conditions subtypes or variations of existing diagnostic entities? The question rests on the premise that these specific syndromes are not new diagnostic entities and that they are, in fact, similar to syndromes already known in the West. Consequently, they are suitable for grouping according to conventional psychiatric categories (Kiev, 1972).

The assumption is that primary clinical syndromes may be manifest in a variety of equivalent subtypes. Accordingly, *koro* (impotence panic) is nothing but a form of psychosexual disturbance with cultural variations of castration anxiety (Kobler, 1948), or depersonalization syndrome (Yap, 1965). *Wiitiko,* the cannibalistic psychosis, more or less belongs to the category of schizophrenia, with the exception of the symptoms of animal possession; and, of course, *pibloktoq* is a form of hysterical reaction.

We must, therefore, consider the matter of frequency. To what extent do such subtypes or variations occur in certain areas? If certain subtypes do occur frequently, then investigation should seek the cultural factors which contribute to the phenomena. Furthermore, certain specific syndromes are so different from those of the presently described diagnostic psychiatric groups that it is difficult to categorize them as any "subtype" or variation. For example, "frigophobia" (sensation of chills, excessive tendency to catch cold, wearing over-abundant clothing and overheating surroundings) is a complex of psychophysiological, phobic and hypochondriacal reactions. Thus, it is difficult to categorize it into any one, presently existing, diagnostic group.

We need to devote serious attention to filling the gaps in our current classification systems. In spite of the broad spectrum of emotional reactions that exist, the two commonly used systems list only anxiety disorders and depressive disorders. Surely, a wider range of pathological emotional reactions needs inclusion. Fear, startling, and rage have all been demonstrated in ways that are pathological and can be classified.

Of the two classification systems, Diagnostic and Statistical Manual of Mental Disorders, Third Edition (DSM-III), seems useful only to psychiatrists in the United States or perhaps in some other Western cultures. It elaborates on substance abuse and psychosexual disorders that may not occur so frequently in all parts of the world, but omits certain conditions such as neurasthenia which claim a great deal of attention in non-Western areas. In contrast, International Statistical Classification of Diseases, Ninth Revision (ICD-9), with its more expansive listings of psychiatric disorders, is more useful around the world. However, there are plenty of psychiatric conditions still waiting for classification. These include impotence panic, possession psychoses, and various pathological rage reactions. Cultural psychiatrists should be included in the planning of the ICD-10.

The last question is: What are the culture-related psychiatric disorders in Western society? Most culture-related disorders are described as occurring in other than Western societies. It then becomes pertinent to ask what kinds of psychiatric disorders are culture-related and more specific for our contemporary Western society? Perhaps we can answer by pointing out what kinds of psychiatric disorders are currently more prevalent in contemporary Western society but relatively rare, or of less concern, in non-Western society. Homosexual panic, alcoholism, drug abuse, and possibly borderline states may be considered Western society-related psychiatric disorders.

SUGGESTIONS FOR FUTURE STUDY

To understand more fully culture-related, specific psychiatric conditions, we suggest that research should begin with sound clinical investigation. For a better nosological and differential diagnosis, this should include detailed descriptions of the patient's mental status, clinical dynamic case study, and comprehensive reporting and analysis of both the psychological situation and the stress and environmental factors involved with the disorder. We strongly recommend using videotape to record case examples and interviews with patients. These tapes amount to a kind of "living case history" of a condition. They can give visiting psychiatrists from a different culture the next best thing to personal observation of a patient with a certain disorder; the vocal and facial nuances that words (especially in translation) cannot quite describe are present on tape. The recorded case presentation can increase the recognition of phenomena that are similar across cultural boundaries and emphasize the cultural differences that exist.

It is also desirable that research include epidemiological findings that denote how frequently a condition occurs in certain areas. Speculation on why a given condition occurs so often in one place, but not in another, might also be valuable. If such information were available for cross-cultural comparison, then we could better hypothesize the role of cultural factors in specific psychiatric conditions.

REFERENCES

Burton-Bradley, B. G.: The amok syndrome in Papua and New Guinea. *Med. J. Australia,* 1:252–256, 1968.

Carothers, J. C.: A study of mental derangement in Africans, and an attempt to explain its peculiarities, more especially in relation to the African attitude to life. *Psychiatry,* 11:47–86, 1948.

Cawte, J. E.: Malgri: A culture-bound syndrome. In: *Culture-Bound Syndromes, Ethnopsychiatry, and Alternate Therapies.* W. P. Lebra (Ed.), Honolulu, Hawaii: University Press of Hawaii, 1976.

Chiu, T. L., Tong, J. E., and Schmidt, K. D.: A clinical and survey study of latah in Sarawak, Malaysia, *Psychol. Med.,* 2:155–165, 1972.

Cooper, J. M.: The Cree witiko psychosis. *Primitive Man,* 6:20–24, 1933.

Ellis, W. G.: "Latah," A mental malady of the Malays. *J. Ment. Sci.,* 43:33–40, 1897.

Geertz, H.: The vocabulary of emotion. A study of Javanese socialization processes. *Psychiatry,* 22:283–295, 1959.

Geertz, H.: Latah in Java: A theoretical paradox. *Indonesia,* 5:94–104, 1968.

Gillin, J.: Magical fright. *Psychiatry,* 11:387–450, 1948.

Gobeil, O.: El susto: A descriptive analysis. *Int. J. Soc. Psychiatry,* 9:38–43, 1973.

Gussow, Z.: Pibloktoq (hysteria) among the polar Eskimo: An ethno-psychiatric study. In: *Psychoanalysis and the Social Sciences.* W. Muernsterberger (Ed.), New York: International Universities Press, 1960.

Gwee, A. L.: Koro—A cultural disease. *Singapore Med. J.,* 4:119–122, 1963.

Gwee, A. L.: Koro—Its origin and nature as a disease entity. *Singapore Med. J.,* 9:3–6, 1968.

Hippler, A. and Cawte, J.: The malgri territorial anxiety syndrome: Primitive pattern for agoraphobia. *Journal of Operational Psychiatry,* 9:23–31, 1978.

Kasahara, Y.: Fear of eye-to-eye confrontation among neurotic patients in Japan. In: *Japanese Culture and Behavior, Selected Readings.* T. S. Lebra and W. P. Lebra (Eds.), Honolulu, Hawaii: University Press of Hawaii, 1974.

Kiev, A.: *Curanderismo: Mexican-American Folk Psychiatry.* New York: The Free Press, 1968.

Kiev, A.: *Transcultural Psychiatry.* New York: The Free Press, 1972.

Kobler, F.: Description of an acute castration fear, based on superstition. *Psychoanal. Rev.,* 35:285–289, 1948.

Lambo, T. A.: Malignant anxiety in Africans. *J. Ment. Sci.,* 108:256–264, 1962.

Landes, R.: The abnormal among the Ojibwa Indians. *Journal of Abnormal Social Psychiatry,* 33:14–33, 1938.

Lin, T. Y.: A study of the incidence of mental disorder in Chinese and other cultures. *Psychiatry,* 16:313–336, 1953.

Maldonado-Sierra, E. D. and Trent, R. D.: The sibling relationship in group psychotherapy with Puerto Rican schizophrenics. *Am. J. Psychiatry,* 117:239–243, 1960.

Mehlman, R. D.: The Puerto Rican syndrome. *Am. J. Psychiatry,* 118:328–332, 1961.

Meth, J. M.: Exotic psychiatric syndromes. In: *American Handbook of Psychiatry, 2nd Edition, Volume 3. Adult Clinical Psychiatry.* S. Arieti and E. B. Brody (Eds.), New York: Basic Books, Inc., 1974.

Murphy, H. B. M.: History and the evolution of syndromes: The striking case of "latah" and "amok." In: *Psychopathology: Contributions from the Biological Behavioral and Social Sciences.* M. Hammer, K. Salzinger, and S. Sutton (Eds.) New York: John Wiley and Sons, 1972.

Murphy, H. B. M.: Notes for a theory of latah. In: *Culture-Bound Syndromes, Ethnopsychiatry, and Alternate Therapies.* W. P. Lebra (Ed.), Honolulu, Hawaii: The University Press of Hawaii, 1976.

Parker, S.: The wiitiko psychosis in the context of Ojibwa personality and culture. *American Anthropology,* 62:603–623, 1960.

Rin, H.: A study of the aetiology of koro in respect to the Chinese concept of illness. *Int. J. Soc. Psychiatry,* 11:7–13, 1965.

Rubel, A. J.: The epidemiology of a folk illness: Susto in hispanic America. *Ethnology,* 3:268–283, 1964.

Simons, R. C.: The resolution of the latah paradox. *J. Nerv. Ment. Dis.,* 168:195–206, 1980.

Stevens, H.: Jumping Frenchmen of Maine. *Arch. Neurol.,* 12:311–314, 1965.

Still, R. M. L.: Remarks on the aetiology and symptoms of a young-dah-hte with a report on four cases and its medico-legal significance. *The Indian Medical Gazette,* 88–91, February, 1940.

Tan, E. S.: Amok: A diagnostic consideration. *Proceedings of the Second Malaysian Congress of Medicine,* 22–25, 1965.

Tan, E. S.: Sexual symptoms in anxiety. *Proceedings: Fifth Malaysia-Singapore Congress of Medicine,* 5:146–148, 1970.

Tan, E. S.: Personal communication. 1972.

Teicher, M. I.: Windigo psychosis: A study of relationship between belief and behavior among the Indians of Northeastern Canada. *Proceedings of the 1960 Annual Spring Meeting of the American Ethnological Society.* V. Ray (Ed.), 1960.

Teoh, J. I.: The changing psychopathology of amok. *Psychiatry,* 35:345–351, 1972.

Thorne, F. C.: Startle neurosis. *Am. J. Psychiatry,* 101:105–109, 1944.

Tousignant, M.: An ethnopsychiatric study of espanto. Ph.D. Dissertation. Department of Anthropology, University of Chicago, 1974.

Westermeyer, J.: A comparison of amok and other homicide in Laos. *Am. J. Psychiatry,* 129: 703–709, 1972.

Westermeyer, J.: On the epidemicity of amok violence. *Arch. Gen. Psychiatry,* 28:873–876, 1973.

Winiarz, W. and Wielawski, J.: Imu—A psychoneurosis occurring among Ainus. *Psychoanal. Rev.,* 23:181–186, 1936.

Yap, P. M.: Mental diseases peculiar to certain cultures: A survey of comparative psychiatry. *J. Ment. Sci.,* 97:313–327, 1951.

Yap, P. M.: Koro—A culture-bound depersonalization syndrome. *Br. J. Psychiatry,* 111:43–50, 1965.

Zaguirre, J. C.: Amuck. *Journal of Philippine Federal Private Medical Practice,* 6:1138–1148, 1957.

CHAPTER 5

Epidemic Mental Disorders

INTRODUCTION

Epidemic and endemic mental disorders have been demonstrated, if not defined, since before the Middle Ages. We will detail some of these demonstrations later; first, a definition is in order. Epidemic mental disorders—and their smaller scale endemic kin—are social-cultural-psychiatric phenomena in which a group of persons through social contagion, together as well as individually, manifest for a short time various psychiatric conditions. The symptoms are usually similar to those of hysterical or panic states; however, some spreading mental-emotional states are a mixture of various disturbances. For example, in 1962, 217 natives of Tanganyika, East Africa—most of them schoolgirls—suffered sudden, often incapacitating episodes of uncontrollable laughing and crying. No physical reasons were found for the attacks of *endwara yokusheka* (the illness of laughing). The diagnosis was mass hysteria (Rankin and Philip, 1963). But, when one of us personally investigated eight members of a family in Taiwan who believed they, as a group, were being persecuted and poisoned, the illness was quite different. This was group, or endemic, paranoia (Tseng, 1969).

Epidemic group disorders, such as hysteria, panic, or delusion, are contagious, disorganized, and uncontrolled. Thus, they differ from ritualized and institutionalized contagious behaviors often related to group religious or civil customs. Consider two contrasting situations: In the Middle Ages, dancing mania swept parts of Europe. People, swayed by an irresistible excitement, jumped, "danced," and ran around until fatigue overcame them. This was epidemic hysteria (Kagwa, 1964.) But, in the present day, men of the Hasidic sect of the Jewish religion dance together to the point of ecstasy. This dancing is no mental disorder. Spontaneous, sometimes almost frenzied though it may seem, it is a ritualized expression of a tenet of faith: that devotion to God should be happy; that "evil desire can be overcome by joy and not by melancholy" *(The Standard Jewish Encyclopedia).*

Most psychiatrists tend to neglect epidemic-endemic mental conditions, perhaps because they consider them so rare. However, a review of the literature—including some accounts of music, dance and religion, along with psychiatric reports—indicates that epidemic mental disorders often were, and are, seen in many parts of the world. Certainly, these conditions merit our concern and investigation. Studying these epidemic-endemic illnesses enlarges our knowledge of psychiatric disorders in general. We can see them as influenced by mass psychology and by the contributions of society, culture, and environment. With this more encompassing view, the clinician can note how certain psychiatric disorders he commonly diagnoses and treats can be contagiously transmitted to others. He will observe that a group of people can simultaneously develop emotional disturbances when a particular sociopsychological atmosphere exists. Finally, such thoughtful study may challenge clinicians to discuss and evaluate the role and function of psychiatrists in relation to such social-psychiatric phenomena. Inevitably, the clinician must ask himself, "What is the contribution of psychiatry in the intervention and management of mass mental disorders?"

HISTORICAL SURVEY

The Western world has witnessed group exhibitions of "peculiar behavior" for centuries. From the early 1300s down through the 16th century, dancing epidemics erupted. Metz, Cologne, and Aix-la-Chapelle saw dancing manias come and go in 1377; Strasbourg residents danced in 1412 (Kagwa, 1964). Burton's *Anatomy of Melancholy* gave a different description: "Tis strange how long they will dance, and in what manner, over stools, forms, tables; even great bellied women sometimes . . . will dance so long that they can stir neither hand nor foot, but seem to be quite dead."

Western Europe called the frenzied activity St. John's Dance or St. Vitus' Dance. The epidemic traveled to Italy by the late 1600s. In 1844, Hecker wrote that one with this condition first became morose, withdrawn, and apathetic, but at the sound of music, he began to dance and jump (Tan, 1963). In Italy, the mania inspired folk accounts of cause and cure. It was supposed to be caused by the bite of a tarantula, was relieved only by the spirited music called *Tarantella,* and was, accordingly, called Tarantism. Outbreaks in Spain were called *Jota* (Ivanova, 1970). Psychiatry calls it mass hysteria.

Hysterical outbreaks in a religious framework happened in the 17th century. Several involved nuns; the episode at the convent at Loudun, France, is conspicuous. The hysteria centered on beliefs in *incubi* and possession. The lore of the times held that demoniac spirits could take the form of a man, obtain semen (some said from a corpse), and actually impregnate a sleeping victim. The very word "nightmare" comes from the Latin *incubo* and its literal meaning, "to lie upon." A 1651 prayer ended with the supplication that the devil would not molest one during sleep, "especially in those members designed for procreation" (Robbins, 1959).

The possession-by-demon belief made possible what seems to have been a blend of deliberate, malicious acting and genuine hysteria. The drama began with a plot to punish a priest, Father Grandier, who had insulted the powerful Cardinal Richelieu. Several nuns were persuaded to pretend they were possessed. Father Grandier was forced to exorcise them in public because, the nuns said, he had caused their possession. Other sources say one nun who cherished an unrequited love for the priest told her *incubi* possession story to the other nuns and they became convinced they, too, were possessed (Sirois, 1974). The public exorcisms inspired their own mass hysteria. Before the episodes ended, Father Grandier had been tried for witchcraft, tortured, and burned alive; two other priests who had tortured him died insane, and a third was later banished from France. A doctor who functioned as "witch hunter" died in delirium. As for the nuns themselves, were they acting only at the beginning? Or, cloistered in their sisterhood, caught up in their own dramatics, given appreciative—and hysterical—audiences, did they become genuinely hysterical themselves? History suggests that hysteria prevailed among both performers and onlookers who recorded the events, for reports tell that the nuns' faces became "so frightful one could not bear to look at them," that they uttered loud cries and obscenities, that "their eyes remained open without winking," and that one young nun was "in convulsions" and, falling on the ground and "lifting her petticoats," she "displayed her privy parts without shame" (Robbins, 1959).

A half-century after the Loudun incident, Louis XIV issued an edict to end witchcraft trials in France. But in the young American colonies, Salem, Massachusetts, was yet to know its infamous chapter in hysteria. Here, in this dull village in 1692, a few bored teenage girls fueled a cycle of suspicion, accusation, revenge, and panic. The girls put on some exhibitions of "fits" and eccentric behavior. They then named a few community scapegoats as causes—a

Negro slave, a pipe-smoking woman beggar, a crippled woman had "bewitched" them. Brought to trial, one of the scapegoats named another as the witch behind the trouble. The cycle had begun. Neighbor with a grudge accused neighbor. In panic, some of the accused confessed to witchcraft; some named others as witches and thereby aligned themselves with the "innocent." Accused became accuser; pursued became pursuer. By the time the last witchcraft trial ended, more than 30 men and women and even two seven-year-old children had been put to death (Robbins, 1959).

Are these examples only historical curiosities or merely evidence of beliefs or ignorance in developing countries? The phenomena of later years and established civilizations provide a decided *no*. For example, Schuler and Parenton (1943) cite Schutte's 1906 description of "trembling disease" that affected children in several schools in Meissen, Germany. In this, the children's hands and arms shook spasmodically for a few minutes, or in some cases for as long as an hour. The seizures lasted for weeks with random, symptom-free periods in which the children felt completely well.

Just before Halloween of 1938, panic threatened much of the United States when CBS Radio broadcast the Mercury Theatre's version of H. G. Wells' *War of the Worlds.* Some of us still remember that Sunday evening. We were lulled at first by a simulated "remote broadcast" of dance music. "News bulletins" interrupted. A strange object—was it a meteor?—had fallen in New Jersey. A news announcer was dispatched to "the scene." His voice, at first professionally calm, rose in convincing mock hysteria as he described a "strange machine." From that machine, he said, came "monsters from Mars," devastating the land. Later "bulletins" came: Neither troops nor air attack could halt the monsters. Then, from the radio sets there came, for a moment, only silence. It was bone-chilling. CBS—so the silence implied—no longer existed.

Thousands of listeners did not wait long enough to hear the reassuring station break announcement. Panic had set in. In New Jersey, hundreds of cars clogged the highways; people were fleeing—but where? Some told police they had *seen* the Martians and their machines; they were ready to wade the Hudson River and take New York City. In Georgia, frantic phone calls to police and newspapers reported that "monsters" had killed—individual reports varied—from 40 to 7,000 persons. A church service in Indianapolis was abruptly ended so that people could go home, while in Virginia, people gathered together to pray. Pennsylvania bridge players fell on their knees to pray. People fainted—five college students in North Carolina; two girls riding in their father's car in Michigan. And in Pittsburgh, genuine tragedy was narrowly averted. A man came home and found his wife ready to swallow poison.

RECENT EPIDEMIC EPISODES

Epidemic mental disorders have continued down to the present; examples that follow are from the 1960s and '70s. We chose them to illustrate possible correlation between elements of a particular culture and the type of mass behavior that occurred.

Epidemic Hysteria in Malaysian Schools

Epidemic hysteria has been frequently observed in the Malay area (Tan, 1963). Teoh, Soewondo, and Sidharta (1975) describe a 1971 episode—one of 17 that year—that concerned girl students in a school dormitory at a small town not far from Kuala Lumpur. The dormitory accommodated 50 adolescent Malay girls. It was initially supervised by a woman teacher, who later resigned from her post because the headmaster constantly interfered with her functioning. After she resigned, the headmaster managed the dormitory himself and made no real attempt to find a new supervisor. Consequently, the girls, their parents, and the entire community became extremely annoyed. The social taboos against a man's entering the living quarters of a Malay female are rigid, and the sexes are separated at an early age; the community felt strongly that it was incorrect and improper for a man to manage a girl's dormitory. Yet, the headmaster appeared in the girl's rooms unannounced, day or night. He pampered and "fussed over" the girls, even telling the younger ones how to wear their sanitary napkins. As a headmaster, he held the key position in the community; no one dared to oppose him directly.

The situation set the stage for an epidemic of hysteria. First, a 15-year-old girl suddenly appeared depressed, complained of difficulty in breathing, and experienced hyperventilation and tetanic spasm. She groaned in severe pain; she complained that someone was calling her from the vicinity of the toilets. Several days later, two dormitory mates developed similar symptoms. Screaming and shouting, one claimed that students had thrown soiled sanitary napkins around the place and had polluted the territory of the local gods. This girl especially made it clear that strong attraction to the headmaster and resulting jealousies existed among the girls.

The sufferers were sent home to rest, but when they returned, the symptoms recurred. More girls then developed attacks. When the chief education officer of the state investigated, he found five girls running around, screaming, hyperventilating, and fainting as each reached the climax of the outbreak. During the attack, one of the girls demanded a human sacrifice. The terrified headmaster bargained with her, and she compromised on the sacrifice of a goat. A local traditional healer was called upon, and the sacrificial ceremony was performed. The outbreak of hysteria finally caused the community to express public dissatisfaction with the headmaster and to pressure him to either change his behavior or be transferred. The headmaster finally agreed to appoint a new dormitory mistress and also promised to improve the physical situation at the school.

Analysis of this epidemic suggested that the outbreak was centered around the schoolmaster's disapproved behavior, primarily his intrusion into the girls' private lives. However, since this culture provides no appropriate way to oppose authority, mass hysteria became the only way to show the headmaster he needed to recognize and change the source of the problem. Only through their dissociated state could the girls express their complaints, protests, and demands. The epidemic also made it clear that Malayan children, traditionally reared in a relatively anxiety-free environment and protected against frustration for years, were not prepared to handle the anxieties and general stresses of life when they reached adolescence (Murphy, 1959). Hysterical reaction is understood as one of the neurotic ways to respond to anxiety. It can easily be utilized by a group of relatively innocent girls as a reaction to a stressful situation.

The epidemic was also greatly colored by the psychosexual issues: the intrusion of the schoolmaster into the dormitory and some of the girls' attraction to and jealousy over him. Current psychodynamic theory of the etiology of hysteria takes the view that early psychosexual development is arrested at the Oedipus level, and the incestuous tie to the loved, opposite sex parent is not relinquished. This leads to conflict in adult life over sexual involvement because it retains its forbidden incestuous quality (Nemiah, 1975). It would be worthwhile to study the usual psychosexual development of Malayan girls, with particular focus on how they relate to their father figures and how they solve the incestuous conflict. Such information would provide a pertinent illustration of how culture may pattern certain aspects of child development to selectively reinforce certain personality traits which, in turn, may predispose to certain stresses.

An Epidemic of Impotence Panic (Koro) in Singapore and Thailand

Koro is an impotence panic; a fear of death is associated with the belief that the penis is shrinking into the abdomen. Ngui (1969) reported a collective occurrence in Singapore in 1967. Swine fever had broken out, and a program to inoculate pigs was carried out and publicized. Several months later, a case of *koro* suddenly appeared. Unfortunately, a rumor that eating inoculated or infected pork could cause *koro* created public panic. Soon the incidence of *koro* assumed epidemic proportions. As many as 100 cases were seen at general hospitals in a single day. Of the total cases, 95% were Chinese males, with only 2.2% Malays and Indians. (The percentage distribution of population by racial groups in Singapore is 74.4% Chinese, 14.5% Malay, 8.1% Indian, 3% Eurasian and others.)

Swine fever with its accompanying rumor may have precipitated the mass occurrence of *koro*. However, Ngui's report points out that the *community-shared* folk concept of *koro* was an important ground for shared panic. Ngui also noted that six cases described as suffering from *koro* were below the age of six years, with one just seven months old. These young children were used psychologically as displaced or projected identifications of their anxious parents. Just as a parent's fears can often be manifest in the behavior of his or her offspring, the psychological atmosphere or mood of a small group within the community can contribute to collective panic.

Shortly after the war in Vietnam, a *koro* epidemic erupted in Eastern Thailand as many Cambodian refugees were migrating across the border. The Thais still feared a communist invasion. In this atmosphere of political-military apprehension, a rumor spread that communists had put a certain herb into the food. The herb was said to make Thai males sexually impotent, thus making it easy for communists to seduce Thai women. Men, allegedly suffering from *koro*, began to ask for treatment. Eventually, more than a thousand cases were reported (Suwanlert, 1977).

Although castration anxiety among the male is universal, intensity and reactions to this anxiety vary among different cultural groups. In a society which allows a boy to be very close to his mother and remain relatively protected, separation and independence from parents are delayed. In young adulthood, facing an adult psychosexual role carries at least potential anxiety.

Many Oriental countries have a folk concept that careful regulation of sexual life, as well as taking foods and tonic to maintain vitality, is necessary for men. Medical advertisements in newspapers and magazines still show this concern. As an extension of such folk orientation, many people still believe that neurasthenia is caused by excessive sexual activity resulting in nervous exhaustion. Clinical cases of neurotic concern over spermatorrhea (leakage of sperm), as well as *koro* (impotence panic), are observed. Both are extreme ways to respond to culturally shared sex-related anxieties. With such beliefs, epidemics of impotence panic can take place.

An Endemic Depression in a Japanese Leprosarium

Ikeda (1966) reported a 1960 emotional disturbance involving 11 nurses in a Japanese leprosarium. The leprosarium, with a staff of 67 nurses, accommodated about 1,200 patients.

A new head nurse, inexperienced in leprosy nursing, began duty on the ward. In the same month, a young male patient killed an aged, female patient; the two had been having a love affair. Two months later, a patient beat a ward housekeeper. Soon after this, another patient attempted suicide. In connection with the suicide attempt, the patients' governing body accused a staff nurse of negligence, and the new head nurse severely reprimanded her. Several days later, a patient attempted to escape, and the same staff nurse was again criticized by the patients' group. This nurse then began to suffer from sleeplessness, loss of appetite, and headaches. She feared that patients might persecute her or attack her sexually and became so depressed that she was hospitalized for psychiatric treatment. Very soon, a second nurse, a close friend, complained of similar symptoms and attempted suicide. Within a short time, 11 nurses, one after another, suffered various kinds of emotional disturbances, with symptoms of somatic complaints, depression, fear of persecution, and visual hallucinations. Several nurses attempted suicide by drug overdose. When the public learned this, an official investigation resulted.

According to Ikeda's analysis, the collective emotional disturbances were due to several factors: The sanatorium was an isolated and closed society; the nurses' daily lives were monotonous and unrewarding; there were almost no social gatherings or recreational activities for the nurses as a group, even for those who lived in the same dormitory. Important elements were the significant changes in the relationship between nurses and patients that came after World War II. Patients had developed community government, were encouraged to protest for their rights, and made more demands of the nursing staff.

The nurses were understaffed; morale was low. The new head nurse constantly criticized the nurses and gave them little support. In this setting of low morale, insufficient staff, and militant patients, the traditional, conservative nurses—faced with constant situations of frustration—found no other alternative except this rampant outbreak of fear and depression.

Paranoid Delusions Among Relatives

Paranoia, like depression, can spread from person to person. Such "mental contagion" was personally investigated by one of the authors (Tseng,

1969). The affair involved three adults and five children. The key figure, Mr. Chong, developed the delusion that he was persecuted by the communists. He transmitted his delusion to his sister, then to her husband (Mr. and Mrs. Wang), and later to five of the couple's children, forming a paranoid family. (There were seven children in all. Both partners had been previously married and divorced; this was Mr. Wang's third marriage.) The time and place are significant. This was Taiwan in the early 1960s. Among the many mainland Chinese who migrated to Taiwan, memories of communist oppression were still fresh. In Taiwan the political and social situation was unstable, and the infiltration of communists was probable.

Mr. Chong, 36, was the youngest son of a successful, strong-willed father. The father was first a merchant in northern China, and later, a Protestant lay preacher. Mr. Chong and his sister, Mrs. Wang, had been very close since childhood. As a child, Mr. Chong loved stories of intrigue and fighting. As a young adult, he became a military policeman, and when this failed to give him a sense of authority and superiority, he became a civilian policeman. In 1949, communists imprisoned his father. Chong rescued him and brought his parents and sister to Taiwan, where he married a local Chinese woman. There, as a policeman, he was so overzealous that his superiors finally fired him. He then became a lay preacher and lived in the church compound. Soon he was publicly criticizing the church elders, and personality conflicts resulted. Mr. Chong told his sister that the elders were "looking at him" and "talking about him." The sister, remembering mainland China days, warned him that the elders might have a communist sympathizer or agent in their ranks. Mr. Chong's paranoia increased. His house was burglarized, and he accused the elders. With this, his church employment ended. He viewed this as "enemy persecution." With his church quarters gone, he went to live with his sister and her family. (His wife lived in another town.)

Soon both Mr. Chong and his sister believed that they were being watched and harmed by communists, the family maid, church elders, neighbors, and even strangers. They quarreled with their neighbors, who they thought were saying the brother and sister had an "abnormal relationship."

Uncomfortably in the middle of this was the brother-in-law, Mr. Wang. No wonder he was uneasy; his neighbors were also his business colleagues. Mr. Wang had also known danger and intrigue. During World War II, he was in the Chinese underground. There he learned to poison the (Japanese) enemy. At first, Mr. Wang refused to believe his wife's and Chong's suspicions. Later, when the colleague-neighbors grew unfriendly, he, too, became suspicious. This reached a climax when he drank some tea in his office and then felt ill. "My colleagues are poisoning me," he thought. "My wife, brother-in-law, and I really *are* being persecuted."

One by one, four of the five children succumbed to the contagion of fear-suspicion-and-delusion. Only Sen, 19, the eldest son of Mr. Wang, held out. It is interesting that Sen was a rigid, rebellious youth, a poor student, and not as bright as his siblings. Long, the timid and obedient 10-year-old, was the first to accept the family delusions. He found some candy on the street, ate it, and became ill. Father and son then decided that the "enemy" had poisoned them. Half-sisters Mei, 13, and Hwei, 15, followed suit within a month. They decided that strangers were talking about them and making fun of them. At their father's order, both girls quit school. Ten, the 17-year-old boy, was allowed to stay in school because his father believed he could cope with the "enemy." Ten, intelligent and curious, fond of arguing and desirous of power, had even anticipated his father's conclusion that communists were the persecutors. Eventually, even the rebellious Sen yielded to pressure and quit school. Four young persons were now home every day, cut off from companions. Daily the family discussed the "enemy," watched for "suspicious-acting" persons, believed the water was poisoned, and quarreled with the neighbors.

Mrs. Chong, the only adult born in Taiwan, formerly had agreed with her husband that all things conspired against him. However, listening to repeated stories of persecution, she began to be skeptical. At this point, her husband asked her to give up her job and live with him and the brother-in-law's family to fight against the enemy; she flatly refused. Mr. Chong then believed that even his own wife was being persuaded to side with the enemy. The next move was dramatic. Mr. Chong, Mr. and Mrs. Wang, and the children all went to the President's residence to seek protection against their "enemies." This brought the paranoid family to psychiatric attention.

The case meets almost classically the diagnostic criteria for psychosis of association: evidence that participants are in close contact; that the delusional content of everyone concerned is similar; that the partners support, accept, and share each other's paranoid ideas. Besides the paranoid personality trait which the individual members had in common, there existed a family dynamic which led to the occurrence of such a paranoid family situation. For a family to have so many stepchildren as the result of many divorces and subsequent remarriages is very unusual among Chinese. Thus, under the reality stress of unemployment, the burglary, and sickness, a crisis for this family occurred which necessitated externalization of their anger. Above all, the environment was the most crucial factor for the development of such a group-shared, political-persecutory delusion. The sociopolitical situation in Taiwan at that time made it easy to label the enemy "communists." Such an invisible enemy was so available, plausible, and probable that anyone might easily believe in it and so succumb to a paranoid endemic mental disorder.

A BRIEF COLLECTION OF OTHER EXAMPLES

A review of the literature indicates that, in the past decades, Western society has had its share of epidemic or endemic mental disorders. Some of these deserve a brief review.

The case of the "phantom anesthetist" of Mattoon, Illinois, was described by Johnson (1945). A woman alleged that both she and her daughter were gassed and attacked by an intruder. The local newspaper played up the story, and within two weeks 29 women claimed similar attacks. Police failed to find any evidence, and medical examination of the women revealed that they were all cases of hysteria.

Schuler and Parenton (1943) reported an epidemic situation in Bellevue, Louisiana, involving a group of high school girls. The authors stressed the academic prominence of the coeducational school and the intelligence and achievement of the students involved. A few days before the onset, the school had converted physical education classes into classes to teach social dancing. The outbreak started with one of the most popular and prominent girls in the senior class. However, she did not dance well. At the school's homecoming dance, she merely watched the others. It was then she suddenly developed a nervous twitching and jerking in her legs. The spasmodic twitching recurred occasionally at school during the next several weeks. Three weeks later, two other girls developed similar symptoms. After several days, more girls followed suit. The investigator interpreted the first case as a somatic expression of avoiding the stress of trying to dance. The other girls may have unconsciously identified with the first girl and, as a result, developed the same symptoms.

In 1958, Taylor and Hunter gave an account of an hysterical epidemic in a hospital ward of female neurotic patients. The epidemic generated from the fears and nightmares of one woman who felt her professional future would be jeopardized by motherhood. Discussions of childbirth circulated the ward for three weeks. Then several patients demonstrated hysterical behavior resembling birth and rebirth experiences. The women took turns "giving birth" and "being born." Other patients who were not a part of the "birth experience" had strong emotional reactions to this; they suspected the first group of being lesbians and of having homosexual relationships in the ward. The authors speculated that the essence of such mental epidemics often lies in group emotions and close emotional attachments.

In 1965, overbreathing became epidemic among girls at a secondary school at Blackburn, England. The episode began after 20 girls fainted during a ceremony which kept the entire student body standing for three hours. (A polio outbreak had happened just the year before; fear quickly swept the community.) The students' discussions of the faintings and dizzy feelings promoted a massive outbreak of complaints. The very next day, 85 girls were sent by ambulance to the hospital. Before the episode ended, approximately a third of the 550 girls enrolled had been affected (Moss and McEvedy, 1966).

GENERAL VIEW

Because most epidemic mental disorders manifest themselves as mass hysteria, the term "mass hysteria" has been mistakenly used as being synonymous with any epidemic mental disorder. Yet, strictly speaking, emotional disorders can become epidemic in many other forms. Examples (some previously described) indicate this. There have been: group panic with the fear of sexual impotence (Ngui, 1969); hysterical attribution of accidental cuts or bleeding scratches to a razor-wielding "slasher" (Jacobs, 1965); the Illinois cases who believed they were being gassed by a "phantom anesthetist" (Johnson, 1945); collective delusions (Medalia and Larsen, 1958); epidemic depressions (Ikeda, 1966) or suicides (Anonymous, 1977); psychosomatic disorders, such as skin rash and irritation (Barnes, 1972; Levine et al., 1974); and even group behavior disorders, such as an outbreak of connected arson episodes (Boling and Brotman, 1975).

As for epidemic hysteria itself, Sirois (1974) found 78 episodes of outbreaks in the world literature during one hundred years (1872–1972). Probably many episodes were not reported. At any rate, it is fair to say that the disorder is not a rare phenomenon. According to Teoh et al. (1975), 29 episodes involving school students were reported between 1962 and 1971 in Malaysia. This indicates that epidemic hysteria may occur as frequent phenomena in certain areas predisposed by cultural conditions and their influence on personality development and character formation.

Most contemporary episodes seem to take place in an institutional setting, such as a school, factory, or hospital, in which a group of people are interrelated and associated in a very special manner, rather than in a group or crowd with no special affiliation. In most outbreaks of hysteria, those affected are predominantly young females (Sirois, 1974), although some forms of disorder, such as *koro*, or impotence panic, by definition involve only men.

The first person affected in an outbreak usually has an ordinary onset of mental disorder. Soon others manifest similar symptoms; eventually a large-scale incidence is triggered. Occasionally, the initial sufferer has special status in the group and thus functions as a model of identification for others (Taylor and Hunter, 1958). Sometimes a special event that attracts attention, especially one imbued with shock and horror, kindles a kind of emotional storm which precipitates subsequent episodes. Such events have included the accidental shooting of a boy by another (Helvie, 1968) and the physical assault of a nurse by a patient (Ikeda, 1966). A more important condition seems to be the presence of some preexisting stress or group apprehension caused by a variety of sources, e.g., an authority-submission conflict (Teoh et al., 1975), academic or achievement stress (Muhangi, 1973), or fear of enemy infiltration (Suwanlert, 1977). In other words, some unusual tension, fear, or anger among the group becomes a fertile ground for such outbreaks.

Certainly tension and fear existed in the United States on the 1938 evening when an estimated one million persons believed Martian monsters would destroy them. The precipitant was the previously described radio drama which presented an invasion from Mars as a here-and-now reality. The background for massive panic had been building for some time. Depression still hung over the land. Unemployment blighted lives. Fascism and communism were feared. Science was a mystery, especially to those who were frightened. (A CBS survey found that half as many people with college degrees, as compared to those with grammar school education, believed the broadcast was a true news report.) The stage had been set for panic; more immediate events pulled the curtain. Only two weeks before, news of the European war crisis had filled the airwaves; news bulletins interrupted radio programs at any time (Cantril, 1940). This technique was used on the *War of the Worlds* broadcast. The interrupted program and fears of war were, perhaps, linked in the minds of many listeners.

Without this existing climate of fear, the "invasion from Mars" might have been just another interesting radio program. For when persons grouped together are essentially free of such preexisting states, one individual can publicly exhibit hysteria, and the others will remain calm. The group has a higher resistance to emotional upsets. Each individual's stability contributes to group stability. But when the group shares, for the most part, disquieting emotions, group resistance to seeing (or hearing about) mental disorder is already weakened. This group is ready to accept hysteria; this group is prepared to decompensate.

From a sociological point of view, several mechanisms—including group influence, social isolation, or crowd response—should be considered in group contagion (Kerckhoff and Back, 1965). Investigators hypothesize that the group involved is an in-group (Chew et al., 1976), or is socially isolated from others (Ikeda, 1966), so that its members maintain a particular cohesiveness and identification in which they readily share, transmit, and react to the stress in a collective manner. Today, mass communication by newspaper, radio, and especially television, may facilitate the rapid spreading of information and help create an atmosphere of excitement, frenzy, or fear. In this way, a whole community may become very quickly and deeply involved (Johnson, 1945). However, it is important to note that the precipitating ideas, beliefs, or false beliefs (delusions) transmitted or shared by members of the group must seem so true and/or familiar that the group readily accepts or adopts them without hesitation. Group members then transform these ideas into conflicts to which they are already vulnerable, or which are latent in them. Conflicts are then expressed as disabling symptoms. It does not matter whether the information concerns a "scientific" explanation, such as a gas intoxication or radiation from H-bomb tests as the cause of "pitting marks" on car windshields (Medalia and Larsen, 1958), or a supernatural explanation, such as obeying the spirits of dead ancestors as the cause of agitated behavior (Ebrahim, 1968); the important factor is that the reaction is expressed within a social experience to which men respond and collectively react.

From a dynamic point of view, the occurrence of such epidemics may serve as a coping defense that helps the group deal with problems they are facing. The epidemic may develop as a "group protest" against authority, as in the case of girl students angered by the rumor that school officials would force them to submit to pregnancy tests to check for sexual promiscuity (Knight et al., 1965). The epidemic may provide a channel to express a complaint when no other alternative exists (Adomakoh, 1973). However, it may also be merely a collective reaction to the emotional frustration (helplessness) of losing a school football game (Levine, 1977).

When any collective mental disorder begins or threatens, it is important to establish a diagnosis quickly so that an organic cause, such as infection or intoxication, can be ruled out. When the nature of an epidemic occurrence is expressed in psychological manifestations, an explanation of the real cause should be given publicly as soon as possible. This will lessen the panic atmosphere which usually occurs as a response to alarming phenomena. Public attention to the first case should be kept to a minimum to reduce subsequent outbreaks.

So far, the psychometric study of individual victims has not contributed much to our understanding of the causes of epidemics. Unfortunately, many investigators are concerned only about the demographic description of the occurrence; few have investigated the sociopsychological and cultural aspects of such phenomena. These aspects demand additional study.

REFERENCES

Adomakoh, C. G.: The pattern of epidemic hysteria in a girls' school in Ghana. *Ghana Med. J.*, 12:407–411, 1973.

Anonymous: A suicide epidemic in a psychiatric hospital. *Diseases of the Nervous System*, 38:327–331, 1977.

Barnes, R.: An unusual "epidemic" in a clothing factory. *Society of Occupational Medicine Transactions*, 22:137–139, 1972.

Boling, L. and Brotman, C.: A fire setting epidemic in a state mental health center. *Am. J. Psychiatry*, 132:946–950, 1975.

Cantril, H.: *The Invasion from Mars: A Study in the Psychology of Panic.* Princeton: Princeton University Press, 1940.
Chew, P. K., Phoon, W. H., and Mae-Lim, H. A.: Epidemic hysteria among some factory workers in Singapore. *Singapore Med. J.,* 17:10–15, 1976.
Ebrahim, G. J.: Mass hysteria in school children. Notes on three outbreaks in East Africa. *Clin. Pediatr.,* 7:437–448, 1968.
Helvie, C. O.: An epidemic of hysteria in a high school. *J. Sch. Health,* 38:505–509, 1968.
Ikeda, Y.: An epidemic of emotional disturbance among leprosarium nurses in a setting of low morale and social change. *Psychiatry,* 23:152–164, 1966.
Ivanova, A.: *The Dance in Spain.* New York: Praeger Publishers, 1970.
Jacobs, N.: The phantom slasher of Taipei: Mass hysteria in a non-Western society. *Social Problems,* 12:318–328, 1965.
Johnson, D. M.: The "phantom anesthetist" of Mattoon: A field study of mass hysteria. *Journal of Abnormal and Social Psychology,* 40:175–186, 1945.
Kagwa, B. H.: The problem of mass hysteria in East Africa. *East Afr. Med. J.,* 41:560–565, 1964.
Kerckhoff, A. C. and Back, K. W.: Sociometric patterns in hysterical contagion. *Sociometry,* 28:2–15, 1965.
Knight, J. A., Friedman, T. I., and Sulianti, J.: Epidemic hysteria. A field study. *Am. J. Public Health,* 55:858–865, 1965.
Levine, R. J., Sexton, D. J., and Romm, F. J.: Outbreak of psychosomatic illness at a rural elementary school. *Lancet,* 2:1500–1503, 1974.
Levine, R. J.: Epidemic faintness and syncope in a school marching band. *J. A. M. A.,* 238: 2373–2378, 1977.
Medalia, N. Z. and Larsen, O. N.: Diffusion and belief in a collective delusion: The Seattle windshield pitting epidemic. *Am. Sociol. Rev.,* 23:180–186, 1958.
Moss, P. D. and McEvedy, C. P.: An epidemic of overbreathing among school girls. *Br. Med. J.,* 2:1295–1300, 1966.
Muhangi, J. R.: A preliminary report on "mass hysteria" in an Akole school in Uganda, *East Afr. Med. J.,* 50:304–309, 1973.
Murphy, H. B. M.: Cultural factors in the mental health of Malayan students. In: *The Student and Mental Health: An International View.* D. M. Funkenstein (Ed.), Cambridge: Mass Riverside Press, 1959.
Nemiah, J. C.: Hysterical neurosis, conversion type. In: *Comprehensive Textbook of Psychiatry-II, Vol. 1.* A. M. Freedman, H. I. Kaplan, and B. J. Sadock (Eds.), Baltimore, Maryland: Williams and Wilkins, 1975.
Ngui, P. W.: The koro epidemic in Singapore. *Aust. N. Z. J. Psychiatry* Special Issue II, on Anxiety, 3:263–266, 1969.
Rankin, A. M. and Philip, P. J.: An epidemic of laughing in the Bukoba District of Tanganyika. *Transcultural Psychiatric Research Review,* 2:128, 1963.
Robbins, R. H.: *The Encyclopedia of Witchcraft and Demonology.* New York: Crown Publishers, 1959.
Schuler, E. A. and Parenton. V. J.: A recent epidemic of hysteria in a Louisiana high school *J. Soc. Psychol.,* 17:221–235, 1943.
Sirois, F.: Epidemic hysteria. *Acta Psychiatr. Scand. (Suppl.),* 252:1–46, 1974.
Suwanlert, S.: Personal communication, 1977.
Tan, E. S.: Epidemic hysteria. *Med. J. Malaya,* 28:72–76, 1963.
Taylor, F. K. and Hunter, R. C. A.: Observation of a hysterical epidemic in a hospital ward. *Psychiatric Quarterly,* 32:821–839, 1958.
Teoh, J. I., Soewondo, S., and Sidharta, M.: Epidemic hysteria in Malaysian schools: An illustrative episode. *Psychiatry,* 38:258–268, 1975.
The Standard Jewish Encyclopedia. C. Roth (Ed.), Garden City, New York: Doubleday, 1962.
Tseng, W. S.: A paranoid family in Taiwan: A dynamic study of *folie à famille. Arch. Gen. Psychiat.,* 21:55–65, 1969.

CHAPTER 6

Alcohol-related Problems

Good ale is meat, drink, and cloth.
Drunkenness is nothing but voluntary madness.
Drink wine, and let water go to the mill.
Drink and carouse; you live but once.
Drunkenness is an egg from which all vices are hatched.

So, throughout centuries and in many countries, folk sayings have expressed man's divergent attitudes towards drinking, his attempts to understand excessive drinking ("the drunkard is afflicted," went an old English proverb), and his awareness of addiction ("he who has drunk will drink," said the French). There have been early legal attempts to control alcohol abuse. In the England of Queen Anne's reign, *whetters* ("people . . . who drink themselves into an intermediate state of being neither drunk nor sober") were forbidden "to give or endorse any note or execute any point of commerce after the third half pint before the hour of one" (Ashton, 1968). Korea prohibited wine between 1726 and 1775. In wealthy circles in Florence of the early 1700s, snobbishness cut down on alcohol as "parties became more sober since sherbet and lemonade replaced wine, which was much cheaper" (Cochrane, 1973). In other places and eras, alcohol consumption increased. In ancient Greece, the "earliest wine . . . usually mixed with 20 parts water, in Pliny's time [was mixed with] only eight parts of water (Brewer, 1891). There has always been the attempt to avoid a hangover. England's antidote in about 1710 was "the essence of prunes . . . [which] prevents any liquor from intoxicating the brain'' (Ashton, 1968).

Humans' attempts to define, understand, and control the problems of drinking in each group's particular society have continued on to the present. Today, it is more nearly possible to take a dual view of alcohol-related problems—to observe what happens outside, as well as within, our cultural boundaries. Data (still incomplete and not too reliable) give us some knowledge of alcoholism in at least the developed nations. In fact, the Alcoholism Subcommittee of the WHO Expert Committee on Mental Health (1952) has framed a general definition: ''Alcoholics are those excessive drinkers whose dependence upon alcohol has attained such a degree that it shows a noticeable mental disturbance or an interference with their bodily and mental health, their interpersonal relations, and their smooth social and economic functioning; or who show the prodromal signs of such development. They therefore require treatment.''

Yet this definition is subject to culturally dictated interpretations. What one society may perceive as an interference in functioning or a mental disturbance, another society may not. In many ways, the culture shapes drinking consumption and recognition of drinking as a problem. The rates of alcoholism among different cultural areas may vary enormously. Even the rate within a culture is not necessarily fixed; the prevalence of alcoholism may double or triple within a decade with social changes.

Jellinek (1962) gave an interesting example of cultural differences in the meaning of alcohol problems. He contrasted Finland with France. In Finland, alcoholic drinks were sold mainly in urban areas. Finnish workers from isolated camps came to town and had a few drinks. Their consumption did not suggest a ''drinking spree,'' yet they became so violent and caused such damage that the Finns considered this their alcoholism problem. (The Finns who slowly and steadily drank themselves to death did not arouse such concern.) In contrast, French drinking at that time was not a matter of addiction or occasional excesses. The French saw in their country an alcoholism without drunkenness; the problem for a large proportion of French drinkers was physical damage, such as liver cirrhosis. The cirrhosis remains a problem in France, but the drinking pattern now includes drunkenness (Associated Press, 1980).

Negrete (1973) postulated that heavy drinkers in cultures which condone a high ''social'' consumption of alcoholic beverages are less psychologically disturbed than heavy drinkers in cultures with a tradition of temperance. By studying Anglo-Protestant, Anglo-Catholic, and French-Catholic alcoholics in Montreal, Canada, the author reported that poor social functioning associated with drinking, as indicated by unemployment, marital maladjustment, and law-breaking, is not equally experienced by alcoholics belonging to these three different subcultures. He believes that cultural attitudes not only affect the social manifestations of alcoholism, but may even shape specific roles for alcoholics. The Catholic alcoholics tended to take the sick, or "incapacitated" role; the Protestants, the sociopathic one.

ANTHROPOLOGICAL INSIGHT ON DRINKING BEHAVIOR

Bales (1949) analyzed three general ways in which culture and social organization can influence rates of alcoholism. The first is the degree to which the culture brings out inner tensions and acute needs for adjustments in its members. The second comes in the attitudes towards drinking which the culture produces. The third is the degree to which the culture provides suitable means of satisfaction other than drinking. Bales distinguished four different types of attitudes represented in various cultural groups which seem to have different effects on the rates of alcoholism. They are:

A. *Complete Abstinence.* For various reasons, often religious, drinking alcohol is not allowed for any purpose. Moslems provide an outstanding example, although in practice the taboo has been unevenly observed.
B. *A Ritual Attitude.* Alcoholic beverages are used only as part of religious ceremonies. The beverage may be regarded as sacred; drinking it is a ritual act of communion with sacred powers. This is a characteristic attitude toward drinking among many aboriginal people and also among Orthodox Jews.
C. *A Convivial Attitude.* Drinking is a "social" ritual; it symbolizes social unity or solidarity and releases emotions which further social ease and good will. The American attitude toward drinking belongs to this type.
D. *A Utilitarian Attitude.* This includes drinking for medicinal reasons and drinking designed to further self-interest or gain personal satisfaction. It is often, though not necessarily, "solitary" drinking. Since there is no counter-anxiety attached, the individual is apt to adopt drinking as the means of dealing with his particular maladjustment. This attitude is most likely to lead to widespread, compulsive drinking.

Drinking has concerned, and been investigated by, many anthropologists. By utilizing anthropological profiles, Horton (1943) intensively studied the functions of alcohol in primitive societies and revealed that: a) a release of sexual and aggressive impulses accompanies drinking; b) response to drinking tends to vary in intensity in direct relationship to the level of anxiety in the society; c) the intensity of this response tends to vary inversely with the degree of counter-anxiety caused by unpleasant experiences while, or after, drinking. (The release of sexual or aggressive impulses can bring social punishment, for example, or drunkenness itself can cause physical discomfort or injury.) Horton concluded that in all primitive societies the primary function of drinking is to reduce anxieties.

Later, Field (1962) examined Horton's classic study. In this, he had the advantage of more recently developed scales of measurement. He measured the levels of six fears in these societies (fear of sorcerers, spirits, both combined, ghosts, animal spirits, and ghosts at funerals) and compared them with degrees of drunkenness. He found that variations in the level of these fears showed no relationship to drunkenness. He also confirmed Horton's observation that more drunkenness exists in tribes with very primitive hunting and gathering systems than in tribes with more advanced agricultural and herding economies. The types of societies may exert different social controls on individual conduct.

In addition, Field found that less drunkenness seemed to exist in patrilineal tribes than in matrilineal ones and that drunkenness was strikingly associated with bilateral descent. A strong relationship was shown between degree of drunkenness and the type of marital residence (and its significance in patterns of living). Well above the median of drunkenness were tribes with "bilocal" residence (newlyweds make their own decision to live either near the bridegroom's or bride's parents; the society does not decree living at either place), or "neolocal" residence (the couple lives in a new location). Here, personal decision-making, no institutionalized constraints, and the individual's and nuclear family's separation from a corporate kin structure apparently relate to the drunkenness. Also well over the median were the tribes with "uxoripatrilocal" residence (the couple lives with the bridegroom's family only after an obligatory period of residence with the bride's family). In this system, the husband is virtually "on trial" by the bride's family; he must have their permission to make the move to his family's home; his male authority is weakened, and the authority over him shifts from father to father-in-law. In contrast, the tribes in which the bride leaves her home to live near the groom's family ("patrilocal" residence) showed less drunkenness. This was thought to be linked with male dominance and more centralized family authority. However, Field advised caution in applying these conclusions on primitive drunkenness to ethnic variations in alcoholism.

EPIDEMIOLOGICAL DATA ON ALCOHOL CONSUMPTION

Unfortunately, comparing rates of alcohol drinking in various cultural areas does not give us much reliable information. It is assumed that per capita consumption is directly related to the proportion of heavy drinkers in each population. However, differences in definitions of alcoholism and in methods of estimating consumption and varied drinking patterns make epidemiological data open to inquiry. Yet the search for information must begin with some basis; we cannot wholly disregard these data.

Most data come from developed countries. WHO published a report (Moser, 1974) on per capita consumption of alcohol (as 100% ethanol) in adult (over 15 in some countries; over 18 in others) populations. Consumption was high for France (26.1), Yugoslavia (17.3), Chile (14.0), Switzerland (13.6), and Australia (13.4). Countries with relatively low consumption were Sweden (7.2), United Kingdom (6.0), Japan (5.7), Finland (5.6), and the Netherlands (4.3). Because statistical data for underdeveloped or developing countries are not available, comparison is not possible.

Adomakoh (1976) studied the African scene and reported on drinking behavior, particularly in black African countries. He found that even though drinking has always been important in traditional African social life, drinking habits and attitudes are not uniform among Africans. Some Animists and Christians, for example, are permissive; others, such as Moslems, are repressive.

Adomakoh noted other reports on Africa by German (1972), Wood (1968), and Asuni (1974). German found that alcohol addiction and resulting psychoses were extremely common in East Africa. Wood studied 1965 admissions to the mental hospital in Kampala and disclosed that, in 13% of all admissions, alcohol was an important cause of acute mental disorders. However, in Nigeria, West Africa, Asuni found that alcoholic psychoses were very rare. Evidently, problems linked with drinking vary greatly among developing countries.

ETIOLOGICAL CONSIDERATIONS

Possible racial differences in alcohol sensitivity once provided only a subject for speculation. More recently, biological investigations have been reported by Wolff (1972, 1973), Ewing et al. (1974), and Wilson et al. (1978). The investigations indicate that the Oriental tends to have more significant cardiovascular sensitivity, such as skin flushing and general discomfort, with alcohol than the Occidental. Hanna (1978) found that both Chinese and Japanese metabolized alcohol at a much higher rate than did Europeans. Possibly the low rates of alcoholism common to Oriental people have physiological rather than cultural origins.

It has also been demonstrated that American Indians have a faster rate of alcohol metabolism than Caucasians (Farris and Jones, 1978).

The pattern of physiological reactions to chemical substances, coupled with cultural sanctions on certain behavior patterns, may determine the choice of a society's intoxicant. For example, Singer (1974) has speculated that traditional Chinese culture sanctions subservient and yielding traits which determine choosing narcotics rather than alcohol.

Accessibility may help bring about alcoholism. De Lint and Schmidt (1971) supported this view with a study based on epidemiological data. They found that in France, Italy, and Portugal, countries which rank highest in the overall level of alcohol consumption and its epidemiological indicator, liver cirrhosis, alcoholic beverages are both available and inexpensive. The authors suggest that prohibiting the sale of alcohol is a way to reduce or prevent alcoholism. In fact, Poland is considering laws to close bars on pay day (Associated Press, 1980).

DRINKING PATTERNS AND PROBLEMS IN VARIOUS AREAS

Alcoholism in the United States

For the most part, the literature on alcoholism in the United States tends to focus on the drinking patterns and problems of ethnic or geographic groups. This is due to the relative ease and practicability of studying small, homogeneous populations. However, the United States includes thousands of subcultures and subgroups and so the literature on alcoholism in America can only be broad and general.

Cahalan and Cisin (1976) give the most detailed overview of drinking behavior and problems in the United States. They conclude that the Americans most likely to be drinkers are: men under 45 years of age; men and women of higher social status; professional, business, and other white collar workers; college graduates; single men; residents of the Middle Atlantic, New England, East North Central, and Pacific regions; residents of smaller cities; residents of towns; Americans whose fathers were born in Ireland or Italy; and Jews and Episcopalians.

Cahalan and Cisin define relatively heavy drinkers as those who drink nearly every day, with five or more drinks on each occasion at least once in a while, or those who drink about once a week, usually with five or more drinks each time. Among drinkers, they listed those most likely to drink heavily as: men aged 45–49; people of lower social status; operatives and service workers; men who have completed high school, but not college; single, divorced, or separated men and women; residents of the Middle Atlantic, New England, and the Pacific regions; residents of the larger cities; Americans whose fathers were born in Ireland, Latin America, the Caribbean, or the United

Kingdom; Protestants of no specific denomination; Catholics; and people without religious affiliation. (The Latin-American or Caribbean descent groups included a high proportion of abstainers as well as a high proportion of heavy drinkers.)

Falk (1970) states that the excessive use of alcohol in the United States is not so much a disease as it is a social condition promoted by cultural and economic pressures which tend to reward heavy social drinking.

Alcohol and Native Americans

Although there is general agreement that alcohol has a disruptive effect on North American Indians, a review of the literature shows that there is yet no understanding of why this problem exists. Yet unknown are whether or not these native Americans see alcoholism as a problem in their own communities, and what approach would be the most effective in treating their heavy drinkers.

Brod (1975) believes that the ambiguity in our understanding is due to several factors. We do not know to what extent problems of Indians are related to alcohol. We do not have a reliable idea of alcoholism incidence among these people. We do not have a consistent definition of alcoholism or an objective way of diagnosing alcoholism, especially cross-culturally. Finally, we do not have the information to determine whether motives for heavy drinking and subsequent "drunk Indian" behavior are pathological.

Brod cites studies documenting several phenomena. The alcohol-related arrest rate for Indians is 12 times the national average; Indians display more severe withdrawal symptoms than other groups; and the alcoholism death rate for Indians is 4.3 to 5.5 times the U.S. all-races rate.

Many studies, including that of Dailey (1968), note the traditional use of hallucinogens and other intoxicants in the spiritual ceremonies of native Americans. Westermeyer (1972) reports that Chippewa Indians in Minnesota recognize and practice two types of drinking which they themselves call "white" (drinking with restrained behavior, usually among whites) and "Indian" (drinking which, after one or two drinks, results in noisy, "drunken" behavior and often proceeds to fighting, "crying jags," or stupor). "Indian" drinking, Westermeyer wrote, is an accepted, expected way to maintain in-group relationships and tribal or family loyalties. The Chippewa, who must ordinarily behave according to majority white mores, can restate his Chippewa values by "Indian" drinking.

Brod (1975) and Whittaker (1963) agree that two influential factors place Indians in a state of transition. They are the stress of deculturation as the historic culture is lost, and the stress of acculturation as Indians integrate with the dominant American culture. Alcohol is commonly used as a buffer by groups undergoing this transition.

Attempts to control alcohol use among American Indians have led to some interesting conclusions. Kunitz and Levy (1974) believe that attitudes are changing in Navajo communities where native, paraprofessional educators emphasize the disadvantages of alcohol as understood by the majority American society. The authors feel that, as heavy drinking is seen as dangerous and inappropriate, communities will themselves exert pressures that modify drinking.

Latin America

Negrete (1976), who extensively reviewed alcoholism in Latin America, defines Latin America as the part of the Americas that extends from Mexico south to the Antarctic, a region including 21 independent nations demographically and socio-characteristically classified as developing countries.

According to him, Latin American drinking customs are, in general, exceedingly liberal. All kinds of stores and public places sell alcoholic beverages. The culture not only tolerates heavy drinking, but also promotes it. Festive occasions are characterized by drinking, and drunkenness is common. Cultural pressure to drink is particularly directed at men. In some areas, heavy drinking is considered a sign of virility, and men who can "hold their liquor" enjoy a certain prestige.

Negrete notes direct field inquiries that revealed that 23.2 per 100 adults in Argentina—nearly one-fourth of the adult population—are problem drinkers, as are 12.9 in Chile, and 10.3 in Brazil. "Adult" is 21-plus in the United States; 15-plus in Latin America. If age difference is adjusted, the Latin American figures correlate closely with the 31.5 figure for the United States. However, the average of the three Latin American studies showed 10.4 males to every one female problem drinker, while the United States has a five male to one female ratio, or twice as many women problem drinkers. The women of Latin America do not tend to be problem drinkers as much as their United States counterparts do.

Figures for mortality with alcohol-related causes in some Latin American countries are among the highest in the world. Countries with larger urban-industrial centers (Chile, Argentina, and Mexico) have rates for deaths from alcohol-linked external causes (accidents, homicides, violence) that are much higher than those for the United States and Canada. Argentina and Chile have the highest per capita alcohol consumption in Latin America; all three Latin American countries also have high incidence of liver cirrhosis, highway and non-vehicular accidents, suicide, and violent behavior.

Marital breakdowns due to alcohol are far less frequent in Latin America than they are in other cultures, Negrete writes. Spouses and other relatives seem to have greater tolerance for the problem drinker, even though he may neglect his family and behave violently. The Catholic faith, with its disapproval of divorce and prohibition of subsequent remarriage, probably keeps many alcohol-damaged unions intact.

Australia

During 1968–1969, Encel et al. (1972) conducted a survey of drinking practices and attitudes in the Sydney metropolitan area. This disclosed that 48% of the men and 15% of the women were heavy drinkers, and 19% of the men and 12% of the women were moderate-to-frequent drinkers. Drinking was shown to be widespread in the general population with heavy drinking normative behavior among men. Moon (1976) found that total alcohol consumption throughout Australia has been increasing for several decades. Per capita consumption has increased from 7.32 liters in 1949, to 11.41 liters in 1968, to 13.23 liters in 1972. In the view of Encel et al., alcoholism in Australia is a major health hazard, probably ranking just under heart disease, mental illness, and cancer.

Union of Soviet Socialist Republics

Drinking has always been a part of Russian life. Drinking specifically to get drunk has long been a cherished practice of Russian men. Yet, even within this broad framework of alcoholic tradition, time has brought changes. According to Segal (1976), alcoholism in pre-Revolutionary times was common, primarily among workers and artisans; drunkenness was limited to ritual occasions; peasants got drunk only on church holidays to celebrate the harvest and on a few specially festive days. Today, both city dwellers and farmers drink heavily; no special or ritual occasion is required. Approximately 94% of all Russians over 15 years drink; 19% are heavy drinkers, and 11.6% are alcoholics. There are 8.5 alcoholic men to every alcoholic woman.

Segal compared Russian drinking patterns to those in the United States and found both common causes and points of difference. He notes similar influences, such as urbanization, the weakening of social control and cultural taboos, adoption of positive attitudes towards drink, peer pressure, and the examples of drinking provided to adolescents. However, he finds Russian drinking is more particularly motivated by psychological characteristics of ambivalence, lack of self-confidence, and a concealed dependency need. In Soviet society, he writes, there is little opportunity for self-realization or creativity. A spiritual wasteland exists for many Russians. Traditional religious-ethical beliefs are gone; Communist ideology is seen through disillusioned eyes. Drinking, once essentially a social ritual, is now a release. An almost totally permissive attitude towards drinking to get thoroughly drunk makes this release quickly and easily attainable.

Italy

In Italy, drinking wine with meals is taken for granted. The average Italian lives most of his life with a certain amount of alcohol in his body, yet he is not often, nor seriously, drunk. Even the Italian who, at times, may show signs of intoxication is not considered to be an alcoholic. Drinking is, and always has been, a part of Italian culture. Acceptance of the wine-with-food kind of drinking is complete. Attitudes are also tolerant towards alcoholism, a condition recognized in Rome before the time of Christ.

Yet Bonfiglio et al. (1977) find that this traditional Mediterranean wine drinking is now being overshadowed by alcoholism of the Northern European and Anglo-Saxon type. Drinking wine (sometimes even diluted with water) is being supplemented (or replaced) by drinking hard liquor. In the 30 years between 1941 and 1972, Italy's wine consumption has increased almost 100 percent, beer consumption has increased by more than 600 percent, and drinking spirits has jumped by approximately 700 percent. During this same period, deaths from cirrhosis of the liver increased from 9.32 per 100,000 to 29.90. Italy, Bonfiglio and his colleagues believe, has a problem of vast proportions that has not yet been given the attention it demands.

France

In neighboring France, drinking patterns have also changed in recent years. Twenty years ago, alcoholic intake was 95% wine. Today wine accounts for only 6% of total consumption; whiskey, vodka, and gin consumption has doubled in a decade, and beer drinking has risen. Today, *la défonce du samedi soir,* "the Saturday night bender," drinking oneself into a stupor on hard liquor, has entered the French way of life. Government statistics state that alcohol kills 55 persons each day (Associated Press, 1980).

Jews Outside the United States

Jews have always enjoyed a reputation for sobriety. Two investigators within the last decade have studied the exceptions, Jewish alcoholics. We summarize their findings here:

When Schmidt and Popham (1976) looked for the exceptions in Toronto, Canada, they searched the ten-year records of two alcoholism treatment centers—one private and one public. From 6,000 admissions, they found only 29 Jewish patients listed. Jews make up 6% of Toronto adults, but they represented only 0.5% of alcoholic cases in the two centers. The very rarity of the exception supports, if not proves, the premise that Jews remain sober.

The authors had surmised that, because of strong Jewish views against drunkenness, only very vulnerable, unstable Jews would be alcoholics. When they studied the case records, they found "anxiety," "anxiety state," and "anxious" were the terms most often used. They noted three different modes of adjustment. Patients with an Orthodox background denied they were alcoholic. Patients who accepted the alcoholism diagnosis denied their Jewishness and identified with non-Jewish social values and institutions. Three patients disagreed with the widely held view on Jewish sobriety and argued that Jewish drunkenness was common.

Hes (1970) studied drinking habits of Yemenite Jewish immigrants in a rural settlement in Israel. Of 57 heads of households, 30—more than half—were heavy drinkers. The finding does not disprove Jewish sobriety; it does shed some light on contrasting drinking patterns among various groups of Jews, for Hes points out that, even in their native Yemen, the group studied had been considered unusual. Other, especially urban, Jews in Yemen had castigated these regional Yemenites as being rough, uncultured, and aggressive.

Japan

In Japan, the small bottle of *sake* has long accompanied the festivity of weddings and the gravity of mourning. Social drinking is a Japanese tradition, but drinking as a real problem is a post-World-War-II development. Before the war, per capita consumption was 2.3 liters of absolute alcohol; in 1969, it had increased to 4.3 liters (Yamamuro, 1973). In 1963, Japanese alcoholism incidence was estimated roughly at 3% of the population (Moore, 1964).

Chinese in Various Areas

The use of alcohol in China is as old as her history. Drinking, in the past and the present, is limited to certain occasions. It accompanies ceremonies and enlivens social occasions. Toasts and drinking games are a part of banquets. Men are encouraged to drink at these parties; women often quietly pour tea in their small cups and pretend to drink alcoholic toasts. The sociability of drinking at the proper time and place is valued; drunkenness is an embarrassment for a man, disgrace for a woman. The incidence of chronic alcoholism is low, and alcoholism as a social problem is relatively unimportant in mainland China (LaBarre, 1946), in Taiwan (Lin, 1953), and in Hong Kong (Singer and Wong, 1973).

A similar drinking pattern exists among overseas Chinese in the United States (Wang, 1968; Chu, 1972). It is interesting that, according to Singer and Wong (1973), Chinese alcoholics in Hong Kong showed certain differences from their Western counterparts. The Chinese were more introverted and neurotic, and less aggressive in terms of violent tendencies or crimes of drunkenness.

The Meo of Laos

Westermeyer (1971) studied the Meo people of Laos and found that they distill a strong whiskey from rice or corn mash. Each household makes its own supply; alcohol is readily available. However, social custom regulates where and when it is drunk. Every adult must drink at specific times and in specified amounts according to age, sex, and social role. Drinking takes place at festivals of the New Year, weddings, and the rice harvest, for example, and at animal sacrifices and funerals. As a result of these social regulations and constraints, non-sanctioned drinking and alcoholism in the usual sense do not occur among the Meo.

Micronesia

When the inhabitants of Micronesia first tasted alcoholic beverages is not known. Certainly they witnessed drinking through centuries of Spanish, German, and Japanese rule. Micronesians, however, had little need for intoxicating drinks. Their traditional drink, originally restricted to feasts and ceremonial occasions, was *kapa,* or *sakao,* made from the roots of the *Sakau* plant *(Piper methysticum).* This acts on the central nervous system, inducing passivity; the *kapa* drinker does not become aggressive. Yet at some time, Micronesians learned to distill an alcoholic drink from the milk that oozes from a cut coconut flower stalk. This is called "toddy" or "tuba," and possibly other regional names. Its alcoholic content varies. One Micronesian writes that some persons need a half-gallon to get drunk; others only two cups (*Some Things of Value,* 1975).

When Germany gained control of Micronesia, making "toddy" was prohibited to safeguard the coconut industry. Evidently, some Micronesians were also drinking imported alcohol, for the Germans also prohibited this. The Japanese continued the prohibition and forbade drinking any liquor with more than 3% alcohol (Yanaihara, 1940). Yanaihara writes that this was to "protect the native population" from the health hazards of "foreign liquors." Drinking as a problem seems to have emerged after World War II, when many young men began to drink beer and hard liquor. Usually, drinking was done at public bars, during weekends, or on pay day. Characteristically, many men would get drunk quickly, and quarrels and fighting followed. As a result, in Truk, Caroline Islands, the people voted in 1978 to stop the importation of alcohol. As a personal informant from Micronesia reports, drinking of home-distilled liquors continues among some men, but this is done quietly in private homes to avoid legal punishments. Violence in public and injuries related to drunkenness have shown a marked decline in Truk. In at least this one island society, sociopolitical policy worked towards the solution of an alcohol problem.

SUMMARY COMMENT

Though alcohol problems are substance-induced and sometimes physiologically influenced, they are more closely linked with culture. It is the society that shapes the pressures to drink or to abstain, that suggests or even dictates the occasions for drinking, and, to an extent, the choice and volume of alcohol ingested. A whole complex of social changes, tensions, pressures, examples, and attitudes influence the sex and age of those allowed to drink (the pre-teenage alcoholic was virtually unknown in the United States a few decades ago). So, too, does the society define and recognize alcoholism as a problem, or a "sin," or a disease, or merely a condition of little importance. Individual factors, both physiological and psychological, cannot be disregarded. Yet, in general, alcohol-associated problems are best considered a socioculturally related disorder and should be approached from a sociocultural point of view.

REFERENCES

Adomakoh, C. C.: Alcoholism: The African scene. *Annals of the New York Academy of Science,* 273:39–46, 1976.

Ashton, J.: *Social Life in the Region of Queen Anne.* London: Chatto and Widnus, 1968.

Associated Press: Alcohol is killing 55 drink-loving Frenchmen a Day, by Marcus Eliason. *Honolulu Star-Bulletin.* April 17, 1980.

Asuni, T.: *Pattern of Alcohol Problems as Seen in the Neuro-Psychiatric Hospital, Aro, Abeokuta 1963–1973.* Association of Psychiatrists in Africa, Workshop. Nairobi, Kenya. International Council on Alcohol and Addictions. Lausanne, Switzerland, 1974.

Bales, R. F.: Cultural differences in rates of alcoholism. *Q. J. Stud. Alcohol,* 6:480–499, 1949.

Bonfiglio, G., Falli, S., and Pacini, A.: Alcoholism in Italy: An outline highlighting some special features. *Br. J. Addict.,* 72:3–12, 1977.

Brewer, E. C.: *The Historic Notebook.* Philadelphia: J. B. Lippincott, Co., 1891.

Brod, T. M.: Alcoholism as a mental health problem of Native Americans. A review of the literature. *Arch. Gen. Psychiatry,* 32:1385–1391, 1975.

Cahalan, D. and Cisin, I. H.: Drinking behavior and drinking problems in the United States. In: *Social Aspects of Alcoholism (Vol. 4 of the Biology of Alcoholism).* B. Kissin and H. Begleiter (Eds.), New York: Plenum Press, 1976.

Chu, G.: Drinking patterns and attitudes of rooming-house Chinese in San Francisco. *Q. J. Stud. Alcohol,* Supplement 6, 58–68, 1972.

Cochrane, E.: *Florence in the Forgotten Centuries (1527–1800).* Chicago: University of Chicago Press, 1973.

Dailey, R. C.: The role of alcohol among North American Indian tribes as reported in the Jesuit relations. *Anthropologica,* 10:45–57, 1968.

De Lint, J. and Schmidt, W.: Consumption averages and alcoholism prevalence: A brief review of epidemiological investigations. *Br. J. Addict.,* 66:99–107, 1971.

Encel, S., Kolowicz, K. C., and Resler, H. E.: Drinking patterns in Sydney. *Q. J. Stud. Alcohol,* Supplement 6, 1–27, 1972.

Ewing, J., Rouse, B. A., and Pellizzari, E. D.: Alcohol sensitivity and ethnic background. *Am. J. Psychiatry,* 131:206–210, 1974.

Falk, G.: The contribution of the alcohol culture to alcoholism in America. *Br. J. Addict.,* 65:9–17, 1970.

Farris, J. J. and Jones, B. M.: Ethanol metabolism in male American Indians and whites. *Alcoholism: Clinical and Experimental Research,* 2:77–81, 1978.

Field, P. B.: A new cross-cultural study of drunkenness. In: *Society, Culture, and Drinking Patterns.* D. J. Pittman and C. R. Snyder (Eds.), New York: John Wiley and Sons, 1962.

German, A.: Aspects of clinical psychiatry in Sub-Saharan Africa. *Br. J. Psychiatry,* 121:461–479, 1972.

Hanna, J. M.: Metabolic responses of Chinese, Japanese and Europeans to alcohol. *Alcoholism: Clinical and Experimental Research,* 2:89–92, 1978.

Hes, J. P.: Drinking in a Yemenite rural settlement in Israel. *Br. J. Addict.,* 65:293–296, 1970.

Horton, D.: The functions of alcohol on primitive societies: A cross-cultural study. *Q. J. Stud. Alcohol,* 4:199–320, 1943.

Jellinek, E. M.: Cultural differences in the meaning of alcoholism. In: *Society, Culture and Drinking Patterns.* D. J. Pittman and C. R. Snyder (Eds.), New York: John Wiley and Sons, 1962.

Kunitz, S. and Levy, J. E.: Changing ideas of alcohol use among Navaho Indians. *Q. J. Stud. Alcohol,* 35:243–259, 1974.

LaBarre, W.: Some observations on character structure in the Orient. II. The Chinese, Parts I and II. *Psychiatry,* 9:215–237 and 375–395, 1946.

Lin, T. Y.: A study of the incidence of mental disorder in Chinese and other cultures. *Psychiatry,* 16:313–336, 1953.

Moon, J. R.: Alcoholism in Australia in 1975. *Annals of the New York Academy of Science,* 273:47–77, 1976.

Moore, R. A.: Alcoholism in Japan. *Q. J. Stud. Alcohol,* 25:142–150, 1964.

Moser, J.: *Problems and Programmes Related to Alcohol and Drug Dependence in 33 countries.* Geneva: World Health Organization, Offset Publication No. 6, 1974.

Negrete, J. C.: Culture influences on social performance of alcoholics: A comparative study. *Q. J. Stud. Alcohol,* 34:905–916, 1973.

Negrete, J. G.: Alcoholism in Latin America. *Annals of the New York Academy of Science,* 273:653–658, 1976.

Schmidt, W. and Popham, R. E.: Impression of Jewish alcoholics. *J. Stud. Alcohol,* 37:931–939, 1976.

Segal, B. M.: Drinking patterns and alcoholism in Soviet and American societies: A multidisciplinary comparison. In: *Psychiatry and Psychology in the USSR.* S. A. Corson and E. D. Corson (Eds.), New York: Plenum Press, 1976.

Singer, K. and Wong, M.: Alcoholic psychoses and alcoholism in the Chinese. *Q. J. Stud. Alcohol,* 34:878–886, 1973.

Singer, K.: The choice of intoxicant among the Chinese. *Br. J. Addict.,* 69:257–268, 1974.

Some Things of Value: Micronesian Customs as Seen by Micronesians. G. Ashley (Ed.), Saipan: Education Department, Trust Territory of the Pacific Islands, 1975.

Wang, R. P.: A study of alcoholism in Chinatown. *Int. J. Soc. Psychiatry,* 14:260–267, 1968.

Westermeyer, J.: Use of alcohol and opium by the Meo of Laos. *Am. J. Psychiatry,* 127:1019–1023, 1971.

Westermeyer, J.: Chippewa and majority alcoholism in the Twin Cities: A comparison. *J. Nerv. Ment. Dis.,* 155:322–327, 1972.

Whittaker, J. O.: Alcohol and the Standing Rock Sioux Tribe: Psychodynamic and cultural factors in drinking. *Q. J. Stud. Alcohol,* 24:80–90, 1963.

Wilson, J. R., McClearn, G. E., and Johnson, R. C.: Ethnic variation in use and effects of alcohol. *Drug Alcohol Depend.,* 3:147–151, 1978.

Wolff, P. H.: Ethnic differences in alcohol sensitivity. *Science,* 175:449–450, 1972.

Wolff, P. H.: Vasomotor sensitivity to alcohol in diverse mongoloid populations. *Am. J. Hum. Genet.,* 25:193–199, 1973.

Wood, J. F.: A half century of growth in Ugandan psychiatry. In: *Uganda Atlas of Disease Distribution.* Kampala, Uganda, 1968.

World Health Organization: Second Report of the *Alcoholism Subcommittee of the World Health Expert Committee on Mental Health.* WHO Technical Report Series No. 48, 1952.

Yamamuro, B.: Alcoholism in Tokyo. *Q. J. Stud. Alcohol,* 34:950–954, 1973.

Yanaihara, T.: *Pacific Islands Under Japanese Mandate.* London: Oxford University Press, 1940.

CHAPTER 7

Suicide

How, when, and for what reasons man attempts or succeeds in ending his own life are grave subjects well suited to cross-cultural comparative study, for in most societies suicide is well-defined abnormal behavior. Even the layperson can often identify a person likely to commit suicide. The study of suicidal behavior presents fewer problems of diagnostic criteria than are encountered in studying other psychiatric conditions. Furthermore, suicidal behavior, because it is predominantly related to psychological factors, can be understood as emotion-related, rather than biologically determined behavior; thus, examining the sociocultural aspects of suicide is especially important.

VARIATIONS OF FREQUENCY

The epidemiological study of suicide is affected and limited by factors usually found in any epidemiological study, such as community attitudes toward the phenomena investigated and medical and official willingness to report occurrences. Yet, if there is an adequate reporting system, it is relatively easy to obtain data which represent a fairly true picture of the occurrence of suicide in a particular society.

A study of suicide incidence in different countries gives an impression that frequency may vary widely in different places. Figures compiled by the World Health Organization in 1973 (Table 1) show that in developed countries the suicide rates per 100,000 population for the period of 1959–1969

TABLE 1

Suicide Rates of Developed Countries as Reported by WHO, 1973
(Per 100,000 Population, 1950–69)

		Period			
	Countries	50–54	55–59	60–64	65–69
1.	Japan	20.0	24.5	18.0	
	Denmark		22.0	19.2	19.2
	Germany		18.8	19.1	20.6
	Switzerland	22.1	20.9	18.0	17.8
2.	U.S.A.			10.7	10.9
	Belgium		14.2	14.2	15.0
	France		16.6	15.5	15.4
	United Kingdom	10.5	11.6	11.7	9.8
	Australia	10.2	11.3	13.4	13.7
3.	Canada	7.4	7.4	7.6	9.4
	Venezuela	4.9	5.9	5.6	6.6
	Italy			5.5	5.3
	Netherlands	6.1	6.4	6.5	6.8
	Norway			7.3	7.6
	New Zealand	9.6	9.2	8.8	9.6

were: high in Japan, Denmark, Germany, and Switzerland; moderate in the U.S.A., Belgium, France, United Kingdom, and Australia; relatively low in Canada, Venezuela, Italy, Netherlands, Norway, and New Zealand.

There is no simple way to explain why frequency in a fairly short period, is relatively fixed in one country, while the rate often varies considerably among other nations at similar levels of socioeconomic and technical development. This is particularly true for Scandinavia: Suicide rates are very high in Sweden and Denmark, but strikingly low in their neighboring country, Norway.

According to this WHO report, the *committed* suicide rate does not fluctuate dramatically within a decade in a socially economically stable country. However, according to Weissman's review (1974), in Great Britain, Australia, and the United States, the suicide *attempt* rate increased from about

60–80/100,000 to 140–180/100,000—more than twice, to nearly three times—during one decade, from 1960 to 1971, while the *committed* rate remained the same. Weissman further reported that the attempters are usually young (under 25), divorced or single females who attempted suicide primarily because of interpersonal conflicts. He speculated that in most Western countries, strong family ties and religion, which once integrated the individual within a social group, are no longer effective resources for young persons. Geographical mobility, which contributes to social isolation, and the changing roles of women may be additional factors in the increased attempts. These findings seem to support the clinical impression that committed suicide and suicide attempt have different natures, and that frequency of attempts, more than of committed suicides, changes in response to variations in sociocultural pressures. We may speculate that committed suicides are more or less associated with severe psychiatric conditions, such as psychotic depression or schizophrenia, which have predominantly endogenous determinants. These suicides are consequently less subject to fluctuation caused by external conditions. However, attempted suicides usually occur on impulse, among a young (predominantly female) population with interpersonal conflicts which reflect emotional frustrations. Consequently, attempts may fluctuate widely in association with sociocultural conditions.

Yet these general conclusions carry exceptions and question marks. Can the committed suicides of Japan, which maintain an even rate, be attributed to endogenous causes—or to cultural forces? Perhaps the most striking exception to conclusions on committed suicides comes from two regions of the Marshall Islands of Micronesia, Majuro and Ebeye. There, medical colleagues from the area report, suicide was virtually unknown until after World War II. A slight increase was noted in the next two decades, but between 1975–1980 suicides rose sharply. In five years there were 39 suicides, 12.8 per 100,000 (Rubinstein, in preparation). The suicides follow an almost identical pattern. Young men between 14 and 22 years, most of them school dropouts, become frustrated when their parents don't give them spending money. They become angry, get drunk, and kill themselves. What is the cause for such recent endemic suicides among the youth? A youth's reaction to the rapid cultural change?

In the United States suicides have recently risen sharply among young people, too. In 1968, the suicide rate among the 15–24 age group was 7.1. A decade later, it had risen to 12.7 (U.S. National Center for Health Statistics Annual Summaries). (In the same decade youth joined cults, drug abuse increased, and violence became a national problem.)

Though the WHO report gives suicide rates in developed countries, little information from newly developing or underdeveloped countries is available (Table 2). Data that are provided from any area should be carefully interpreted; community attitudes toward suicide and the sources of information, including the reporting system, may influence the statistics.

Popular belief of the past held that suicide was a product of civilization and development, and was rare in preliterate cultures (Zilboorg, 1936). More current reports show considerable variation. Some indicate that the rate of suicide is generally low among less developed cultural areas. For example, Asuni (1962) estimated that the suicide rate in Western Nigeria was extremely low, less than 1 per 100,000. According to German (1972), in 1937 Laubscher

TABLE 2

Suicide Rates of Developing and Underdeveloped Countries as Reported by Various Investigators
(Per 100,000 Population)

Areas	Period	Source of Information	Reporters	Suicide Rate
Taiwan	1960–70	Post-war Government Data	Rin (1975)	15–16.0
Hong Kong	1955	Government & Hospital Data	Yap (1958)	12.0
Thailand	1960–69	Autopsy Data	Eungprabhanth (1975)	3.52
Singapore	1971	Hospital Data	Chia & Tsoi (1974)	11.0
Kabul/Afghanistan	1955–64	Government Data	Gobar (1970)	0.25
Madurai/India	1958–62	Autopsy Data	Ganapathi & Rao (1966)	43.0
Tikopia/Western Pacific	1929–51	Field Information	Firth (1961)	37.0
Western Nigeria	1957–60	Coroner's Report	Asuni (1962)	21.0
Busoga/Uganda	1952–54	Inquest Report	Fallers & Fallers (1960)	7.0

reported an incidence of less than 1 per 100,000 among South African pagan natives. But Orley (1970) wondered whether the figures may have been underreported among African peoples, at least by the Baganda who consider suicide a terrible act. The Baganda fear the body of a suicide; burial is done in great haste, and law-enforcement agencies are too inadequate to monitor the true incidence of occurrence. Thus, the figures are somewhat suspect.

Interestingly enough, Hoskin et al. (1969) reported a high incidence in a preliterate, primitive society. They estimate from research data that the suicide rate in Southwest New Britain, New Guinea, is about 23 per 100,000 annually—nearly double the 12 per 100,000 rate for Australia or the United States. Though the New Britain society is characterized by the extended family with its adequate support, ample opportunity to express grief and loss through elaborate mourning rituals, and adequate outlets for hostility and frustrations, nevertheless, the suicide tendency is high. In their field work, Hoskin et al. found that there were few villagers who could not recall the name and the story of one or more persons who had hanged themselves. Every village had several men who could describe in detail the best way of knotting the rope. Even the children—who now go to school— were fully aware of suicide. When they were asked to write "projective tests," one out of every 12 referred to shame, and one out of eight mentioned death and suicide. The investigators commented that the ritualization, acceptability, and familiarity of the suicide option as a response to life's difficulties might be factors in the conspicuous presence of suicide.

In the United States, it is generally believed that the suicide rate is very high among American Indians, who, as a group, have lost much of their traditional life-style and have had difficulty adjusting socioculturally as a marginal group. However, Webb and Willard (1975) reviewed the available literature and found varying patterns of suicide among different American Indian groups. Though there are fewer than 5,000 Shoshone Indians, they are frequently investigated, and their suicide rate of 100 per 100,000 (ten times the U.S.A. national average) has been mistakenly attributed to all American Indian groups. Yet among the Navajos, the largest (more than 100,000) U.S. tribe, the suicide rate of 8 per 100,000 is not high. This is considerably lower than for Caucasians in the same geographical area; Arizona has a rate of 14 per 100,000 and New Mexico, a 12 per 100,000 rate. Navajo reservations are in both states. As Shore (1975) pointed out, high suicide rates among Indian tribes with a relatively small population have received widespread publicity, have been generalized to include all American Indians, and, consequently, have created the stereotype of "the suicidal Indian"; examples of lower suicide rates from larger tribes have received little or no emphasis.

METHOD OF SUICIDE

The method of suicide is relatively easy to investigate because information is usually available from hospital records and government reports, or through field work. A review of the literature indicates that methods vary greatly in different areas of the world; also revealed are certain patterns in the choice of method (though they are as subject to change as clothing fashions). For example, many investigators have reported hanging as the most frequent method of suicide in Africa. Beattie (1960) wrote that 90% of the suicides among the people in Bunyoro were committed by hanging. Fontaine (1960) noted the same tendency in Gisn (64 out of 68 cases), as did Fallers and Fallers (1960) for Busoga (96%).

Thailand shows a decided contrast. There, poisoning is the most common method (58%), with parathion usually chosen because of its wide use as an insecticide (Eungprabhanth, 1975). Ganapathi and Rao (1966) reported that in Madurai, India, 45.5% of the suicides took organophosphorus compounds after these insecticides began to be sold in there in 1958. Nalin (1973) reported a similar situation in Guyana, where, from December, 1962, through May, 1965, 68% of all fatal suicides were from malathion poisoning. The term "malathion epidemic" has even been used. Quite obviously, what is available may determine what is used. Farberow and Simon (1975), who studied suicide in Los Angeles and Vienna, found that in Vienna, 38% of the total suicide cases used domestic gas, and only 4% guns. In Los Angeles, where household gas is non-lethal, guns were used in 39% of all suicides.

Yamamoto (1974) explored Japanese-American and non-Japanese-American suicides in Los Angeles. He revealed definite correlations between ethnic-cultural background and the method used for suicide. The Japanese-American still tends to use traditional Japanese methods of hanging (38%), cutting (10.8%), and burning (2.4%); non-Japanese-Americans use barbiturates (38.8%) and guns (28.6%). Among Japanese-Americans, most of those using "Japanese" methods of suicide had Japanese first names, while the majority of those using "American" methods had American first names; acculturation seems to influence even the mode of suicide.

Firth (1961) examined suicide behavior in Tikopia, a Polynesian community in the Western Pacific, and recorded three "customary" methods which are differentiated broadly according to age and sex. The middle-aged and elderly hang themselves; women only, especially young ones, swim to open sea; men only, especially young men, put out to sea in a canoe.

As time passes and generations change in a society, suicide methods chosen may also gradually change. One example: For traditional Chinese women, hanging or drowning by jumping into a well or river was the customary method; later—at least in Taiwan—rat poison was frequently taken; recently, overdoses of sleeping pills were chosen. Hanging is still used to some extent, but drowning in a well or taking rat poison is almost unheard of now. Whitlock (1975) reviewed 1956–1973 suicide patterns in Brisbane, Australia, and reported a sharp rise in barbiturate overdosage. The same period showed a marked decline in carbon monoxide poisoning; the country had changed to non-toxic gas for domestic use.

In general, a society tends to adopt a certain preferred method or methods during a given period. Not only availability of means (weapon, rope, poison, etc.) but also familiarity with and knowledge of methods influence the decision. Within the range of available methods, the suicidal one chooses a method recognized and, in a sense, acceptable to his group or culture. The method chosen often illustrates or is determined by differences in age or sex; men tend to use more aggressive and more surely fatal methods, while women choose less aggressive though often fatal ones. In most societies, the method also reflects social custom or "fashion," even when no overt meaning is attached to the chosen procedure.

In the civilized world of high-rise apartment houses and speeding cars, two types of possible suicide are now prominent: the "fall" from an upper story to pavement below and the car "accident." Whether these deaths are suicides, homicides, or due to sudden vertigo or genuine accident is often open to question. However, the plunge to the pavement is accompanied by a suicide note or previous suicidal statements often enough to mark this method as an increasing choice in many large cities.

SUBTYPING AND CLASSIFICATION OF SUICIDE

The disciplines of cultural psychiatry, anthropology, and sociology are particularly useful in a study of suicide in different cultural settings. In these disciplines, specialists have outlined and described many variations of self-killing behavior; a review of their work provides an initial framework for an expanded classification system.

The sociologist Durkheim, back in 1897, described three basic types of suicide that stem from a man's relationship to his society:

a) *Altruistic suicide* is literally required by society as the customs or rules of the group demand suicide under certain circumstances.
b) *Egoistic suicide* occurs when an individual has too few ties with his community and fails to become integrated within the society.

c) *Anomic suicide* is undertaken when the accustomed relationship between a person and his society is suddenly shattered, either by loss of a job or a friend.

Farberow (1975) also identified two main threads of self-destruction—socially (or institutionally) influenced suicide and individual (or personal) suicide.

For further cultural-psychiatric study, a classification system that combines sociocultural and psychiatric points of view is needed. With this, psychiatry can focus on and better understand the nature of self-killing and the conditions which may influence this behavior. The broad classifications which follow are an attempt to categorize possible similarities in suicide behaviors and compare the different cultural contexts in which suicides occur.

Sociocultural Suicide

This broad category encompasses suicides which take place primarily to fulfill some group or societal function, rather than as the result of an individual emotional concern. Sociocultural suicide can be further classified as codified suicide and suicide for a social purpose.

Codified Suicide

This is predetermined, demanded, or expected by the society to fulfill a certain institutional purpose. In this obligatory self-killing, rules govern the place, the day, and the specific manner in which the suicide should take place. An individual's decision may be voluntary or virtually forced, but it is determined by a sense of responsibility to the established cultural system. Usually the person who performs such a suicide does not suffer from any psychological disorder; he acts in the predetermined situation and in the prescribed manner (Carstairs, 1956–57). An example—no longer prevalent—of codified suicide in Indian culture was *suttee,* the old Hindu custom in which a widow cremated herself upon her husband's funeral pyre. In Japanese *kamikaze* missions during World War II, many—but not all—of the pilots committed suicide in an attempt to prevent their country's defeat. However, other *kamikaze* pilots went to their deaths unwillingly; some had been shackled into their planes (Clark, 1967). Personal acquaintances knew pilots who flew around in circles until they ran out of gas and their planes crashed into the ocean. These men chose passive suicide rather than homicide-suicide (Meguro, 1966).

Suicide to Serve a Social Purpose

Without really obeying cultural dictates or being motivated by moral responsibility, a person may turn to suicide or communicate a socially significant message. Suicide of this type is usually a means to a social end. A soldier who kills himself to avoid being captured or a woman who commits suicide to "preserve her chastity" dies willingly rather than face compromise and disgrace. Others kill themselves as a reproof or ultimate protest to authority (as illustrated by the monks who burned themselves to protest against the government during the Vietnam War). In some cultures, people believe that ghosts have the power to torment and punish the living. Here, suicide as "revenge" is known (Jeffreys, 1952). The reasoning goes: "Someone has insulted or injured me. Therefore, I will kill myself so I can become a ghost and come back and punish my enemy." It is, in a sense, a preventive concept; no one wants to let such a prospective ghost-avenger die. In other societies, suicide is one way to expiate mistakes; the belief is that legally and morally one is thus pardoned for errors.

Personal-Psychiatric Suicide

This is primarily at a personal level; it comes from individual psychiatric-emotional causes, rather than from any cultural or societal stimulus. It can be subdivided as suicide associated with psychotic conditions and suicide associated with emotional frustration.

Suicide Associated with Psychotic Conditions

This type of suicide has little culture influence; it is a result of influences in a psychotic condition. A person "instructed" by a voice (auditory hallucination) may take his own life. One who has not had any previous depression, but suddenly becomes preoccupied by guilt and is severely depressed, has a persecutory delusion which prompts suicide.

Suicide Associated with Emotional Frustration

In this instance, an individual may be suffering from a mild psychiatric disorder or may be considered "normal"; then some experience causes extreme emotional upheaval or frustration, and suicide—or the attempt—follows. Involved here is some dimension of culture. The decision to die is often connected with some aspect of the individual's community or social interactions. He or she acts from one of the following motivations: a) to escape from the stress or frustration; b) to eliminate feelings of desperation and hopelessness; c) to end prolonged psychological or physical suffering; d) to act out a personal revenge, or to show anger or disappointment; e) to cry out for help or attention; or f) to be reunited with some deceased loved one. Most of the attempted suicides stem from this stress or frustration-linked behavior.

Special Forms of Suicide

These are types of suicidal behavior which warrant special categories because each has either a unique nature or is a mixture of a sociocultural manifestation and a personal-psychiatric suicide.

Couple Suicide

This form of suicide usually takes place in a culture with rigorous social and cultural regulations governing mate selection and marriage. If a couple cannot marry because of parental or family disapproval, differing backgrounds, or existing social taboos (e.g., marrying a person of the same surname in China is forbidden even if there is no blood relationship), and there is no alternative solution to their situation, the couple may decide to die together. Such unhappy couples may take poison, or bind themselves together and jump into a river or the ocean. This is a practice still occasionally observed in Oriental countries such as Japan and Taiwan.

Family Suicide

This describes the phenomenon in which a whole family jointly commits suicide. One of the parents suggests suicide because of an unbearable personal situation: severe debts, an incurable disease, a problem which seems insurmountable; the spouse then consents to die with his or her mate. Together the parents kill their young children and finally kill themselves. Homicide and suicide are combined. One motivation is the assumption that no one will care for the orphaned children; thus, it is better for the entire family to die. Family suicide occurs in a society which values greatly the tie between parent and child, and believes that children are best cared for by parents. Blood relationship and emotional ties are equally important in such societies.

Mass Suicide

In this phenomenon, members of a large group commit suicide together. Underlying this unusual group action is often a strong sense of patriotism or a unique communal spirit. Prompted by a shared experience and a common belief system, the group decides it is better to die together than to confront the disgrace and mistreatment of a surrender, or the loneliness and grief that follow the death of a revered leader.

During World War II, hundreds of Japanese civilians committed mass suicide when United States forces wrested the island of Saipan from the Japanese. There were many reasons for choosing suicide. Surrender and—to the Japanese mind—sure disgrace awaited them. Pride, personal and national, motivated self-destruction. So did their culture in which suicide is honorable and, at times, expected. Fear, too, played a part. The people expected to be mistreated or tortured. Obedience also may have shaped the decision to die; the Japanese military government expected everyone to resist until death. A saying expressed the people's agreement that, "We prefer to be a broken jade rather than remain as a whole brick." Mass suicide was the inevitable climax. Men, women, and children jumped from the cliffs of Marpi Point to certain death on the knife-edged rocks below (Crowl, 1960).

In the Saipan incident, some homicide where young children were concerned was also involved. In 1978's occasion of horror, the mass deaths at Jonestown, Guyana, mass homicide was more certainly joined with mass suicide. In this tragedy, approximately 900 United States citizens, members of the People's Temple, swallowed potassium cyanide and potassium chloride at the command of their cult leader, Jim Jones. Survivors from the jungle-fringed settlement in South America told of cult members who swallowed the poison voluntarily and of those who were forced to take it; of the protesting and the drug-tranquilized; of those who believed they would be castrated and tortured if they refused to die; of mothers who poisoned their children and then themselves; of those who lined up, cafeteria-style, for their cup of poison-laced soft drink (News accounts, 1978). The Jonestown deaths and their complex motivations are discussed in detail in Chapter 11 on "Culture, Religion, and Psychopathology."

Homicide as a Means of Suicide

This sequence begins as homicidal behavior and ends with one's own death. From the Moros of the Philippines comes the example called *juramentado.* At one time, this was a planned, violent action against oppressors and enemies (the term means "taking a vow," with the connotation of defending one's country). As Ewing (1955) describes it, it is an institutionalized suicidal process. A man becomes sick of life. Perhaps his marriage is unhappy; perhaps his fellows shun him. He decides on *juramentado.* First, he must get permission from his parents. He then prepares his weapon, has his head shaved and his eyebrows plucked. He chooses a certain place, usually a crowded market place, and begins a mass execution of Christians. He intends to kill as many Christians as possible. Eventually, of course, he is killed. The whole bloody event is a way to give up life without actually committing suicide. Suicide is forbidden for the Moro; *juramentado* allows one to get into heaven. It is also highly esteemed as "going out like a man". *Juramentado* has characteristics of both the psychiatric and the sociocultural suicide.

Suicide as a "Rational" Way of Ending Life

In the United States and England it is possible that a new cultural trend to accept suicide as a coping mechanism is underway. In both countries there is increasing public discussion favoring suicide as a way out of terminal illness. In England, a 6,000-member organization called Exit has compiled a booklet on how to commit suicide "without bungling," and a similar organization exists in California. Television talk shows present discussions on self-inflicted death. Aiding and abetting suicide in both countries is still illegal, but the open consideration of the suicide option may predict a social phenomenon to come.

MOTIVES FOR SUICIDE

Although the dynamics of suicide have been intensively explored clinically at the individual level, very little systematic study of suicide motives has been done at the cross-cultural level. Such study would be limited by the varying styles and degrees of sophistication of different investigators who explore the psychological causes for suicide in different cultural areas.

Among the cross-cultural studies that have been done is the very interesting one (Hendin, 1967) that compares suicides, their types and causes, in three Scandinavian countries. The comparisons clearly illustrate the vastly different cultural attitudes and psychosocial pressures of each country.

In Sweden, suicide brought about by concern over performance is prevalent. The Swedish people have high standards of performance and great self-hatred for failure. For the men, success or failure has a life-or-death meaning. Another factor, repressed anger, seems involved. This has a childhood origin. A child is taught not to show feelings, but to develop a reasonable, unemotional manner. Thus, the Swedes learn their characteristic affectivity: to handle anger through withdrawal and detachment. Significantly, there is a Swedish idiom that means "to kill someone by silence."

In contrast, Denmark has few "concern over performance" suicides.

There, self-killing might be classified as "dependency-loss" and guilt-instilling suicides. These, too, seem to stem from cultural ways of child care. The Danish child is cuddled, fondled, and encouraged to remain long dependent on his mother. Later frustration of dependency needs, connected with separation loss or abandonment, then precipitates "dependency-loss" suicides. Childish aggression is handled in ways that instill guilt; suicide is also used as a way to make others feel guilty.

In Norway—with strikingly few suicides—the mother's focusing her emotional life on the child is to some extent counterbalanced by her desire for an independent one; an attempt is made to minimize the development of dependency problems that threaten the Danish child. Also, the Norwegian child is not taught to suppress emotional expression, as the Swedish child is; consequently, the Norwegian tends to be emotionally free as an adult. This partially explains why Norwegians seem less susceptible to suicidal acts. The fewer Norwegian suicides are usually a quite different type, a "moral" form of suicide. These suicides follow aggressive, antisocial behavior with subsequent intense guilt.

Sporadic reports on causes suggest that the reasons for suicide within particular cultures often vary according to age, sex, and occupation or position in the community. For example, for people in Madurai, India, failure in examinations and disappointment in love affairs were, in the 1960s, very common factors in suicides of younger persons, while poverty, unemployment, and physical diseases seem to have caused older individuals to kill themselves (Ganapathi and Rao, 1966). Bourne (1970) found that, among Chinese in San Francisco, physical illness prompted most suicides for men, while among women, interpersonal conflict was associated with a history of psychiatric illness. For Chinese in Hong Kong, economic insecurity and uncertainty were significant causes for suicide in such disparate groups as the unemployed, businessmen, and prostitutes. Poverty and illness contributed to suicides among Hong Kong's aged. Interpersonal conflicts caused young women to take their lives. This was particularly so among women away from their families and trapped in socially disapproved occupations or sexual liaisons (Yap, 1958). Chinese women in Taiwan took their lives because of frustrated love affairs, marital discord, or conflicts with a family member. Legal-criminal problems and social maladaptation were outstanding causes among the men (Rin, 1975).

In Thailand, socioeconomic factors and chronic illness played a significant role in male suicides, while emotional factors seemed to be primary reasons for suicide in females. Pregnancy without marriage was sometimes involved.

In general, in economically developing countries, financial problems may become a direct cause for many individuals to kill themselves. However, lack of money and material well-being are not predominant problems in all cultures. Sampath's 1969 report of the situation at St. Thomas, Virgin Islands, makes this clear. According to him, in this multi-ethnic society, North Americans, the most economically comfortable persons on the island, have a high suicide rate; the least economically secure group, one of Negro origin which came from the neighboring British islands to work, has very few cases.

Suicide behavior among Japanese in Japan is unique in many aspects. The rate is high and many forms of suicide are represented. Iga and Tatai (1975) described types which Japanese identify and recognize. Suicide is identified by method as: *Dokuyaku Jisatsu* (suicide by poisoning); *Tosui Jisatsu* (drowning); *Tooshin Jisatsu* (jumping from a high place); and *Hara-Kiri* or *Seppuku* (self-disembowelment). Motives are also recognized and classified into very particular categories. *Jun-shi* is suicide following the master's death (exemplified by General Nogi and his wife after the death of the Meiji Emperor in 1912). *Kan-shi* is suicide to remonstrate; an inferior kills himself to communicate a criticism to his superior. *Kashitsu-shi* is suicide as a way to pay for a mistake one has made. *Fun-shi* is suicide to express indignation toward authority. Such a diversified terminology not only denotes a cultural familiarity with suicide as a part of daily life, but also reflects underlying causes for problems in this particular cultural system. In the authoritarian society of Japan, a man learns how to serve a master (or employer) and is expected to do so as long as he lives. This system originated in the ancient eras of feudalism and continues, to a certain degree, even in contemporary society. When a man graduates from school or college, he very carefully selects the company he wants to join. Once employed, he is prepared to serve that company the rest of his life without changing his job or superior. Within such a system, his relationship with authority is characterized by obligation, obedience, and a psychological dependency. If the relationship becomes difficult and uncomfortable, he is not able to express his opinion and anger openly. This unique inferior-superior relationship may be a background for various kinds of special suicide, such as the suicide which follows the master's death, or the suicide to remonstrate against one's superior.

Among North Alaskan Eskimos, suicide behavior patterns changed as their social structure and stresses did. Kraus (1971) describes this. In the traditional pattern, middle-aged and older men committed suicide; they were motivated by sickness, old age, and bereavement. In more recent years, as Eskimo life knew new stresses (cash economy, alcohol, breakdown in family ties), the young (15 to 25) committed or attempted suicide. For these young people, now including women, motives are unclear, but are often linked with intense, unbearable affective states. The suicidal behavior comes abruptly and unexpectedly; alcoholic intoxication is often involved.

There are presently as many questions as answers in connection with suicide and social stress. Very much unanswered is the question of how to identify the degree and nature of this stress. The American Indian is a case in point. Dizmang and his colleagues (1974) noted that Indian suicides occur in the under-35 age group, with unemployment, inadequate job training, and the dissolution of traditional family life all primary cases. Shore (1975) and other investigators found that frequency of suicide varies greatly among different Indian tribes; some have extremely low rates compared to Caucasians in the same area. Yet, all Indians face the same situation of acculturation.

Instead of focusing merely on minority groups, Parkin (1974) compared three cultural groups in Fairbanks, a small city in the interior of Alaska. He reported that Caucasians account for the great majority of both attempted and completed suicides, as compared to Eskimos and American Indians. He commented that, to many Caucasians, Alaska is the last frontier, the final place in which a person can prove himself. Thus, a great many persons who were unable to manage satisfactorily in other places came to Alaska in search of opportunity. The travel, isolation, and prolonged confinement during the winter months—particularly for housebound women—were additional factors which contributed to the high suicide rate.

The premise that social disruption is an underlying cause of self-destruction requires further investigation. The focus needs to be on fairly recent history (personal-social-political) of the suicide phenomenon. Two countries, Japan and Taiwan, present interesting links between suicide trends and national events. Wen (1974) reviewed data from both countries. He found—in addition to the increase in older suicides common to developed countries—another peak age period. Suicides rose sharply in the 15-to-30 age group. In both countries, these youthful suicides also occurred during a very particular time period. For the Japanese, the peak for the younger group came during the period of 1955–1958 and declined shortly thereafter. A very similar peak occurred in Taiwan from 1962 through 1964. Both Wen (1974) and Lin (1969) believed this unusual correlation could be traced back to the closing era of World War II, when these same youths were either very young children or pre-adolescents. Both Japanese and mainland Chinese knew trauma then; only the form of suffering varied. In Japan, a nation felt emotional and political turmoil. For millions of Chinese refugees, tragedy in their homeland was succeeded by the anxieties and adjustments of a new setting, new customs, and often a new language. Children, even very young ones, knew or sensed this was a time of trouble. The authors speculated that the traumatic experiences of childhood may be extremely crucial in the development of self-destructive behavior in adulthood. This, of course, is a hypothesis; additional information and cross-cultural data are needed to test its validity.

CULTURAL IMPLICATIONS OF SUICIDE

It is usually thought that suicide occurs when a person suffers emotional stress. This premise is often extended from the individual to the sociocultural level, i.e., a society has a large number of suicides; therefore, that society is under a great deal of social stress. This view needs reexamination with particular attention given the nature of the suicide. From a cultural point of view, at least three aspects of suicide behavior should be analyzed: suicide as a reaction to stress; as a socially known and familiar coping mechanism; and finally as a help-seeking mechanism.

We can conceptualize social stress—or its extreme of social disruption—as a condition in which society as a whole experiences great changes in the social structure, value system, role-status, or economic situation. In some cases, a whole society may seem to lose its sense of direction or purpose; this may contribute to stress in its people. Individuals in that society often react to social stress with the manifestations of various emotion-related responses, such as neurotic conditions, psychosomatic disorders, alcoholism, drug abuse, criminality, and riots. Suicide is only one such manifestation. Therefore, suicide should not be considered the only index for indicating social stress. One example: Although Sweden and Japan have much higher rates of suicide than that of the United States, the rates of criminality or alcoholism in those countries are much lower. Therefore, the evaluation of stress which exists in a society should be carefully approached, preferably by examining the total situation, rather than relying on a single index. By analyzing the various motives for suicide and the groups which become involved in suicide, it will be possible to speculate on what type of stress is most prevalent in a society and who most feels its impact.

In Western society, the failure of a love relationship or a marriage, death of a mate, and loneliness are the most significant emotional reasons for suicide. Certainly this illustrates that, within this society, emotional support from relatives, lifelong friends, and members of an extended family is diminishing. The tendency is to invest emotion intensively in one love partner or spouse. When this one-to-one relationship is severed, the main source of emotional support is gone. The resulting frustration can be severe. In contrast, unemployment, poverty, and debt become dominant causes for suicide where economic conditions are unstable and no effective social welfare system exists. Just as a frustrated person copes in various ways, so does a society. Although no one yet clearly understands why a particular group tends to become suicidal rather than homicidal (or alcohol- or drug-addicted), it seems clear that certain groups prefer particular kinds of coping mechanisms.

In the psychodynamic theory of aggression, suicide is viewed as an expression of "inner-directed" negative aggression, and homicide as the "outer-directed" manifestation of anger. If we agree with this theory, it is tempting to speculate that the frequencies of suicide and homicide exist in an inverse relationship within a society. A high occurrence of homicide with a relatively low suicide rate in the Philippines is often quoted to support this hypothesis. However, reports from other areas indicate this inverse relationship does not always exist. Gobar (1970) noted that in the Kabul Province of Afghanistan, a less than usual difference is found between homicide and suicide rates. Based on a 10-year average, the suicide rate is 0.25, and the homicide rate, 3.44. Both rates are low in comparison to other countries. Asuni (1962) found both suicide and homicide rare in Western Nigeria.

Palmer (1965) correlated the rates of murder and suicide in 40 non-literate societies with degrees of structure in each society. He used the prevalence of severe punishment for crimes as an inverse measure of the degree to which the society is structured. He found that both murder and suicide increased with an increase in overall punishment. This seems to disprove the theory that the more highly structured a society is, the lower the homicide rate and the higher the suicide rate.

Collomb and Collignon (1974) pointed out that traditional African cultures have in common strong familial and social cohesion, fidelity to traditional customs and beliefs, and religions which link man with the world and his ancestors. In these cultures, destructive, aggressive behavior, criminality, and severe delinquency are rare. Interpersonal conflicts between two individuals are resolved by mediation of a third party—the magician or priest who invokes the aid of institutionalized rituals. Thus, hostile aggression is not necessarily present, either in the form of suicide or homicide.

In the study of culture and coping mechanisms, we need to consider to what extent members of a society are familiar with a particular coping mechanism and how they sanction and utilize it. This is especially important in trying to interpret the relationship between culture and suicide. As illustrated by Hoskin et al. (1969), one preliterate tribe in New Guinea has many suicides because of the familiarity with suicide among the villagers. Everyone knows about the past and current suicides in the village; many know how to knot the rope for hanging.

The familiarity with various socially defined types of suicide in Japanese society is usually given as one of the reasons for the high incidence of suicide among even the youngsters in Japan. Perhaps Japan is the only country which would design the "suicide submarine" to attack Pearl Harbor, not in desperation at the end of the war, but before the declaration of war upon the United States. This illustrates how self-killing, with a society's sanction, operates as a way to achieve a goal of success and triumph.

Finally, the nature of suicide behavior should be carefully studied and differentiated in terms of the purpose behind the act. Suicidal behavior may be help-seeking, rather than self-destructive. Kato (1970) has pointed out that the ratio of committed to attempted suicide is 1 to 0.4 in Japan, while in California, U.S.A., it is quite different, 1 to 7.7. Clearly, suicidal behavior for self-destruction or for help-seeking will vary greatly in different cultures. In a society which tends to have loose family ties and to be highly mobile, it is difficult for people to signal for help, except in a very drastic way. Instead of showing manifestations of apparent physical illness (hypochondriacal complaints), suicidal gestures become a very powerful way to get attention from the medical-social system; consequently many suicidal attempts may actually be cries for help. What the behavior of suicide implies in any society should be carefully evaluated.

OVERVIEW AND SUGGESTIONS

To summarize: The behavior of suicide varies widely in different sociocultural environments in terms of frequency, method, and motivation. It appears to be universally true that men tend to commit suicide by more aggressive methods, while women tend to "attempt" with less aggressive, less certainly fatal methods. Another general trend is that the frequency of suicide increases with age, with the peak occurring after the middle years. The exceptions are some groups in Taiwan and Japan (Wen, 1974) and the American Indian (Dizmang et al., 1974), where there is another peak around the late teen years.

The term "suicide" actually covers various kinds of self-destructive actions, with causes which range from sociocultural conditions to personal-psychiatric ones; thus, there is a strong need to differentiate between suicidal behaviors when we analyze the relation of suicide to culture. Generally speaking, when a society has a low suicide rate, the suicide action is more or less associated with some psychotic condition. The society which has a higher rate, has suicides associated with emotional frustration or socially related stress (Asuni, 1962). In other words, the suicides for personal and emotional reasons, often attempts, are subject to extreme fluctuation when linked to some sociocultural condition or situation (Stainbrook, 1954), while the suicides due to psychotic conditions are relatively fixed (Weissman, 1974).

The general belief that suicide behavior occupies the realms of civilization and that self-destructive behavior is observed less frequently among uncivilized people (Hoskin et al., 1969) is questionable and necessitates further investigation. The parallel between the rate of suicide and social disruption is not a definite one; it, too, depends on many other variables.

If we are to understand the impact of culture on self-destruction, data must no longer be grouped under the blanket term "suicide." To make significant cross-cultural comparisons possible, reporting systems must make careful distinction between various types of suicide. Sociocultural suicide versus personal-psychiatric suicide; suicide associated with psychotic conditions versus suicide associated with emotional frustration; committed versus attempted suicide—these differences must be known and recorded. Then these data can be studied for contrasts (or similarities) of age, sex, causes, and conditions, for the need is not merely to study suicide frequency and suicidal behavior in different cultures; it is equally important to study the dynamics of suicide from many cultural vantage points.

REFERENCES

Asuni, T.: Suicide in Western Nigeria. *Br. Med. J.,* 11:1091–1097, 1962.

Beattie, J. H. M.: Homicide and suicide in Bunyoro. In: *African Homicide and Suicide.* P. Bohannan (Ed.), Princeton: Princeton University Press, 1960.

Bourne, P. G.: Suicide in the Chinese of San Francisco. *Transcultural Psychiatric Research Review,* 7:210–212, 1970.

Carstairs, G. M.: Attitude to death and suicide in an Indian cultural setting. *Int. J. Soc. Psychiatry,* 1-2:33–41, 1956–57.

Chia, B. H. and Tsoi, W. F.: A statistical study of attempted suicides in Singapore. *Singapore Med. J.,* 15:253–256, 1974.

Clark, J. J.: *Carrier Admiral.* New York: D. McKay Co., 1967.

Collomb, H. and Collignon, R.: Suicide behavior in Africa. *Psychopathologie Africaine,* 10: 55–113, 1974.

Crowl, P. A.: *Campaign in the Marianas,* Vol. 9 of *The War in the Pacific.* Washington, D.C. Office of the Chief of Military History, Dept. of the Army, 264–265, 1960.

Dizmang, L. H., Watson, J., May, P. A., and Bopp, J.: Adolescent suicide at an Indian reservation. *Am. J. Orthopsychiatry,* 44:43–49, 1974.

Durkheim, E.: *Le Suicide.* Paris: Libraire Felix Alcan, 1897.

Eungprabhanth, V.: Suicide in Thailand. *Forensic Sci.,* 5:43–51, 1975.

Ewing, J. F.: Juramentado: Institutionalized suicide among the Moros of the Philippines. *Anthropology Quarterly,* 28:148–155, 1955.

Fallers, L. A. and Fallers, M. C.: Homicide and suicide in Busoga. In: *African Homicide and Suicide.* P. Bohannan (Ed.), Princeton: Princeton University Press, 1960.

Farberow, N. L.: Culture history of suicide. In: *Suicide in Different Cultures.* N. L. Farberow (Ed.), Baltimore: University Park Press, 1975.

Farberow, N. L. and Simon, M. D.: Suicide in Los Angeles and Vienna. In: *Suicide in Different Cultures.* N. L. Farberow (Ed.), Baltimore: University Park Press, 1975.
Firth, R.: Suicide and risk-taking in Tikopia society. *Psychiatry,* 24:1–17, 1961.
Fontaine, J.: Homicide and suicide among the Gisn. In: *African Homicide and Suicide.* P. Bohannan (Ed.), Princeton: Princeton University Press, 1960.
Ganapathi, M. N. and Rao, A. V.: A study on suicide in Madurai. *J. Indian Med. Assoc.,* 46: 18–23, 1966.
German, A.: Aspects of clinical psychiatry in Subharan Africa. *Br. J. Psychiatry,* 21:461–479, 1972.
Gobar, A. H.: Suicide in Afghanistan. *Br. J. Psychiatry,* 116:493–496, 1970.
Hendin, H.: Suicide. In: *Comprehensive Textbook of Psychiatry.* A. M. Freedman and H. I. Kaplan (Eds.), Baltimore: Williams and Wilkins, 1967.
Hoskin, J. O., Friedman, M. I., and Cawte, J. E.: A high incidence of suicide in a preliterate-primitive society. *Psychiatry,* 32:199–210, 1969.
Iga, M. and Tatai, K.: Characteristics of suicides and attitudes toward suicide in Japan. In: *Suicide in Different Cultures.* N. L. Farberow (Ed.), Baltimore: University Park Press, 1975.
Jeffreys, M. D. W.: Samsonic suicide or suicide of revenge among Africans. *African Studies,* 11:118–122, 1952.
Kato, M.: Self-destruction in Japan: A cross-cultural epidemiological analysis of suicide. *Transcultural Psychiatric Research Review,* 7:14–15, 1970.
Kraus, R.: Changing patterns of suicidal behavior in North Alaskan Eskimo. Paper presented at the 22nd International Symposium on Circumpolar Health, Nordic Council for Artic Medical Research, Oulu, Finland, June 1971.
Lin, T. Y.: Some epidemiological findings on suicides in youth. In: *Adolescence: Psychological Perspectives.* G. Caplan and S. Lebovici (Eds.), New York: Basic Books, 1969.
Meguro, K.: Personal communication, 1966.
Nalin, D. R.: Epidemic of suicide by malathion poisoning in Guyana. Report of 264 cases. *Trop. Geogr. Med.,* 25:8–14, 1973.
News Accounts, 1978. *Time Magazine,* December 4, 1978. *Honolulu Advertiser, Honolulu Star-Bulletin,* November 20, 1978.
Orley, J. H.: Culture and mental illness: A study from Uganda. *East African Studies No. 36, Nairobi.* East African Publishing House, 1970.
Palmer, S.: Murder and suicide in 40 non-literate societies. *Journal of Criminal Law, Criminology and Police Science,* 56:320–324, 1965.
Parkin, M.: Suicide and culture in Fairbanks: A comparison of three cultural groups in a small city of interior Alaska. *Psychiatry,* 37:60–67, 1974.
Rin, H.: Suicide in Taiwan. In: *Suicide in Different Cultures.* N. L. Farberow (Ed.), Baltimore: University Park Press, 1975.
Rubinstein, D. H.: *Preliminary Research on Suicide in Micronesia.* Manuscript in Preparation.
Sampath, H. M.: A cross-cultural study of St. Thomas, U.S. Virgin Islands. Paper presented at the Joint Meeting of the Carribean Psychiatric Association and the American Psychiatric Association, Ocho Rios, Jamaica, May 1969.
Shore, J. H.: American Indian suicide: Fact and fantasy. *Psychiatry,* 38:87–91, 1975.
Stainbrook, E.: A cross-cultural evaluation of depressive reactions. In: *Depression.* P. H. Hoch and J. Zubin (Eds.), New York: Grune and Stratton, 1954.
Webb, J. P. and Willard, W.: Six American Indian patterns of suicide. In: *Suicide in Different Cultures.* N. L. Farberow (Ed.), Baltimore: University Park Press, 1975.
Weissman, M. M.: The epidemiology of suicide attempts, 1960–1971. *Arch. Gen. Psychiatry,* 30:737–746, 1974.
Wen, C. P.: Secular suicidal trend in postwar Japan and Taiwan: An examination of hypotheses. *Int. J. Soc. Psychiatry,* 20:8–17, 1974.
Whitlock, F. D.: Suicide in Brisbane, 1956–1973: The drug-death epidemic. *Med. J. Australia,* 1:737–743, 1975.
World Health Organization: *Epidemiological and Vital Statistics Report,* Mortality from Sui-

cide 1950–1969. 1973.

Yamamoto, J.: Japanese and American suicide in Los Angeles. *Transcultural Psychiatric Research Review,* 11:197–199, 1974.

Yap, P. M.: *Suicide in Hong Kong with Special Reference to Attempted Suicide.* London: Oxford University Press, 1958.

Zilboorg, G.: Suicide among civilized and primitive races. *Am. J. Psychiatry,* 92:1347–1369, 1936.

CHAPTER 8

Depression

It would be pleasant to report that, with new drugs and improved treatment methods, depression might soon cease to be a serious problem. That utopia is yet a long way off. Better treatment methods are not the same as prevention. The dark shadows that haunt man's spirit and damage his health are still very much with us. As Sartorius (1974) notes, depression is highly prevalent and carries serious consequences in many parts of the world. Many more cases of depression will undoubtedly occur in the future. Life spans are being extended. Long life also means more exposure to stresses that can precipitate depression and increases chances of acquiring chronic diseases that are often accompanied by depression. Around the world, psychosocial environments are rapidly—often traumatically—changing. This, too, can ultimately bring about depression. As depressive illness becomes more recognizably a worldwide problem, it must be explored in all its possible aspects—biological, psychological, and sociocultural.

For any sort of mental exploration, we need to know exactly what we are studying. We need an exact and standard terminology. Yet in both clinical medical practice and research investigation, confusion surrounds the very word depression. The term is used loosely for a wide range of conditions. It may be used to denote normal everyday mood variations or mild but pathological depressive disorders or severe psychotic depression. All have very different etiological natures and varying clinical implications.

According to the International Statistical Classification of Diseases, Ninth Revision (ICD-9), affective diseases are subclassified into manic-depressive psychoses and neurotic depression. However, according to the American Psychiatric Association, Diagnostic and Statistical Manual of Mental Disorders, Third Edition (DSM-III), depressive disorders are classified in a very different manner, namely either as bipolar disorder, major depression, cyclothymic disorder, dysthymic disorder, and atypical affective disorders. Many clinicians have also retained the differential concepts of endogenous depression versus reactive depression, or psychotic depression versus neurotic depression. Obviously the nosological terminology and concept of depression continue to be complicated, and cross-comparison research is often hampered by the diversity of terminology.

From the viewpoint of cultural psychiatry, distinguishing between endogenous depression and psychogenic (reactive) depression is still a useful conceptual framework. If the depression is caused primarily by biological factors, the sociocultural factor will influence the condition only on a secondary level and is less important as an etiological factor. In psychogenic or reactive depression, presumably mainly related to a psychological cause, the sociocultural contribution to the occurrence of the depressive condition is greater. However, in each case there is an interaction between biological and psychocultural factors. To elaborate on the sociocultural aspects of depression, the emphasis should be on the psychogenic or reactive depression rather than on the endogenous type.

FREQUENCY OF OCCURRENCE

Although prevalence rates of depressive disorders have been reported in the literature throughout the world, the cross-cultural comparison of these data is difficult and its usefulness thus far has been rather limited. It is necessary to evaluate such reports very carefully for the following reasons:

1) Any existing data have presented depression as either "affective disorder" or "manic-depressive illness" (as total, or depressive type only), which may or may not include "depressive neurosis," or "psychotic depressive reaction."
2) The nature of investigations and sources of data differ remarkably. Most of the information is taken from hospital registration data, while a small portion is derived from census survey data; inevitably, the depth of study varies. As a result, the validity of the data as showing prevalence rate of depression for cross-comparison is questionable.
3) The diagnostic concept of depression among different investigators is not standardized, so that the pattern of diagnosis is not the same. Some investigators tend to "over-diagnose" depression, while others "under-diagnose."

In past discussions of the frequency of the depressive condition, Sub-Saharan Africa has always been quoted as an example of a culture area where depression is rare. However, Prince (1968), who reviewed literature on depression in Africa, gives a different view. He noted that hospital data during the Colonial era (1890–1956) showed that instances of depression of a psychotic nature were either absent or rare, or, if present, were less intense and shorter in duration. In contrast, during the era of independence from 1957 on, reported instances of depression were common. The radical difference may reflect advances in case-finding as well as changes in concepts and terminology. It has been attributed to new observations made in so-called "open hospitals" and to the reliance of the researcher on newer concepts of depression covering psychiatric conditions which previously may have been labeled as "neurasthenia" or "hypochondriasis." Such tendencies have been observed not only in Africa, but in many other places, as Sartorius (1975) pointed out. He reported that, in addition to the genuine increase in prevalence, several other factors explain the last two decades' increase of depression as a diagnostic category. These reflect changes in clinical medical and psychiatric practice. They are:

a) A change in the diagnostic habits of physicians with greater willingness to diagnose depression.
b) A broader acceptance of the concept of depression as a diagnostic entity (including "masked depression").
c) A change in patients' complaining patterns. More patients are able to describe symptoms of depression more accurately.
d) Increasing availability of improved health services for depressive disorders, even for mild forms.

VARIATIONS IN CLINICAL PICTURES

Modern psychiatrists are fully aware that many factors influence the clinical picture of depression. The *level of severity* is the first to be considered. The essential features of depression, a distressed or saddened demeanor and loss of interest or pleasure in activities, are to be found in any episode of depression, especially in its mildest form. More distinct elements, such as excessive guilt or contemplation of suicide, are present in the moderate form of the disorder. Delusions are associated with the severe form.

In clinical experience, another dimension is the *age factor*. Depression may manifest itself in young children as separation anxiety or negativistic or antisocial behavior; in the adolescent, as withdrawal from social activities or as substance abuse; and among the elderly, as pseudo-dementia, mild disorientation, and memory loss.

Whether the *cultural factor,* as a third dimension, does influence the clinical picture of depression is a pertinent question. Murphy, Wittkower, and Chance (1967) asked psychiatrists around the world for their "impressions" of the symptomatology of depression in their cultural areas. The replies to the questionnaire indicated that there is a basic depressive disorder which in all cultures exhibits certain primary symptoms: a depressed mood, diurnal mood change, insomnia with early morning wakening, and diminution of interest in one's social environment. Other symptoms, such as thought retardation and self-depreciation, appear to be culturally determined.

This "clinical impression" type of survey was criticized as "instant research" (Carstairs, 1967) and as "statistics of impressions" (Pflanz, 1967). Nevertheless, it is one of the initial attempts to use the concept of primary and secondary symptoms in an exploration of possible cultural variations of depressive manifestations (Murphy et al., 1967).

Pfeiffer (1968) and Sartorius (1973) reviewed many articles about depression in various non-European cultures. They agreed that the "core" symptoms of depression—changes of mood, disruption of physiological functions such as sleep and appetite, and hypochondriacal symptoms—in these cultures were the same as in Europe. However, other symptoms, such as feelings of guilt and suicidal tendencies, showed variations of frequency and intensity among cultures. This view is supported by many investigators (Binitie, 1975).

Waziri (1973) provides an example. From clinical observation of depressive illness in Afghanistan, he found that while the biological symptoms of depression were similar to other ethnic groups, the majority of depressed patients expressed "death *wishes*" instead of suicidal intentions or thoughts. In Afghanistan, most religions believe suicide is a sin. According to Waziri, 54% of the depressed individuals who were asked how they viewed life answered that they "wished they were dead" or that they had "prayed to God to take their life away." Twenty percent of the patients had only passing thoughts of suicide, which they banished by thinking of the great sin they would commit. Actually, the suicide rate among the general population had earlier been reported as one of the lowest—0.25/100,000 (Gobar, 1970). A point is well illustrated: Even though suicidal tendency is associated with depressive conditions, cultural attitude—whether a culture sanctions or forbids self-destruction—can swing the balance from death to life.

How a patient presents his depression may be culturally influenced. Bazzoui (1970) wrote that the average depressed patient in Iraq usually seemed quite unaware of his mood. Instead, patients complained of air hunger, of a feeling of pressure on the chest, or of feeling hemmed in. Even with striking physical symptoms and incapacity, retardation or agitation of social functioning, many of the Iraqi patients neither presented externally nor complained of depressed and/or dejected moods. Teja et al. (1971) reported that anxiety, somatic symptoms, hypochondriasis, and agitation were present in a significantly larger percentage of Indian depressives than in British depressives. They believe that both the group's assignment of certain symptoms to illness status and the patient's anticipation of what the local medical practitioners consider illness determine the choice of symptoms.

Notable in cross-cultural study of depression is the presence or absence of self-depreciation, self-blame or guilt. According to Prince's (1968) review, in Africa, mental-emotional self-castigation is rare or absent in the early stages of depressed patients. Earlier, Murphy and his associates (1967) had proposed that the higher incidence of guilt feelings in Western cultures was due to the influence of Christian religion. However, El-Islam (1969) also studied the relationship of guilt, religion, and depression in his observation of depressed Christian and Moslem patients in Cairo. He concluded that the presence or absence of guilt feelings was often associated with the level of education or literacy and the degree of depression (especially in psychotic or severely depressed patients) and was not significantly related to one's religious background. His conclusions suggest that guilt and Christianity are not necessarily closely linked.

These findings naturally stimulate the question of how the idea of sin will manifest itself among depressed patients from a shame-oriented society in contrast to those from a guilt-oriented society. This poses a methodological problem: how to define such terms as shame, guilt, or sin for relevant cross-cultural comparative study. El-Islam (1969) broadly outlined the criteria he used in his Cairo study of depressed Arab patients. He cited as minimal evidence for diagnosing guilt: self-reproach, imagined inadequacies on the job, a feeling of having neglected family affairs or failed one's friends, and a sense of having harmed others through some small offense. Death wishes that arose from a sense of being worthless or sinful caused the most intense guilt. However, other investigators may not agree with these diagnostic guidelines.

We may speculate: Guilt is associated with the severity of depression; it tends to occur when the patient is severely depressed. Guilt is related to the personality structure of the patient: how he develops his internal regulatory system. Guilt is related to the patient's tendency to introject or project anger and hostility. Certainly, if a society emphasizes strong internal control, which encourages the internalization of anger and hostility, then its members will be more apt to experience and express feelings of guilt.

Consider a few societies where strong internal controls are not stressed. In

Iraq, open hostile aggression is often a part of depression. There Bazzoui (1970) found that aggressive behavior (and paranoid ideas) were relatively common in depressed patients. He believed this was because the primitive mechanisms of defense in the form of attack and escape were not yet deeply suppressed in Iraqi culture. In an affective illness, the less civilized or socialized the individual is, the more such mechanisms (escape-attack, denial-projection) appear in the clinical picture. The *amok* syndrome may provide another case in point. *Amok* is reported to occur frequently in the Malay peninsula and other parts of Southeast and Southern Asia. It is apparently a culture-related way of handling a depressive situation. One typical case: After a depressive episode following the experience of being insulted, a man suddenly bursts into a manic homicidal frenzy and kills anyone in his presence.

In Hawaii, Lum et al. (1979) made a pilot study of depression in patients with depressive neurosis or reactive depression from three contrasting ethnic groups: Caucasian, Japanese, and part-Hawaiian. The three groups varied in past adjustment problems, and though life events prior to depression showed differences, no discernible pattern was disclosed. There was little evidence of ethnic differences in types of clinical symptoms, though the Japanese manifested fewer symptoms than the other two groups. However, psychological conditions associated with depression were quite different.

A high percentage of Hawaiian women manifested hopelessness, anger, insecurity, and loss. Half the Hawaiian men suffered from a feeling of failure. Hawaiians in the study and in the general population tend to be in a lower socioeconomic bracket with much unemployment and heavy dependence on welfare. These economic factors with their accompanying feelings of inadequacy can create susceptibility to depression. Only a fourth of the Hawaiian men and slightly less than a third of the women manifested shame or guilt, but approximately 40% of both demonstrated anger, with aggressive behavior on the part of the men.

There are obvious cultural factors involved in the depressions of the Japanese in Hawaii. This group was in general fairly well educated, self- or family-supported, with low reliance on welfare. Most of the men had no drastic life adjustment problems. Yet they were troubled by a feeling of lack of achievement (40%), a sense of failure (35%), and insecurity (35%). (There was little anger or hostility.) This sense of "not measuring up" is associated with the high value Japanese place on family-social obligations and achievement. The depressed Japanese women had had severe adjustment difficulties with family (80%) or in marital relationships (60%). Unlike the men, the depressed Japanese women had broken family ties by hasty or disapproved marriages or running away from home. Breaking with traditional ties, especially in Japanese culture, often leaves the rebel completely rejected. This can certainly contribute to depression.

Where the Caucasians are concerned, we are skating on much thinner speculative ice. This group is probably not representative of Caucasian culture in the United States. This culture emphasizes individual freedom and independence and allows frequent changing of occupation and residence. However, the Caucasians studied, all quite recent arrivals to Hawaii, seem to have changed locale for impulsive or escapist reasons. The Caucasian sample seems unduly marked by psychopathology. Though approximately half had gone beyond high school, unemployment and dependence on welfare or family support characterized about half the group. Life styles of both men and women had been chaotic, with broken marriages or romances and multiple adjustments which related to the occurrence of depression.

On the continental U.S., a commonly held belief is that clinically depressed blacks have less guilt feelings and suicidal trends but more somatic complaints than Caucasians. However, Tonks, Paykel, and Klerman (1970) contradicted this in their comparison of black and white depressed patients in Connecticut. When they controlled for differences in severity of illness between blacks and whites, they found no difference in symptoms with one marked exception: the variable of helplessness. The black group had a significantly lower mean for helplessness than the Caucasian group. It was suggested that the difference may have come from the disparities in living experiences of the two groups. If life is a greater struggle for American blacks, they may necessarily become more self-reliant and less inclined to feeling helpless.

Raskin, Crook, and Herman (1975) studied symptom differences in black and white depressed inpatients. When the two groups were controlled for age and social class differences, they showed marked similarities in the presentation of symptoms, especially core symptoms. The only differences found concerned hostility. Blacks showed a greater tendency toward negativism and the introjection of anger. However, black males, more than whites, also indicated they would attack verbally or physically if they felt their rights were being violated. Among the black males was a high incidence of suicide attempts or threats. This may have been linked with the competing urges to strike back and to internalize anger. Seeking an analysis of sociodemographic variables and depressive scores, Warheit, Holzer and Schwab (1973) surveyed adults in a community in the Southeastern part of the United States. They found that socioeconomic class, rather than race, was largely responsible for differences in depressive symptomatology between blacks and whites.

Apparently, the psychopathology of depression is influenced by multiple factors. These include the severity of the depression; a patient's race; personal background, including age, personality, and educational level; and finally, social class. In general, the primary symptoms—depressed mood and decreased, vegetative functions—form the core pathology fairly well shared by patients across cultures. The secondary symptoms, such as the tendency to self-reproach or self-destruction, are more or less subject to cultural influence.

EMOTIONAL EXPERIENCE OF DEPRESSION

The very breadth of issues raised by a cross-cultural study of depression stimulates questions that demand exploration: Do all people, regardless of their cultures, experience emotion in similar ways? Does the description of the experience of emotion change from culture to culture, or is it the same? Many investigators believe that patients from less culturally developed areas are apt to express depression by somatic complaints, while those of more culturally developed areas use psychological complaints. This is based on the general assumption that, from a developmental point of view, primitive emotion is characterized by syncretism, i.e., affective experience is closely bound up with physical responses. Later, in higher mental life, emotion is gradually differentiated from the somatic response (Werner, 1948).

Furthermore, it has been assumed that if people of a group are concerned with a particular kind of emotional state they will develop many ways to differentiate and express such an emotional state. One suggested way to study the degree of the differentiation of certain emotional states is to analyze the degree of diversity of language used to express a particular state or condition (Leff, 1973).

To explore cross-cultural variations in the meaning and subjective experience of depression, Tanaka-Matsumi and Marsella (1976) asked Japanese and American college students to associate a word with "depression." Of the Japanese students in Japan, 44% gave "rain" and "cloud" and 22% gave "dark" and "gray." Nearly 19% supplied words related to somatic functioning and illness: "disease," "tiredness," "headache," "fatigue." Most of the Japanese-American students in Hawaii gave responses which reflect internal moods ("sadness," 56.3%; "loneliness," 25.3%). The Japanese-American associations were very similar to those given by Caucasian-American students on the United States mainland. The authors conclude that Japanese do not experience depression in the same way Westerners do. Nor do they express feelings as Westerners do. For the Japanese, concrete images from nature allow personal emotions to be expressed impersonally.

Since this particular study utilized normal college students as subjects, a basic question arises: Are the tendencies revealed in this type of cross-cultural study applicable to clinically depressed groups? At any rate, the normal students do illustrate how the somatic expression of emotion may be patterned by a cultural system.

CULTURAL CONTRIBUTIONS TO CAUSES OF DEPRESSION

More and more investigators now study cross-culturally the phenomenological aspects of depression. Yet, surprisingly, relatively few researchers explore sociocultural factors as etiological contributions to the occurrence of depression. Dynamic psychiatrists view depression as a reaction to loss, deprivation, a change in the level of self-esteem, conflict over the aggressive drive, or as a threat to a preexisting personality structure marked by narcissism or dependency. However, within the framework of these clinical theories, depression's psychological causes can also include social-cultural determinants. In fact, cultural and social attitudes and practices can shape emotional responses to the trials and tragedies of life.

Many clinicians believe that childhood separation produces a vulnerability to depression that can be triggered by separation in adult life. For example, a Philadelphia study of psychiatric inpatients revealed a significantly higher incidence of childhood loss of a parent in the "high depressed" groups than in the "non-depressed" groups (Beck et al., 1963). Not only a parent's death during one's childhood can precipitate later depression, but separation, divorce, or prolonged absence of parents may also cause the same delayed or repeated result. Psychological stress, if severe and prolonged, may trigger a biological depression. So these and cultural factors are interconnecting, not separate.

Another, admittedly speculative, consideration enters the picture. It is not always the loss itself that plants the seed of later depression. The circumstances of the original loss and the provision or lack of alternative relationships or supportive figures also influence the emotional impact of the initial trauma. From the social-cultural viewpoint, family structure, child-rearing practices, and the presence or absence of parental substitutes all must be considered as causes or deterrents to a later depression. In societies which discourage divorce or parental separation, and in those which provide a satisfactory substitute for the dead parent, perhaps a future depressive episode may not happen. In such cases, when a child is reared with care, support, and concern, the early separation experience carries less potential for mental-emotional trouble later on.

How a community views death and how it ritualizes its mourning may also affect the occurrence of depression. In Samoa, death is seen as a natural event in life experiences; behavioral patterns in the Samoan family and community provide effective support when someone dies (Ablon, 1971). This helps reduce the occurrence of depression associated with grief. North American societies provide a marked contrast. Here, the grief-stricken often seek impersonal sources of comfort, such as a psychiatrist, social worker, or minister. Fernando (1975), who compared Jewish and Protestant depressives, suggests a kind of cultural cause-effect-cause-effect chain: Cultural factors are apt to determine how a family handles a death; in turn how the death is handled can affect the child's future potential for adult depression.

Though community support can alleviate grief's impact, conversely, community practice can nourish depression. Lewis (1975) reported a culturally patterned depressive episode in an American Indian group in Surinam near Brazil. A young child died. The mother, age about 24, then lost interest in everything. She stopped eating. She simply lay in her hammock and waited for death. She was—in her culture—doing the proper thing, for, according to tribal belief, even after an infant dies, an invisible cord attached to the umbilicus binds child to mother. The dead baby misses its mother and keeps pulling on the cord; consequently the mother is "expected" to die.

In other ethnic groups or social settings, both the rituals of mourning and less specific religious practices may lessen or perhaps prevent depression. Rather surprisingly, studies of depression in American blacks report that the prevalence of clinical depression, particularly in the South, is extremely low. Yet, Southern blacks are traditionally accustomed to loss, disappointment, and stress. A possible explanation is suggested: These people find solace in strong group solidarity. Also, their spirituals and emotion-filled, emotion-discharging religious ceremonies provide an outlet for the feeling aroused by death, separation, and social rejections. Opler and Small (1968) favor this interpretation of a "group ethos" and alleviation in a culturally recognized form. However, they state that this is more applicable to older blacks, and less to the present generation.

The size, the growth rate, and the social structure of a community may also shape individual and family lives and so, to some extent, cause or prevent depression. Wechsler (1961) compared the relationships of population growth to the frequency of hospitalized mental illness in 50 Massachusetts (U.S.A.) communities. His data showed that rapidly growing communities tend to produce significantly higher rates of hospitalized cases of depressive disorders and suicide, but not of schizophrenia, alcoholism, or other mental disorders. This seems to illustrate the close relationship of depression and social disorganization associated with rapid growth of small communities.

In a survey in India, Sethi et al. (1973) found that the rate of occurrence of depression was four times greater in urban areas than in rural areas. The investigators speculated that modernization, industrialization, and rapid change of social values in the urban areas may contribute to depression, while the simple life with its intimate social contacts in smaller communities may be deterrents. Yet Chance (1964) hypothesized a different cause-and-effect. He suggested that in a less cohesive community, the individual has greater freedom to pursue his private ends and to direct his hostilities outward; he is thus less susceptible to depression.

Status—social, occupational, or economic—can also help weave the fabric of depression. In fact, minority status felt by an ethnic group may outweigh ethnic characteristics as a contributing cause of depressive illness, as Fernando (1975) suggested after a cross-comparison of Jewish and Protestant depressive patients in the East End of London. He studied familial and social factors and found that increasing paternal inadequacy and weakening ethnic links and religious faith were related to depressive ills among Jews, but not among Protestants. He suggested that mental stress arose from the marginal position of Jews in British society, rather than from specific traits or customs within Jewish culture.

Higher occupational status is sometimes associated with depression. Bagley (1973) found this in a number of American, German, Scandinavian, (and less consistently in British) studies. Bagley's own suggested explanations: Depressed patients from lower classes may not have been properly diagnosed, so that diagnostic bias exists; individuals with certain personality types are predisposed to rise in the social scale and to be prone to depression; the stresses of being in—or moving up to—upper-middle and upper-class life may predispose some persons to depression.

Among Indian patients, Rao (1966) listed occupational or daily-living stresses—retirement, promotion, job transfer, business or financial difficulties—as precipitating depression. These contrast with the loss of mate or failure of an affair so frequently described as precipitants in Western society.

TO SUMMARIZE

Depression, like anxiety or anger, is part of the emotional phenomena that all men have exhibited throughout history. However, it is clear that in different life-styles, individuals react in different degrees to the loss, loneliness, or frustration that may lead to depression. It is also clear that different societies maintain different life support systems to minimize the severity of depression. Therefore, it is logical to assume that different degrees of severity and frequency and different reasons for depression exist in different societies. Yet, so far, a certain type, a certain frequency, a unique reason cannot be reliably attributed to a definite group or culture. A survey of the cross-cultural literature on depression raises more (certainly, stimulating) questions than it provides certainties. We believe there are reasons for contradictions between studies.

In our view, confusion emerges from cross-cultural studies because we address depression so broadly, including, at one extreme, depression as manifested as "emotional disease" with endogenous causes and, at the other, depression as emotional reaction to psychological cause. Thus investigative studies operate with no cross-cultural guidelines and present contradictory results. There is no integration of biological with psychological with cultural factors in the individual or the groups described.

That depression should be investigated across cultures is, in our opinion, certain. However, this will not be done satisfactorily until international definitions of depressive disorders are standard and international criteria for data are agreed on. With this accomplished, with better designed cross-cultural studies, the clues, suggestions, and questions on the links between culture and depression may, before too long, become conclusions.

REFERENCES

Ablon, J.: Bereavement in a Samoan community. *B. J. Med. Psychol.* 44:329–337, 1971.

Bagley, C.: Occupational class and symptoms of depression. *Soc. Sci. Med.,* 7:327–340, 1973.

Bazzoui, W.: Affective disorders in Iraq. *Br. J. Psychiatry,* 117:195–203, 1970.

Beck, A. T., Sethi, B. B., and Tuthill, R. W.: Childhood bereavement and adult depression. *Arch. Gen. Psychiatry,* 9:295–302, 1963.

Binitie, A.: A factor-analytical study of depression across cultures (African and European). *Br. J. Psychiatry,* 127:559–563, 1975.

Carstairs, G. M.: Critical evaluations: The limitations of "instant research." *International Journal of Psychiatry,* 3:15–17, 1967.

Chance, N. A.: A cross-cultural study of social cohesion and depression. *Transcultural Psychiatry Research Review,* 1:19–21, 1964.

El-Islam, M. F.: Depression and guilt: A study at an Arab psychiatric clinic. *Social Psychiatry,* 4:56–58, 1969.

Fernando, S. J. M.: A cross-cultural study of some familial and social factors in depressive illness. *Br. J. Psychiatry,* 127:46–53, 1975.

Gobar, A. H.: Suicide in Afghanistan. *Br. J. Psychiatry,* 116:493–496. 1970.

Leff, J. P.: Culture and the differentiation of emotional states. *Br. J. Psychiatry,* 123:299–306, 1973.

Lewis, T. J.: A culturally patterned depression in a mother after loss of a child. *Psychiatry,* 38:92–95, 1975.

Lum, K. Y., Char, W., and Tseng, W-S., et al.: Psychocultural study of depression: A pilot study. *Hawaii Med. J.,* 38:359–364, 1979.

Murphy, H. B. M., Wittkower, E. D., and Chance, N. A.: Cross-cultural inquiry into symptomatology of depression: A preliminary report. *International Journal of Psychiatry,* 3:6–15, 1967.

Opler, M. K. and Small, M.: Cultural variables affecting somatic complaints and depression. *Psychosomatics,* 9:261–266, 1968.

Pfeiffer, W. M.: The symptomatology of depression viewed transculturally. *Transcultural Psychiatric Research Review,* 5:121–124, 1968.

Pflanz, M.: Critical evaluations: Statistics of impressions. *International Journal of Psychiatry,* 3:21–22, 1967.

Prince, R. H.: The changing picture of depressive syndromes in Africa. Is it fact or diagnostic fashion? *Canadian Journal of African Studies,* 1:177–192, 1968.

Rao, A. V.: Depression: A psychiatric analysis of thirty cases. *Indian Journal of Psychiatry,* 8:143–154, 1966.

Raskin, A., Crook, T. H., and Herman, K. D.: Psychiatric history and symptom differences in black and white depressed inpatients. *J. Consult. Clin. Psychol.,* 43:73–80, 1975.

Sartorius, N.: Culture and epidemiology of depression. *Psychiat. Neurol. Neurchir.* (Amst.), 76:479–487, 1973.

Sartorius, N.: Depressive illness as a world wide problem. In: *Depression in Everyday Practice.* P. Kielholz (Ed.), International Symposium, St. Mortiz, (Huber, Berne/Stuttgart/Vienna), 1974.

Sartorius, N.: Epidemiology of depression. *WHO Chron.,* 29:423–427, 1975.

Sethi, B., Nathawat, S., and Gupta, S.: Depression in India. *J. Soc. Psychol.,* 91:3–13, 1973.

Tanaka-Matsumi, J. and Marsella, A. J.: Cross-cultural variations in the phenomenological experience of depression: I. Word association studies. *Journal of Cross Cultural Psychology,* 7:379–396, 1976.

Teja, J. S., Narang, R. L., and Aggarwal, A. K.: Depression across cultures. *Br. J. Psychiatry,* 119:253–260, 1971.

Tonks, C. M., Paykel, E. S., and Klerman, G. L.: Clinical depressions among Negros. *Am. J. Psychiatry,* 127:329–335, 1970.

Warheit, G. J., Holzer, C. E., and Schwab, J. J.: An analysis of social class and racial differences in depressive symptomatology: A community study. *J. Health Soc. Behav.,* 14:291–299, 1973.

Waziri, R.: Symptomatology of depressive illness in Afghanistan. *Am. J. Psychiatry,* 130: 213–217, 1973.

Wechsler, H.: Community growth, depressive disorders, and suicide. *American Journal of Sociology,* 67:9–16, 1961.

Werner, H.: *Comparative Psychology of Mental Development.* New York: International Universities Press, 1948.

CHAPTER 9

Schizophrenia

Few disorders are more subject to question marks than schizophrenia. Clues to the etiology, pathology, and treatment responses in this psychiatric puzzle have been pursued for years. Researchers have addressed their concerns to genetics, organic factors, birth order, and even climate and season of conception. They have looked to parental influence, child-rearing, and family structure for the answers; they have enlisted sociology to investigate the effects of urban versus rural environment, social class, and migration. Advances in drug therapy have been remarkable, yet the totality of schizophrenia remains an enigma.

In recent decades, the many aspects of schizophrenia have been studied cross-culturally. This approach has also resulted in tantalizing leads and varying theories, but no conclusions that are beyond challenge. To the many questions psychiatry asks about schizophrenia, the cultural psychiatrist must add: Does the cultural factor play a role of any importance in the prevalence, symptom formation, and subtyping of this condition? The literature shows positive and negative views; contradictions abound. Before we attempt to answer this question, we propose a review of pertinent writings.

EPIDEMIOLOGICAL STUDIES

At first glance, trying to compare prevalence of schizophrenia across cultures or time spans is a little like comparing apples to oranges; the only sure fact is that we are considering the broad classification, be it mental disorder or edible fruit. There are good reasons why the epidemiology of schizophrenia is fraught with inconsistencies. One is the varying methodology of diagnosis. Evaluations made by Kramer (1969) and Cooper et al. (1969) make this clear. The authors examined the well-known differences in first admission rates for the major psychoses to mental hospitals in England and Wales with rates in the United States. The age-adjusted rate per 100,000 population in the U.S. in 1957 was 23.8 for schizophrenia and 10.8 for major affective disorders. The England-Wales rate the previous year was 15.8 for schizophrenia and 30.4 for major affective disorders (Kramer). The implication is that the U.S. has more schizophrenia, while England-Wales have more of the affective disorders.

However, when the diagnostic methodology was standardized in a separate U.S. and U.K. study, the picture was different. This separate study (Cooper, et al., 1969) compared the original hospital diagnoses of patients with diagnoses made using a standardized clinical interviewing method, the Present State Examination (PSE). The patients were those admitted consecutively to Brooklyn State Hospital in the U.S. and to Netherne Hospital in England. The original hospital diagnoses showed schizophrenia rates of 56.6 in the U.S. and 35.2 in England. Diagnosed using the PSE, the rate became 29.7, U.S. and 22.8, England. Affective disorders in the original hospital diagnoses were 16.6, U.S. and 46.2, England. With the standard PSE, the rate was 36.6, U.S. and 58.6, England. Although genuine clinical differences still existed between the patient populations, the original cross-national difference by diagnoses was strikingly changed by standardizing the diagnostic instrument.

Unfortunately, studies of prevalence in many cultures during the same time period do not exist. We must be grateful for, if not content with, data which are available. One of the better known studies is that of Lin (1953). In 1946–48, he made a census survey of mental disorders among long-established Chinese in three Taiwan communities, and then compared Taiwan rates for schizophrenia with those of some other countries. The Taiwan rate was 2.1 per 1,000 population. This compared with a 4.6 rate in Sweden and 4.5 in Norway for approximately the same time period (1944). Within this decade, Finland (1936) had a 4.2 rate; two parts of the United States (1936 and 1938) had rates of 2.9 and 1.7; and in three parts of Japan (1940 and 1941), rates were 3.8, 2.1, and 2.2. In a somewhat earlier period, two parts of Germany (1929 and 1930–31) had rates of 1.9 and 1.5; and Denmark (1935) had a 3.3 rate. Lin's comparisons suggest that schizophrenia prevalence is not culturally influenced. There was no marked difference in rates among the populations studied.

Fifteen years later, Lin et al. (1969) made a follow-up survey of the same three communities in Taiwan. The years had brought social and economic changes. Educational levels had increased; many farmers or fishermen had become laborers with the rapid industrialization of the country; personal adjustments had been made to post-World-War-II changing life-styles; and there had been increased out-migration to cities and industrial areas. Yet, schizophrenia had decreased only slightly from 2.1 to 1.4 per 1,000 population, whereas psychoneurosis had risen noticeably from 1.2 in 1946–48 to 7.8 in 1961–63.

The authors point out that non-psychotic disorders are apparently affected by environmental factors much more than psychotic conditions. They also suggest that 15 years is not long enough for changes in the social environment to bring about psychosis in enough people to affect the prevalence rate. Though they recognize their data do not prove the point, they believe the study does support the view that biological factors operate in psychotic disorders more than in the neuroses. Genetic predisposition universalizes the disorder—but what about the variations in prevalence?

From Yugoslavia comes an intriguing study that pinpointed a striking difference in schizophrenia prevalence in one geographical area within a prevailing culture. Yugoslav psychiatrists have long believed that the coastal areas of Istria and Primorje in Croatia had more schizophrenia—in fact more psychotic disorders—than all other parts of Croatia. For at least a century, the area has been known for its high proportion of "insanity." Crocetti et al. (1964) confirmed this in a statistical study of hospital discharge rates and a simultaneous census of mental hospitals and general hospital psychiatric wards throughout Croatia. They found that the schizophrenia rate in this coastal area was more than twice as high as in the rest of Croatia. This high schizophrenia rate was accompanied by higher rates for all psychoses. Even though the area surveyed included people of other cultures (Italian, German, Hungarian, for example), their proportion was small; 82.6% of the Istria-Primorje population was Croatian. Crocetti and his colleagues speculated that people in this coastal area may have a generally lower state of general health and, consequently, are prone to all types of mental and physical disorders. There is apparently no cultural influence that can explain the Istria-Primorje findings. Perhaps local genetic differences explain this sharp variation. But let's look at other possibilities.

Torrey, Torrey, and Burton-Bradley (1974) chose New Guinea for a prevalence study because the area contains sharply contrasting Western-influenced and still-primitive districts. Though they found that four highland (still primitive) districts had a schizophrenia rate approximately one-tenth of the rate in districts exposed to Western civilization, they do not conclude the difference comes from cultural factors, migration, or bias in case-finding. Rather, they ask questions: Has exposure to Western civilization caused brain damage from chemicals and micro-organisms previously not encountered? Do slow or long latent viruses play a part in causing schizophrenia? They note that rubella, measles, and influenza have been unknown or rare in some primitive societies, but become prevalent when people live more closely in towns or cities.

Schizophrenia and Primitive People

A commonly held view of the past was that schizophrenia was rare or absent in primitive societies (Faris, 1934). This impressionistic belief was gradually abandoned as a result of later studies (Benedict and Jacks, 1954; Leighton and Hughes, 1961). However, as Demerath (1942) noted, the societies studied usually were not truly primitive. Further investigation is needed before making any conclusion.

Rin and Lin (1962) compared the prevalence of mental illness among four aboriginal tribes in Taiwan with that of the Chinese in Taiwan. The four tribes (Atayal, Paiwan, Saisat, and Ami) are of Malayo-Polynesian stock. They represent different levels of social development. The Atayal, the most primitive, are at the level of early agricultural settlement; the Ami are the most advanced, and many have daily contact with the Chinese; the Paiwan and Saisat fall between the two extremes. The schizophrenia rate for the aboriginal groups was 0.9 per 1,000 population, compared to 2.1 for the Chinese. However, the rates for organic psychoses, such as malarial psychoses, were higher for the aborigines than for the Chinese. Alcoholism among the aboriginals was also much higher, except for the Paiwan who had no alcoholism at all. Among the aboriginals, schizophrenia was characterized by an acute onset, hyperkinetic excitement, incoherent speech, visual and auditory hallucination, occasional non-systematized persecutory delusions, and a relatively favorable course and prognosis.

The Factor of Migration

A high schizophrenia rate in migrants has been reported by Odegaard (1932). Later, several researchers, including Malzberg and Lee (1956), confirmed this. Among the explanations hypothesized were: Schizophrenia was caused, in part, because migrants were faced with adjustments to a new culture (acculturation hypothesis); a migrant population already contains an undue proportion of pre-psychotic persons (selection hypothesis); migrants move to a new location to find a setting which frees them from social obligations (segregation hypothesis). According to Hare (1967), the selection hypothesis seems presently to account for most of the correlation between schizophrenia and migration.

Social Status and Schizophrenia

Faris and Dunham (1939) concluded from a Chicago study that the highest rates of first hospital admissions for schizophrenia were in the central city areas of lowest socioeconomic status. Rates diminished near or in higher status peripheral areas. This correlation has also been observed in other cities. It has also been noted that the larger the city, the stronger the correlation between rates of schizophrenia and these indices of social class. So far, this relationship of socioeconomic status to schizophrenia has been demonstrated only in urban populations (Kohn, 1968). Several hypotheses have been developed. For example, the "drift hypothesis" suggests that any differences in rates of schizophrenia are the result of social selection: People already predisposed to schizophrenia gravitate into the lower socioeconomic areas. A contrasting view holds that socioeconomic deprivation is a major etiological factor in becoming schizophrenic.

Hollingshead and Redlich (1954) reported an association between social class and the prevalence of schizophrenia in the New Haven, Connecticut, population. Ranking the population in five social classes, they found that among patients under treatment for less than a year, schizophrenia cases for the lowest, most underprivileged class more than doubled those in the two most privileged classes. The difference was even more striking when they compared chronic cases.

The authors propose that the high ratio of chronic cases to low social classes may be related to treatment differences. Lower-class patients enter treatment later than those in upper classes; lower-class patients are more likely to be given less intensive treatment, or no treatment at all, while middle- and upper-class patients receive more intensive therapy; lower-class patients are more likely to remain under custodial care, or are discharged without any support system. Middle- and upper-class patients are more often discharged to their families and receive family and community support.

A similar excess of schizophrenics in lower social class was found in the Goldberg and Morrison (1963) study made in England and Wales. This and the Hollingshead-Redlich study provided an interesting contrast in social mobilities of the patients. Hollingshead-Redlich reported that 91% of the low social class patients had remained in the same class as their parental families. On the other hand, Goldberg-Morrison found that occupational status, both from father to son and in the patient's own life, had declined. Both studies conclude that socioeconomic deprivation is not a major etiological factor in schizophrenia. Goldberg-Morrison believe the downward drift is a result of the disease process.

After assessing epidemiological data relating to social class in the literature, Kohn (1976) formulated the following hypothesis: People of lower social class lead constricted lives and have only limited experiences. This fosters limited and rigid conceptions of social reality. Such a narrow view impairs the ability to deal resourcefully with problems and stressful situations. Though this impairment does not in itself result in schizophrenia, when it is joined with genetic vulnerability and great stress, it can be disabling. In his view, no one factor explains schizophrenia; a combination of conditions, such as stress, genetics and social class, must be present to cause the disorder. We believe that this "total picture" approach to surveying possible causes should also include consideration of cultural elements.

CULTURE AND SYMPTOMS

Past studies have weighed the effects of culture on the symptoms and subtypes of schizophrenia. Or, to put it more formally, many have studied the psychoplastic effect of psychopathology (Al-Issa, 1970).

Two investigators looked to medical history—specifically to London's Bethlem (once named Bedlam) Royal Hospital. Klaf and Hamilton (1961) compared records of the mid-1800s and the mid-1900s to study phenomenological differences in schizophrenia over a time span. The average age, marital status, and familial incidence of the patients proved similar. In phenomenology came the remarkable differences. Nineteenth century patients were more preoccupied with religion, less preoccupied with sex, and more acutely disturbed, with psychomotor agitation on admission, than were their counterparts of the 20th century.

Not only time, but also geography points out symptomatic variations. A few examples: A 1956 study reported that catatonic rigidity and negativism accompanying the stereotypic manifestations of schizophrenia were more common in India than in other countries (Wittkower et al., 1960). In the same decade, schizophrenia in Africa was claimed to be a "poor imitation of the European forms," showing less violence and aggression than in the West (Benedict and Jacks, 1954). In Iraq, schizophrenic patients were termed more aggressive and more expressive than those in the United States and other Western countries (Bazzoui and Al-Issa, 1966). Schooler and Caudill (1964) compared Japanese schizophrenics at Matsuzawa Hospital in Tokyo with American patients at Spring Grove State Hospital, Maryland. They noted that the greatest difference in symptomatology was in the outward expression of illness. The Japanese displayed more physical assaultiveness toward family members; Americans showed more disruption in reality-testing. This was manifested by hallucinations, bizarre ideas, and feelings of perplexity. Both Japanese and Americans evidenced symptoms that attacked standards highly valued in each group's culture. In Japan, physical assaultiveness towards kin violated cultural ideals of self-control and respect toward one's family. In North America, the hallucinating and perplexed patient negated his culture's emphasis on practical, realistic thoughts and actions.

In multi-cultural Hawaii, Katz and his colleagues (1969, 1973) studied hospitalized schizophrenics of various ethnic groups. They noted that the contrast in manifest psychopathology was most marked between the Hawaii-Japanese (born in Hawaii of Japanese ancestry) and the Hawaii-Caucasian (born in Hawaii of Caucasian parentage) patients. The greatest divergence came in the expression of emotional states: hostility, anxiety, depression, and apathy. The Hawaii-Caucasian psychotic was more "emotional," while the Hawaii-Japanese was considered more "schizoid, withdrawn, and retarded." The authors observed that, while the patients' behavior varied by ethnic groups, there was little change in the basic characteristics—in either cognitive or perceptual aspects—of their psychoses. In the authors' opinions, the main impact of culture is seen in the way emotion and behavior are expressed; they support the view that psychosis as expressed through behavior is an exaggeration of a normal pattern.

In New York City, Opler (1959) surveyed matched samples of hospitalized male schizophrenics of Irish and Italian backgrounds. All the Irish traced their ancestry to southwestern parts of Ireland; all but one of the Italians came from the extreme south of Italy or Sicily. Regional cultural variants were virtually eliminated. He found seven significant differences between the two groups. They came in: sexual identification, guilt, behavior disorders, attitude toward authority, fixity of delusions, somatic or hypochondriacal complaints, and alcoholism.

- *Sexual Identification.* The Italian patients were predominantly overt homosexuals; most of the Irish were latent homosexual types. Here, Opler believes, culture played a part in shaping the homosexual tendencies common in schizophrenics. The Italian culture emphasizes masculinity for males and femininity for females; fathers are dominantly male and authoritarian. However, the culture also stresses the expression of sexuality. In their schizophrenic state, the Italian patients refused to imitate this paternal (or elder brother) example; what began as a latent sexual repulsion of this male role became overt homosexuality. The Irish culture is permeated with sexual repression, and the dominant family figure is the mother. The Irish patients feared the male role, felt anxiety and hostility toward females, but repressed homosexual urges.

- *Guilt or Behavior Disorders.* Most of the Irish patients were preoccupied with guilt and a sense of sin; the Italians were not. Instead, the Italians showed behavior disorders marked by impulsiveness and fluctuating or flighty emotions. The author found this in keeping with the Italian expressive, and the Irish repressive, characteristics.
- *Attitude Towards Authority.* The Italians were inclined to verbal rejection or active flouting of authority; the Irish tended to be compliant.
- *Delusions.* Two-thirds of the Italian patients had no delusions at all during the study; the remaining third had only minor, changeable, delusional episodes. The Irish had three times more delusional fixity. The reasons, Opler writes, concern each culture's influence on such specifics as handling sexual misidentification and hostilities and, more generally, on the repression or expression of feelings. The Irish culture not only encourages fantasy and withdrawal, but it also specifically prohibits acting out sexual misidentification and fosters a pervasive feeling that sex is sinful. Thus, the Irish patients were almost literally forced to find their defense against sexual guilts and low self-esteem in delusions. In contrast, the Italian culture allows expression of feelings and impulsive behavior. The Italian patients, therefore, had less need to build emotional shelter or escape hatches from the fabric of fantasy and delusion.
- *Somatic (Hypochondriacal) Complaints.* Here, the difference was less striking. Slightly more than two-thirds of the Italians had such complaints, but less than half of the Irish did.
- *Chronic Alcoholism.* Only one of the Italians was a chronic alcoholic. Of the 30 Irish, 19 were alcoholic.

Opler illustrated the fact that cultural background, including values, family system, personality patterns, and emotional expression, may influence the problems and behavior that schizophrenics manifest during their illness. However, we note that these culture differences come in the patients' peripheral symptoms or behavior problems. Certain basic (or core) symptoms of schizophrenia tend to be similar without regard to ethnic group.

The near universality of certain symptoms was brought out clearly in 1974. Carpenter and Strauss (1974) studied the diagnostic data of nine countries, gathered in the World Health Organization's International Pilot Study of

Schizophrenia. They reported that Schneider's first rank symptoms of schizophrenia all occur with enough frequency across cultures to have potential diagnostic usefulness everywhere. These include auditory hallucinations such as hearing one's own thoughts spoken aloud, hearing voices commenting on one's thoughts or actions, or hearing voices arguing about one; believing one's thoughts are taken away, leaving the mind blank; thinking one's thoughts are being broadcast so everyone knows them; feeling that one is a kind of passive "puppet" and that some other force is directing one's emotions, willpower, and actions; believing that some external force is imposing bodily sensations; and a form of interpretive delusion in which the patient first perceives some phenomenon normally and then interprets it in a personalized, delusional way ("The car stalled on Second Street; this means I have exactly two years in which to save the world").

CHANGING SUBTYPES

Does the passage of time alter schizophrenia subtypes? Morrison (1974) reviewed the admission records of Iowa State Psychopathic Hospital over a 47-year period and found a decided change in subtypes. The diagnosis of catatonic and hebephrenic schizophrenia decreased markedly; that of paranoid schizophrenia remained approximately the same; chronic undifferentiated schizophrenia showed a notable rise. Grinker (1973) also stated his clinical impression that, today, schizophrenic psychoses are less detached from reality, less dramatic, and have shorter durations than in the past.

Several factors should be taken into account for such changes in subtypes of schizophrenia, such as the diagnostic pattern (Kuriansky et al., 1974), the effects of the medical care system, and the results of drug therapy. For example, Zusman (1967) pointed out that the possible effect of chronic, institutionalized life on the psychopathology of the patients was to make them apathetic, depressed, passive, and chronically catatonic.

In 1966, Hogarty and Gross compared first-admission schizophrenic patients of the pre-drug treatment era with their counterparts of the post-drug therapy age. He found that, since the use of psychotropic drugs, more patients were being diagnosed as paranoid and chronic undifferentiated. He suggested that this diagnostic trend might reflect the chronic, persistent quality of symptoms the first-admission schizophrenics present after receiving drug therapy prior to admission.

Ethnic-cultural elements may also account for differences in schizophrenia subtypes. These elements may especially affect the complexity of mental life and its influence on the manifestations of psychopathology. It was Lambo

(1956) who noted that the clinical picture of schizophrenia in the Western region of Nigeria is characterized by the lack of predominance of any subvariety. German (1972) comments that, in Sub-Saharan Africa, transient acute psychoses with mental confusion and a favorable diagnosis are common.

CULTURE AND PROGNOSIS

For years, psychiatrists have speculated that typical cases of schizophrenia may be rare among primitive people; that, instead, an acute psychosis of short duration is common. Though this may be indistinguishable from classical schizophrenia in its initial stages, it runs a much shorter course and carries a better prognosis.

Murphy and Raman (1971) decided to test this theory. They conducted a 12-year follow-up survey of discharged schizophrenic patients on the island of Mauritius in the Indian Ocean. Two-thirds of the population are of Indian origin; the remainder, principally African. They then compared their data with data from a follow-up study made by the M.R.C. and Social Psychiatry Unit in Britain. Their conclusions: that the incidence of schizophrenia on Mauritius was very close to British rates, but the percentage of patients who functioned normally and were symptom-free on follow-up was higher than in comparable British samples; and that the Mauritius schizophrenic patients showed fewer relapses during the follow-up period than the British sample did. The authors do not believe climate or race were factors. They suggest that in less severe cases, the Mauritian culture encourages the disappearance of symptoms, while some European settings encourage them to persist. It is possible, they write, that the European patient is ensnared in an established sick role, but the Mauritian schizophrenic who has many superstitious explanations for his condition may not be trapped in this role. Though the authors point out that the severe cases did not remain symptom-free, their data generally support the theory that schizophrenia in indigenous African and Asian populations runs a less chronic course than among Europeans and North Americans.

For two years, Sartorius et al. (1977) traced the progress of patients included in the WHO International Pilot Study of Schizophrenia. More than a thousand patients from nine widely differing spots on the globe were studied. The follow-up showed that patients in developing countries had a more favorable course and outcome than those in developed countries. The premise that a relationship exists between sociocultural environment and the prognosis of schizophrenia is strengthened.

The authors speculated that the size of the family group, the nature of interaction between its members, the social stereotypes of schizophrenic disorders, and the medical and social welfare services system which might reinforce such stereotypes are examples of the sociocultural variables which may influence the course of schizophrenia. All these factors need further investigation. Certainly it is more difficult for the schizophrenic to function in a complex society. The schizophrenic farmer in a more primitive setting can usually continue to farm; often only his dog witnesses his eccentric behavior. The businessman in the city finds making a living more difficult; his mistakes and eccentricities are noted. In the family structure of more primitive societies, adult relatives—brothers, for example—are apt to retain close ties and give each other mutual support. Family ties for the schizophrenic in a highly developed society may have dissolved early in adult life. In everything from making a living to dealing with housing and transportation and even observing the requirements and regulations of the medical or welfare systems, the schizophrenic in an advanced society faces details, decisions, and stresses that his more primitive counterpart does not. All these can affect prognosis.

CULTURE, FAMILY, AND COMMUNITY

Because the schizophrenic patient withdraws from his environment, psychiatry necessarily looks to that environment to find what in it caused this need for retreat and separation, and to assess the hazards or benefits of returning the hospitalized patient to his environment. We look at parents, siblings, the family constellation, and at the supportive or rejecting character of the community. In more recent years, researchers also have looked at the culture which influences family and social group and, thus, may affect some aspects of schizophrenia.

For example, Brody (1961) studied young American black schizophrenics. He found that the group (nearly all male) came from matriarchal families with dominant mothers. Fathers were absent or remote or passive. There was a tendency to have important relationships with slightly older or more successful male peers and to suffer a break in these relationships before the psychotic break. He found the psychoses were marked by confusion, somatic concerns, and paranoid attitudes. Delusions were absent or poorly organized. Present were past histories of homosexual interest or relationships and overt homosexual concern. Very early in childhood, the young black becomes aware that his father and other father figures are vulnerable in relation to white males, Brody points out.

Sanua (1961) reported a study made by Sperling at Massachusetts Mental

Health Center. The parental cathexes of male and female Jewish, Irish, and Italian patients were investigated. Sperling found that 80% of the Jewish patients, male and female, showed withdrawal and ambivalent hostile-affiliative tendencies toward their mothers and 70% had an affiliative tendency toward their fathers. Of the Italians, male and female, 60% withdrew from their fathers and 50% from their mothers. However, the Irish males withdrew from their fathers and had ambivalent feelings toward their mothers; females also had ambivalent attitudes toward their mothers, but directed their affiliative tendencies to their fathers.

Sanua (1963) explored parent-child relationships in the families of 150 Protestant and Jewish schizophrenics from the Boston area. Represented were lower-class and middle-upper-class patients. Sanua noted that the greatest differences in parent pathology came in the lower socioeconomic class of both groups. The lower-class Protestant fathers were marked by bizarre acting-out, alcoholism, and excessive bad temper; the Jewish lower-class father was more often passive and ineffectual. The lower-class Jewish mothers had more emotional instability, psychotic breakdowns, and dullness than their Protestant counterparts.

Breen (1968) took a cultural-ethnic view of schizophrenic symptomatology when he propounded his exaggeration hypothesis: that schizophrenic behavior may be an exaggeration of normal life-style. For example, in a cohesive, aggression-controlling culture, schizophrenia may take dependency patterns; in the dispersive, aggression-expressive setting, the paranoid pattern is apt to appear. He examined his own assumptions in a comparative study of American black and American Jewish schizophrenics. They proved valid. Patients from the black (dispersive-aggression-expressive) group were predominantly paranoid; Jewish (cohesive, aggression-controlling) patients had dependency forms.

CONCLUSION

Throughout this chapter, we have presented often opposing views on the importance of culture in the etiology, prevalence, manifestations, and prognosis of schizophrenia. Among this seeming confusion of pros and cons, is there any area of agreement? We believe there is.

In our opinion, a review of the literature charts to some extent what is, and what is not, subject to differences of culture and era. Statistical data demonstrate that prevalence does not change to any marked extent. There are no sudden peaks of occurrence. Schizophrenia is more stable across cultures than, for example, alcoholism.

Certain symptoms seem common to schizophrenics in most cultures. We shall call these "core" symptoms, and define them as disturbance of perception, disturbance of thinking, and disturbance of affect. These are apparently universal. Cultural factors, however, operate in the content and expression of delusions and hallucinations. They also influence what we shall call peripheral symptoms and the comparative prominence of symptoms. Whether a patient is more or less withdrawn, more or less violent, the manner in which he detaches himself from society—these are subject to culture. There is evidence that subtyping is somewhat changed by culture and time span, and that prognosis is modified by the environment in which the patient lives.

Schizophrenia remains very much a mystery. We do not know exactly what this disorder is. Yet the very lack of cultural influences on core symptoms brings us closer to understanding what schizophrenia is not. We believe it is not culture-caused. Rather, it appears to be an endogenous disease process which, in its peripheral manifestations, is affected by environmental factors.

REFERENCES

Al-Issa, I.: Cross-cultural studies of symptomatology in schizophrenia. In: *Cross-Cultural Studies of Behavior,* W. D. Al-Issa (Ed.), New York: Holt, Rinehart, and Winston, Inc., 1970.

Bazzoui, W. and Al-Issa, I.: Psychiatry in Iraq. *Br. J. Psychiatry,* 112:827–832, 1966.

Benedict, P. K. and Jacks, J.: Mental illness in primitive societies. *Psychiatry,* 17:377–389, 1954.

Breen, M.: Culture and schizophrenia: A study of Negro and Jewish schizophrenics. *International Journal of Social Psychiatry,* 14:282–289, 1968.

Brody, E. B.: Social conflict and schizophrenic behavior in young adult Negro males. *Psychiatry,* 24:337–346, 1961.

Carpenter, W. T., Jr. and Strauss, J. S.: Cross-cultural evaluation of Schneider's first-rank symptoms of schizophrenia: A report from the International Pilot Study of Schizophrenia. *American Journal of Psychiatry,* 131:682–687, 1974.

Cooper, J. E., Kendall, R. E., Gurland, B. J., Sartorius, N., and Farkas, T.: Cross-national study of diagnosis of the mental disorders: Some results from the first comparative investigation. *American Journal of Psychiatry,* 125(10):21–29, 1969, Supp.

Crocetti, G. M., Kulcar, Z., Kesic, B., and Lemkau, P. V.: Differential rates of schizophrenia in Croatia, Yugoslavia. *American Journal of Public Health,* 54:196–206, 1964.

Demerath, N. J.: Schizophrenia among primitives. *American Journal of Psychiatry,* 98:703–707, 1942.

Faris, R. E. L.: Some observations on the incidence of schizophrenia in primitive societies. *Journal of Abnormal Social Psychology,* 29:30–31, 1934.

Faris, R. E. L. and Dunham, H. W.: *Mental Disorders in Urban Areas: An Ecological Study of Schizophrenia and Other Psychoses.* New York: Hafner Publishing, 1939.

German, G. A.: Aspects of clinical psychiatry in Sub-Saharan Africa. *British Journal of Psychiatry,* 121:461–479, 1972.

Goldberg, E. M. and Morrison, S. L.: Schizophrenia and social class. *British Journal of Psychiatry,* 109:785–802, 1963.

Grinker, R. R., Sr.: Changing styles in psychoses and borderline states. *American Journal of Psychiatry,* 130:151–152, 1973.

Hare, E. H.: The epidemiology of schizophrenia. In: Recent Developments in Schizophrenia, A

Symposium. A. Coppen and A. Walk (Eds.), *British Journal of Psychiatry*, Special Publication No. 1:9–24, 1967.

Hogarty, G. E. and Gross, M.: Preadmission symptom differences between first-admitted schizophrenics in the predrug and postdrug era. *Comprehensive Psychiatry*, 7:134–140, 1966.

Hollingshead, A. B. and Redlich, F. C.: Schizophrenia and social structure. *American Journal of Psychiatry*, 110:605–701, 1954.

Katz, M. M., Gudeman, H., and Sanborn, K.: Characterizing differences in psychopathology among ethnic groups: A preliminary report on Hawaii-Japanese and Mainland-American schizophrenics. In: *Mental Health Research in Asia and the Pacific*. W. Caudill and T. Y. Lin (Eds.), Honolulu, Hawaii: East-West Center Press, 1969.

Katz, M. M. and Sanborn, K. O.: Multiethnic studies of psychopathology and normality in Hawaii. In: *International Collaboration in Mental Health*, B. S. Brown and E. F. Torrey (Eds.), Bethesda: National Institute of Mental Health, 1973.

Klaf, F. S. and Hamilton, J. G.: Schizophrenia—A hundred years ago and today. *Journal of Mental Science*, 107:819–827, 1961.

Kohn, M. L.: The interaction of social class and other factors in the etiology of schizophrenia. *American Journal of Psychiatry*, 133:177–180, 1976.

Kohn, M. L.: Social class and schizophrenia: A critical review. In: *The Transmission of Schizophrenia*. D. Rosenthal and S. S. Kety (Eds.), Oxford: Pergamon Press, 1968.

Kramer, M.: Cross-national study of diagnosis of the mental disorders: Origin of the problem. *American Journal of Psychiatry*, 125(10):1–11, 1969, Supp.

Kuriansky, J. B., Deming, W. E., and Gurland, B. J.: On trends in the diagnosis of schizophrenia. *American Journal of Psychiatry*, 131:402–408, 1974.

Lambo, T. A.: Neuropsychiatric observations in the Western region of Nigeria. *British Medical Journal*, 2:1388–1394, 1956.

Leighton, A. H. and Hughes, J. M.: *Yoruba Concepts of Psychiatric Disorder*. Cornell Aro Epidemiological Study. First Pan-African Psychiatric Conference. Abeokuta, 1961.

Lin, T. Y.: A study of the incidence of mental disorder in Chinese and other cultures. *Psychiatry*, 16:313–336, 1953.

Lin, T. Y., Rin, H., Yeh, E-K., Hsu, G. C., and Chu, H-M.: Mental disorders in Taiwan, fifteen years later: A preliminary report. In: *Mental Health Research in Asia and the Pacific*, Honolulu: East-West Center Press, 1969.

Malzberg, B. and Lee, E. S.: *Migration and Mental Disease*. New York: Social Science Research Council, 1956.

Morrison, J. R.: Changes in subtype diagnosis of schizophrenia: 1920–1966. *American Journal of Psychiatry*, 131:674–677, 1974.

Murphy, H. B. M. and Raman, A. C.: The chronicity of schizophrenia in indigenous tropical peoples: Results of a twelve-year follow-up survey in Mauritius. *British Journal of Psychiatry*, 118:489–497, 1971.

Odegaard, O.: *Emigration and Insanity*. Copenhagen: Levin and Munksgaards Publishers, 1932.

Opler, M. K.: Cultural differences in mental disorders: An Italian and Irish contrast in the schizophrenics—U.S.A. In: *Culture and Mental Health*, M. Opler (Ed.), New York: The Macmillan Company, 1959.

Rin, H. and Lin, T. Y.: Mental illness among Formosan aborigines as compared with the Chinese in Taiwan. *Journal of Mental Science*, 108:134–145, 1962.

Sanua, V. D.: Socio-cultural factors in families of schizophrenics: A review of the literature. *Psychiatry*, 24:246–265, 1961.

Sanua, V. D.: The socio-cultural aspects of schizophrenia: A comparison of Protestant and Jewish schizophrenics. *International Journal of Social Psychiatry*, 9:27–36, 1963.

Sartorius, N., Jablensky, A., and Shapiro, R.: Two-year follow-up of the patients included in the WHO International Pilot Study of Schizophrenia. *Psychological Medicine*, 7:529–541, 1977.

Schooler, C. and Caudill, W.: Symptomatology in Japanese and American schizophrenics. *Ethnology*, 3:172–178, 1964.

Torrey, E. F., Torrey, B. B., and Burton-Bradley, B. G.: The epidemiology of schizophrenia in Papua New Guinea. *American Journal of Psychiatry,* 131:5, 1974.

Wittkower, E. D., Murphy, H. B., Fried, J., and Ellenberger, H.: A cross-cultural inquiry into the symptomatology of schizophrenia. *Annals of the New York Academy of Sciences,* 84: 854–863, 1960.

Zusman, J.: Some explanations of the changing appearance of psychotic patients. *International Journal of Psychiatry,* 3:216–247, 1967.

CHAPTER 10

Minor Psychiatric Disorders

The general impression among cultural psychiatrists is that minor psychiatric disorders, the so-called neuroses, situational adjustment reactions, substance abuse, and personality disorders, are more subject to sociocultural influences than major psychiatric disturbances (Lapuz, 1972; Neki, 1973; Lin et al., 1969). Yet very few studies have focused systematically on the cultural dimensions of these minor conditions. This may be partly because the diagnostic definitions are used loosely in various countries, and cross-cultural comparison thus becomes difficult. Also, to some extent, there is an assumption that we already know the nature of these minor conditions so well that there is little need for further investigation. In the last several decades, we have not made any notable, large-scale progress in understanding these lesser disorders. This chapter presents a few of the specific conditions which have been studied. It is designed to stimulate interest in further cross-cultural investigation in this field.

CULTURE, EMOTIONS, AND PERSONALITY TRAITS

The cultural dimensions of minor psychiatric disorders should be first studied in terms of culture and emotion. To do this one needs to know how people within a certain culture reveal their emotions in words, gestures, and facial expressions. Boucher (1974) notes Ekman and Friesen's proposed neuro-cultural theory of emotion which states that facial expression is one of the "biological substrates" of emotion, but that the individual learns what stimuli trigger specific emotions and thus learns to control the expression. It is a conclusion any poker player will agree with. All people share the same neurophysiological elements that correspond with fear, but they can learn what to be afraid of and how to reveal or conceal their fear. The controlled facial expression is the result of culture. If a certain society dictates that feelings of anger or joy are not to be displayed, an observer from another culture will be less able to interpret correctly the smiling, frowning, or virtually expressionless face. If a society demands that a smiling face be shown to strangers, depression and anxiety may be harder to detect. The learned, controlled expression of emotion may conceal the essence of emotion.

In cultural psychiatry, we have long recognized that the richness or paucity of terms for emotion in the vocabulary of a culture influences the differentiation of emotions. Leff (1977) believes that how an individual differentiates emotional experiences also depends on social context. Using material from the 1974 WHO International Pilot Study of Schizophrenia, he found that speakers of Indo-European languages differentiated anger from depression and anxiety, but made less distinction between anxiety and depression. Those who spoke non-Indo-European languages had trouble distinguishing among all three emotions. He hypothesized that people in developed countries show greater differentiation of emotional states than those in developing countries (Leff, 1973).

Several investigators have turned their attention to the measurement of such emotional states as anxiety. Spielberger (1976) developed the State-Trait Anxiety Inventory (STAI) for the self-reported measurement of both state and trait anxiety. With careful translation, this has proved useful across cultures. Some results show differences in how anxiety is experienced in different environments. For example, LeCompte and Oner (1976) note that STAI data for Spanish, American, Hindi, and Turkish samples show that Turkish adolescents and young adults demonstrated the greatest state and trait anxiety. Rather than suggesting a study of the Turkish culture to explain this anxiety, they suggest instead that various aspects of the testing situation itself may cause anxiety. When these are identified, they should be changed in accordance with the culture. Because the tests were given in a school setting, a question to be considered is: Does the school setting inspire anxiety in certain cultures?

Over two decades ago, in 1957, Cattell, Saunders, and Stice developed a testing method known as the Sixteen Personality Factor Questionnaire. Cattell and Warburton (1961) used this to study the personality patterns of American and British graduate students. Their findings indicated a marked difference in the structure of the self: The British group scored higher on ego strength and on rational control through self-sentiment (attitude toward self; self-esteem). The Americans showed higher superego development. The authors speculated that these differences may be correlated with the more rationalist moral outlook in Britain and the more fundamentalist moral upbringing in America. A similar study carried out by Tsujioka and Cattell (1965) compared American and Japanese students. Though the results showed essential agreement on most of the factor patterns, the Americans were significantly lower in anxiety and higher in Cortertia (cortical activation) level and in Exvia (no brief definition for the latter term is possible; we must be content with "extraversion"). Kelleher (1972) used the Cornell Medical Index and a short version of the Maudsley Personality Inventory to evaluate a group of Irish and English orthopedic patients. He found that the Irish had more obsessional symptoms and traits, and that they were more disturbed by having them, than the English. Bachelor status for the Irish males and rural residence for the Irish females were associated with the highest obsessional scores. All these studies make it quite clear that personality patterns may differ cross-culturally among the non-psychiatric, normal population.

THE STUDY OF PSYCHOLOGICAL STRESS AND DISTURBANCE

In recent years, several studies have attempted to measure psychological stress and disturbance in different cultural settings. In these investigations, the great difficulty is in applying existing measurement instruments and diagnostic criteria transculturally. The difficulty is compounded when cultural groups are markedly divergent. Beiser et al. (1976) solved the problem of measuring psychoneurotic behaviors among the Serer of Senegal, Africa, by first conducting a kind of vocabulary study. They collected terms for folk diseases and locally recognized mental-emotional disturbances as the Serer knew them. With this background, they were able to identify four dimensions in which the Serer expressed neurotic conditions: physiological anxiety, topical depression, preoccupation with health, and episodic anxiety. They were then able to carry out a culturally appropriate survey of psychiatric disorders.

For at least 30 years, studies have linked life events with illness, physical or mental. Hinkle and his co-investigators (1958) found over a 20-year study that, for most persons, illness tends to occur in clusters during periods of "environmental load." These illnesses most often occurred when people felt their lives were unsatisfying, over-demanding, threatening, or conflictual, and when individuals felt they could not adapt.

One instrument that correlates life events more specifically with resulting adjustments is the Social Readjustment Rating Questionnaire (SRRQ). Masuda and Holmes (1967) used the SRRQ to compare samples of Japanese living in Japan and white, middle-class Americans. The result showed great agreement in the adjustment demands of such life events as death of a spouse, marriage, death of a close family member, and divorce. However, cultural differences were apparent in other items. Detention in jail and minor violations of the law brought much more concern to the Japanese than to the Americans. The greater sense of shame, the higher regard for status, and the fear of social disapproval are all Japanese qualities. Getting a mortgage loan also carried greater impact for the Japanese. Borrowing from strangers is uncommon in Japan. Traditionally, the Japanese have borrowed from relatives or close friends in an atmosphere of asking and being granted a favor which, in some way, would later be returned. To be seen entering a money-lending institution was an embarrassment and a public acknowledgment of bad judgment or failure; an aura of shame hung over the formal transaction. In contrast, North America has a "credit card economy" where the mortgage is even valued as a tax deduction. However, the Americans attached much more importance to marital arguments, separations, and reconciliations than the Japanese.

When Kamaroff, Masuda and Holmes (1968) used the SRRQ to compare black, white and Mexican Americans, they found much more difference between responses of the whites and those of the two subculture groups than were evidenced in the Japanese-American study. Events related to labor and income, pregnancy, and changed health of a family member required more adjustment by the subculture groups, with the blacks feeling greater impact than the Mexicans. The authors concluded that the people living in the "pocket of poverty" in the United States are less similar to white American middle-class society than urban Japanese are.

MINOR PSYCHIATRIC DISORDERS AMONG VARIOUS CULTURES

Though the cross-cultural aspect of neurotic disorders has not yet been adequately studied, this does not mean interest in them has been lacking. As early as 1915, Coriat addressed the subject of psychoneuroses among primitive tribes and stated that, because of their less complex mental organization, neurotic disturbances were reduced to the simplest forms. His conclusion followed field study of the Yahgan and Ona tribes of the Fuegian Archipelago, inhabitants of coastal areas from Beale Island to Wollaston in the neighborhood of Cape Horn. These tribes were known to be among the most culturally primitive in the world. Coriat described fairly frequent episodes in which frenzied individuals rushed wildly from the wigwam and ran until almost, or completely, exhausted. The attacks, prevalent among men from 25 to 35 years, were preceded by moodiness. There were no amnesia or conversion phenomena, though the attacks were similar to hysterical episodes. Coriat speculated that these sudden emotional reactions, resembling the Eskimo *pibloktoq* attacks, are a primitive form of neuroses without significant inhibition or repression.

After comparing psychiatric patients who visited psychological medicine units in the multi-ethnic society of Kuala Lumpur, Tan (1969) reported that anxiety neurosis was more common among the Chinese than among Malays or Indians. The Chinese manifested anxiety in physical symptoms and sexual problems far more often than the other ethnic groups. Chinese male patients often focused their concern on spermatorrhea, which they associate with sexual intercourse or masturbation.

Spermatorrhea: A Concern of Chinese Neurotic Males

Mr. Tenn, a deeply worried young man of 20, came to a psychiatric clinic in Taipei with an urgent plea that we examine his urine to see if it contained semen. "Something is wrong in my kidneys," he said, "My urine doesn't look clear. I'm afraid I discharge semen everytime I urinate."

He complained that he felt tired all the time, his back hurt, his legs were weak, he could not concentrate, and his memory had grown bad. He bore with him a referral slip from a urologist who had found nothing wrong with his genito-urinary system.

Questioning revealed that his concern over spermatorrhea had begun six months previously when, on graduating from high school, he faced being drafted in the Army. (In Taiwan men who do not go to college are drafted for three years of military service.) At about that time, he had made his first (and so far, only) visit to a prostitute. It was not a satisfactory experience. Initially, Tenn feared he had contracted VD. This fear was soon overshadowed by the conviction he was losing semen and that this meant a kidney disorder. The focus of anxiety had changed when one of his friends died from nephrosis. He consulted his uncle, an herb doctor, who told him that, "Young men who masturbate too much may have trouble with their kidneys and even die." Grown anxious over his own masturbation, Tenn soon began to think, "My kidneys are affected. I might even die, just like my friend."

He promptly had a complete physical examination which showed no physical abnormality or illness.

Tenn's childhood history and family background provided plenty of clues to the young man's present difficulties. His father was a general in the Army—a strict disciplinarian and a firm believer that boys should be vigorous, athletic, self-confident, and geared to achievement. He was often away on Army duty; when he was stationed at home, he was busy with evening meetings. Tenn's mother came from a lower social class than her husband. The marriage was reasonably harmonious.

Tenn occupied the important place in a Chinese family: He was the eldest son. As a young child, he was considered weak and "sickly." He suffered from frequent attacks of diarrhea. He recovered from these after eating the soup and rice gruel his mother prepared especially for him. When he began school a servant carried him back and forth. While his mother protected and babied him, General Tenn—when he was home—tried to get the youngster to play ball, run, and "act like a real boy." As Tenn went on to grade school, his father lectured him frequently on the need to make high grades. This Tenn never quite achieved.

When Tenn was in junior high school, his father was transferred to another city, and Tenn then stayed in the school dormitory. There he complained so often of trouble in sleeping and eating and the general discomforts of dormitory life, that his mother began to visit him weekly, bringing with her home-cooked food. Finally, the mother persuaded General Tenn to let the son come home. There, his mother cuddled and sympathized with him while his father lectured him on "learning to act like a man."

Throughout Tenn's junior and senior high school, his father repeatedly demanded that his son make high grades so he could go to college or military school. His grades remained mediocre. As high school neared an end, some of Tenn's classmates began dating and talking about girls. Too timid to ask a girl for a date, Tenn summoned up his courage, visited the prostitute, and began to center his anxiety around his genito-urinary system.

The underlying problem is a universal one. But the symptomatic expression as an attempt to cope with the problem differs from East to West. It was clear that Tenn's problem was basically a symptom of disordered psychosexual development. Basically, Tenn suffered from insecurity as a male. Growing up with an overprotective, indulgent mother and a father who was alternately absent or present as a strict, demanding and emotionally distant person, Tenn was unable to relate to or identify with him. When the father expected high performance, his son failed. Where the father showed strength and confidence, his son demonstrated weakness and timidity. Inevitably, the young man grew to feel that "I don't measure up. Not in sports. Not in school. Not (as he viewed the dating of his peers) with the girls." He grew closer and closer to his mother who was sympathetic. But instead of facing his own insecurities, instead of openly acknowledging that "I can't meet father's standards," he dealt with the stress of joining the Army and being like his father by flight into a sexual experience with a woman, which failed to rescue him. He was then forced to develop symptoms such as, "I am weak. Physically, I am ill." He thus found a "reason" for "not measuring up."

On the surface are hypochondriacal concerns and psychosomatic symptoms. On a deeper level operate the doubts and fears centered on growing up and functioning as a man. How these levels are expressed and the ultimate outcome of such male insecurities and/or inadequacies can be quite different in Eastern or Western societies. Tenn's physical complaints came directly from the Chinese belief that losing semen means losing vitality. Intercourse in marriage carries some safeguard: The *yang* and *yin* are balanced. Outside of marriage, e.g., in extramarital intercourse or masturbation, spermatorrhea is thought to bring about weakness and even death. Tenn also followed cultural patterns in expressing mental-emotional distress in terms of bodily ills. Physical complaints in Chinese culture call forth concern and sympathy; psychological suffering does not.

The East-West contrast is marked in the coping mechanisms used. In Western societies, many young men with backgrounds like Tenn's might choose a homosexual orientation in life, a way of rejecting the father and identifying with the mother, or as an arrest of development at an earlier normal stage, one that is safer than the adult heterosexual one. Western culture offers coping choices based on performance, whether hetero- or homosexual. In China, the culture offers respectable physical ailments focused on sexual organs. With sexual equipment somehow "sick," the insecure male need not prove his sexual ability.

Psychosomatically Oriented Disorders in India

The following case, provided by Dr. Erna Hoch (1960), concerns a man who is "too weak to work." In this example, culture dictates family roles which, in turn, shape the direction neurosis takes. The patient's own words illustrate how the culture links mind-emotions-body conditions.

Let us first meet the patient, with no more information than he is a 35-year-old Hindu farmer from an area little touched by Western influence. He has no idea the clinic he has been referred to is a psychiatric one; he has had, says Dr. Hoch, no chance to build up defenses against a psychological approach (or adjust his speech to fit). The interview began thus:

Dr. H: What is your trouble?
Patient: My mind is bad.

Dr. H: How does this express itself?

Patient: I feel some giddiness. My eyesight is not clear. Often there is weakness in my whole body. This happens particularly whenever I try to do any work.

Dr. H: What is your work?

Patient: I am a farmer. I used to work in the fields.

Dr. H: What do you do now?

Patient: Nothing. I cannot work. I just lie all day, feeling restless, anxious. All just looks dark. There is heat in my whole body and my heart beats fast.

Dr. H: When did all this start?

Patient: Four or five years ago.

Dr. H: Who died at that time?

Patient: (His face first showed puzzled surprise. He then grinned broadly.) My father. My father died five years ago. My trouble started ten days after my father's death.

Dr. H: And you are the eldest son?

Again the patient smiles with surprise at the doctor's astute question before he answers "yes."

The clues have been supplied. The death of the father and its impact on the patient seem to be tied in with his position as the eldest son. Dr. Hoch's knowledge of the Indian-Hindu culture and her subsequent questioning affirmed this. In the Hindu tradition, the eldest son is pampered and kept in a kind of extended childhood without responsibilities. When his father dies, he is expected to become immediately the adult, responsible family head. The patient, though there were only two children, had been so pampered. When his father died, he went through the ritual (shaving his head) of accepting family responsibility, and his psychosomatic symptoms began. Dr. Hoch speculates that eldest sons are disproportionately present among Hindu neurotic men.

The case—almost unforgivably condensed here—is rich in other cultural factors. The patient's opening words, "My mind is bad," and his delighted recognition of the psychiatrist's linking of his initial symptoms with the father's death show what Dr. Hoch calls an Indian "natural awareness of psychosomatic unity." It is interesting that the patient also distorted a religious-cultural belief to fit his own dependency needs. Asked about his religion, he made it clear that he considered the godhead Bhagwan a universal provider who, because he had brought him into the world, owed him a living. The misuse or misunderstanding of Indian religious beliefs, not the beliefs themselves, is often implicated in neuroses, Dr. Hoch writes.

Shinkeishitsu (Nervous Temperament) Disorders in Japan

Japanese psychiatrists are familiar with an interesting neurotic disorder called *shinkeishitsu.* This is characterized by anxiety, a persistent sense of inadequacy, and fear of meeting people. The patient may fear encounters with people of intermediate familiarity (phobia of interpersonal relations) and dread eye-to-eye confrontation. There is hypersensitivity about being looked at or looking at others. The patient may be worried about blushing before others (erythrophobia) or be convinced that his body odor is unpleasant. As a result, he often tries to avoid approaching people. *Shinkeishitsu* most often affects the young. The patient is usually introverted, shy, sensitive, and lacking experience in socialization, particularly in a heterosexual setting. Often he has been overprotected by parents. Thus, the disorders tend to occur in adolescence when the patient finds it necessary to form his own social relationships outside the family. The prevalence and severity of *shinkeishitsu* make the condition quite different from the shyness sometimes seen in adolescents of Western cultures.

Shinkeishitsu is a product of Japanese thought, living conditions, and social custom. The Japanese culture is shame-oriented; how one appears to others is of paramount importance. The all-important "others" will be prompt with adverse (if unspoken) criticism if one is socially rude or inept. The culture is also geared to achievement; family as well as personal shame follows failure. There is a demand, indeed a need, for controlled and mannerly behavior, for Japan is a place of group affiliation and crowded living conditions. The small family home with its frail shogi partitions allows little privacy; one's actions are usually within another's sight or hearing.

Yet the Japanese realize that each personality has a dual makeup: *omote* the "front," and *ura* the "rear" natures (Doi, 1973). The "rear," all that is impulsive, aggressive and sexual, must somehow coexist with the "front," the controlled, courteous, agreeable aspects of man. And so, adjustments and outlets are arranged. In the home, there is the polite pretense of not watching and not hearing. In the social system, men are allowed to drink to excess, usually away from home. There is an "outside" and an "inside" language: one for the more formal encounters outside the family; one the relaxed speech suitable for intimates. With these adjustments, many Japanese adults reconcile their "front" and "rear" selves. The adolescent and the adult who has not learned this reconciliation-coexistence process are apt to suffer from *shinkeishitsu.*

Shinkeishitsu patients are often given the Japanese treatment called Morita Therapy. During the course of therapy, the patient is asked to write a diary, which is commented on regularly by the therapist. Segments of a patient's diary, with his therapist's daily comments, illustrate both some characteristics of nervous temperament disorder and how this patient suffers from anthrophobia (Kondo, 1979). The patient is extremely anxious and avoids getting close to other people. Admitted to a Morita-oriented hospital, he is confined to his room for a week of bed rest, followed by gradually increasing activity. His diary begins after the week of complete rest. The psychiatrist's comments, on the righthand side of the page, are written in the patient's diary each day.

Day One (of keeping diary)	*Doctor's Comments*
I did not sleep well last night. I had to make an effort to wake up this morning. After breakfast I swept the yard (he describes other light physical tasks).	It is nice that you have such an interest and such good intentions to work.
In the evening, I mentioned that I wanted to participate in the workroom activities, but I was told that since this is my first day (of activity), I should take a rest. I feel a little unhappy about this.	However, since you have just finished bed rest, go slowly.
I heard that if I did not worry and suffer while I took the one week bed rest, I might not get well. I am concerned that I did not suffer enough. . . . When I talk to other people, I am so tense that I cannot express what I want to. Sometimes I do not have the courage to communicate . . . when I am in the yard and somebody comes close to me, I still try to avoid contact and walk away.	Even while you are trembling, talk as you need to and as well as you can.
Day Two	
. . . I talked with other people in the workroom, but somehow my heart palpitates so strongly that I hesitate a little bit. (He describes physical activity). . . . The farewell party for a discharged patient was quite a bit of fun . . . only I feel a little discomfort in being overstimulated by the excitement . . . whenever I have contact	Try to see your problem of over-concern in an objective way and try to change gradually.

with others, I am concerned about their attitude towards me and worry that they have a bad image of me. . . .

Day Three

(The patient again describes in detail the tasks and wood carving he has done, using the phrases "I did it very carefully" and "I tried to do it very carefully.")

The doctor came to see me and talk to me, and I felt uncomfortable because I asked so many foolish questions. After supper . . . I played the guitar. Whenever people came in, my fingers and knees would tremble, and I could not play well. When I realize that there is no need to worry about how people feel about me, I feel more relaxed.

Our minds have two faces. Even if you are concerned by something, try to play what you want to play. Follow your desires.

I was called by the nurse, and I thought that maybe I did something wrong. . . . I found that my mother had left some money for me. . . . I appreciate that she is very concerned about me. However, as usual, I am afraid that she overprotects me.

It is quite natural for a parent to be concerned. However, do not become dependent.

Day Four

(The patient tells of having a fairly long and animated conversation with another patient.) Then I began to get worried about other people reacting to my laugh and funny faces during the conversation. I began to be concerned with people. Finally, I felt that I am foolish and crazy and disgusting, and I felt very unhappy. I feel very bad at how people look askance at me because I behave strangely. From tomorrow on, I definitely don't want to talk to anyone any more. . . . My symptoms not only do not improve, but look like they are getting worse. . . . I cannot stand it. I need to talk to the doctor tomorrow.

It is quite characteristic of this kind of neurosis to have this kind of attitude, to be concerned about yourself in such a way and to make a decision extremely at 100 or at zero.

Day Five

(After tasks and wood carving) my spirits rose, and I felt more hopeful again. . . . I wiped the window frames. . . . I wiped very hard. In the evening there was a party. . . . I felt uncomfortable, closed-in in the crowd, but sometimes I enjoyed the party. I began to feel intimate and close to some people who seemed cold to me before . . . I am happy that we could be friendly . . . . Yesterday and today I had a very valuable experience. I felt that maybe my illness was improving, but I will try not to expect too much too soon.

This is a good experience. If you decide that they are cold to you and never try to get close to them, then you will never have a chance to get friendly with them.

I tend to have a lot of salivation and feel uncomfortable and nauseated. Tomorrow I will try to encourage myself to work harder.

If things go well, do not become careless; if things get worse, do not get frustrated.

Essentially, Morita Therapy is designed to change the patient's focus of concentration. He is helped to focus on the task at hand, the situation to be faced, instead of on his symptoms. There is no attempt to get rid of the symptom; the goal is to live with the shyness, the trembling, the fear of blushing. In essence, it is a therapy of acceptance, rather than struggle. This acceptance begins in the first of four to five days of isolation when the patient regresses, and experiences all the thoughts, emotions, and anxieties that come with lonely inactivity. By the end of a week's isolation, work is welcome. Then the attention is directed to the task. The wood must be carved carefully, the windows must be thoroughly cleaned, the guitar is played whether or not one trembles, blushes or feels faint. In the daily task-filled routine, in the self-understanding gained through the commented-on diary, and, in many hospitals, in frequent personal consultation and group lectures by the therapist, the message comes through: One does not live by dwelling on one's own feelings and discomforts, but by doing what needs to be done. To greet the acquaintance is important; blushing during the greeting is not. To walk across a room to view a sunset or a flower matters; whether one walks timidly and with embarrassment does not. Seeing the beauty is the important thing. Though Japanese therapists do not all agree that Morita Therapy was inspired by Buddhist teachings, we feel that the theme of accepting self-and-symptoms has its roots deep in the Japanese culture. The "growing up" in a dependent relationship with a directive therapist, an authority or teacher who uses a cognitive or rational kind of approach, is also culturally syntonic. In the United States, it might be resisted as brain washing.

Malignant Anxiety in Africa

In stark contrast to the quiet manifestations of *shinkeishitsu* disorders in Japan is the malignant anxiety of Africa. Lambo (1962) described this as a clinical syndrome sometimes associated with criminal conduct. He coined the term "malignant anxiety" after studying 29 individual cases and analyzing three major epidemics in Kenya, Eastern Nigeria, and the Congo. We include the condition as a minor psychiatric disorder with some reservations. Though Lambo believed the condition lacked psychotic manifestations, the infrequent end result is homicidal acts by men and suicide attempts by women. The disorder is characterized by depersonalization, extreme irritability, intense anxiety with restlessness, intense fear of being bewitched or the conviction that one is bewitched, and psychosomatic symptoms.

Lambo supplies the following case history. The case of E.J., a 48-year-old Nigerian, came to clinical attention when he was convicted of murder. E. J. was born in a small village where his father, an aggressive, unloving man, was chief. E.J. had married three wives and fathered two children. For years he had belonged to a secret cult. After the government banned the cult, E.J. moved to a large town to find work, but "things went from bad to worse." With emotional and financial insecurity, his symptoms developed. He became mortally afraid of being a victim of black magic and began to feel he was gradually changing within himself. He had attacks of shivering, feelings of "emptiness" in his head, and a sense of constriction in his stomach. After unsuccessful moves to two more towns, he returned to his village. There, for the first time, trance states followed episodes of intense anxiety and fear. He then rejoined the secret society. Eventually, he took a leading part in a society murder, though he said the society did not commonly do this. Later, he committed another murder on a night when he suffered from excruciating anxiety, cold sweats, and severe palpitation. After the murder, he felt relieved for a short time.

This case illustrates the occurrence of malignant anxiety among middle-aged Africans who are in the process of renouncing their culture and assimilating a new way of life. The syndrome is rare in an undisturbed sociocultural environment. When adaptation to new and stressful life situations is difficult, anxiety with psychosomatic manifestations and criminal behavior may occur in individuals with unstable, premorbid personalities. Though most cases are sporadic, the disorder sometimes assumes an epidemic form.

SUBSTANCE ABUSE AND CULTURE

Nearly every society has, at different times, known substance abuse. The extent, the causes, and the attitudes concerning the problem may have varying social-cultural foundations. Three divergent examples of abuse, attitudes, and control are presented here.

Post-War Epidemic Use of Amphetamines in Japan

Immediately after World War II, the Japanese were faced with grave problems of social and economic reconstruction. Everyone was forced to work long and hard for food, clothing, and housing. During this period, the central nervous system stimulant, amphetamine, appeared on the market. Many Japanese believed the *kamikaze* pilots had used the drug in their suicidal attacks; now it was being sold with advertising that advised, "Get rid of slumber and be full of energy." At first, only night workers, such as waitresses and bartenders, college students, artists, entertainers, and some writers, took amphetamines. Later, use of the drug spread into the general population. It was probably used as a socially sanctioned antidepressant, but then society reacted against the mass abuse of the drug, and restrictions to control it went into effect. Soon, the drug use virtually ceased; only runaways and juvenile delinquents took amphetamines. The phenomenon was a transient one that reflected the social atmosphere at the time (Hemmi, 1974). It had served its purpose and was no longer needed as Japan became a nation again.

Opium Smoking in Laos

Westermeyer (1974) provides an account of opium use among the Meo people of Laos. For most of these tribal people, the primary value of opium was economic; nearly every household grew opium to trade for silver and iron. Though some Meo smoked opium occasionally and some were addicted, the majority did not use it. Westermeyer found that most addicts were farmers, that women far outnumbered men, and that addiction was not associated with criminality or uniformly related with decreasing social competency. He believes certain cultural factors accounted for this difference from other places where addiction was primarily a city phenomena associated with criminality and low social competency. Because the Meo raised their own opium, no one was driven to crime or violence to obtain it. Addiction was not considered socially desirable, but no great social opprobrium descended on the addict.

Radical Eradication of Opium Abuse in China

In pre-revolutionary China, both the problem and attitudes towards opium abuse were far different from those in Laos. Lowinger (1972) reports that by 1906, more than 15 million Chinese were addicted, and by the 1920s, one-fourth of China's adults used opium. The problem was wiped out by political action. Early in 1950, Premier Chou En-Lai signed an order prohibiting opium. By March 1953, government sources announced that the cultivation, production, and sale of opium had been completely eliminated. This has been confirmed by non-Chinese investigators.

The entire, and successful, program combined medical care for addicts with a massive campaign that labeled addiction a social-political problem. The major thrust was to change the ideology of the young and prevent new addicts while those already addicted were treated. Detection of addicts by local Communist cadres and heavy social censure of users was combined with mass propaganda that presented opium abuse as an offense against the country as well as the individual's health. At the same time, with distribution of the land from landlords to peasants, poppy fields were replaced by food crops. Penalties for those responsible for growing and manufacturing and selling opium included execution; leniency was given those merely employed by opium traffickers. Opium, heroin, and equipment were burned at well-publicized mass meetings. Almost a century of opium use had been relegated to history in three years. Passivity was no longer a desirable or permissible character trait in a newly emerging nation. Its reinforcement with opium was eliminated; national character needed to change.

COMMENT

We have reviewed a few of the minor psychiatric disorders which have been studied in relation to cultural factors. Yet we feel certain that in every inhabited spot in the world, large numbers of people suffer in varying degrees from minor mental-emotional afflictions which are linked to social-cultural stresses, values, and customs. These deserve the attention of cultural psychiatry. Up to now, investigation has centered on the severe disturbances and the clearly culture-specific or culture-bound conditions. In some of these—schizophrenia is a paramount example—the role of biological factors has become more evident; the role of culture has receded. It is time now for a change in direction—time for the systematic study of the neuroses, situation adjustment reactions, and other disorders that clinicians (if not patients) term minor. We need to know to what degree these ills are due to society and culture and in what respects they transcend cultural differences.

This change of direction brings certain requirements. The methodology of investigation needs to be improved. We need better methods to objectively describe manifestations and to identify underlying psychological causes. These descriptions and identifications must conform to a standard methodology to make true cross-cultural investigation possible and conclusions valid. If we are to dig into the great mine of yet unexplored information, we must first refine, sharpen, and test our tools.

REFERENCES

Beiser, M., Benfari, R. C., Collomb, H., and Ravel, J-L.: Measuring psychoneurotic behavior in cross-cultural surveys. *J. Nerv. Ment. Dis.*, 163:10–23, 1976.

Boucher, J. D.: Culture and the expression of emotion. *International and Intercultural Communication Annual Vol. 1,* 1974.

Cattell, R. B. and Warburton, F. W.: A cross-cultural comparison of patterns of extraversion and anxiety. *B. J. Psychol.,* 52:3–15, 1961.

Coriat, J. H.: Psychoneuroses among primitive tribes. *Journal of Abnormal Social Psychology,* 10:201–208, 1915.

Doi, L. T.: Omote and ura: Concepts derived from the Japanese two-fold structure of consciousness. *J. of Nervous and Mental Disease,* 157:258–261, 1973.

Hemmi, T.: Social-psychiatric study of drug abuse in Japan. From: *Proceedings of the 5th World Congress of Psychiatry.* Mexico, D. F., 25 November–4 December, 1974. Reprint from *Excerpta Medica* International Congress Series No. 274, 190–192.

Hinkle, L. E., Christenson, W. N., Kane, F. D., Ostfeld, A., Thetford, W. N., and Wolff, H. G.: An investigation of the relation between life experience, personality characteristics, and general susceptibility to illness. *Psychosom. Med.,* 20:278–295, 1958.

Hoch, E. M.: A pattern of neurosis in India. *Am. J. Psychoanal.,* 20:8–25, 1960.

Kamaroff, A. L., Masuda, M., and Holmes, T. H.: The social readjustment rating scale: A comparative study of Negro, Mexican and white Americans. *J. Psychosom. Res.,* 12:121–128, 1968.

Kelleher, M. J.: Cross-national (Anglo-Irish) differences in obsessional symptoms and traits of personality. *Psychol. Med.,* 2:33–41, 1972.

Kondo, K.: Personal communication, 1979.

Lambo, T. A.: Malignant anxiety in Africans. *J. Ment. Sci.,* 108:256–264, 1962.

Lapuz, L.: A study of psychopathology in a group of Filipino patients. In: *Transcultural Research in Mental Health.* W. Lebra (Ed.), Honolulu, Hawaii: University Press of Hawaii, 1972.

LeCompte, W. A. and Oner, N.: Development of the Turkish edition of the State-Trait Anxiety Inventory. In: *Cross-Cultural Anxiety.* C. D. Spielberger and R. Diaz-Guerrero (Eds.), Washington, D.C.: Hemisphere Publishing Corporation, 1976.

Leff, J. P.: Culture and differentiation of emotional states. *Br. J. Psychiatry,* 123:299–306, 1973.

Leff, J. P.: The cross-cultural study of emotions. *Cult. Med. Psychiatry,* 1:317–347, 1977.
Lin, T. Y., Rin, H., Yeh, E. K., Hsu, G. C., and Chu, H-M.: Mental disorders in Taiwan, fifteen years later: A preliminary report. In: *Mental Health Research in Asia and the Pacific.* W. Caudill and T. Y. Lin (Eds.), Honolulu, Hawaii: East-West Center Press, 1969.
Lowinger, P.: How the People's Republic of China solved their drug abuse problem. In: *Proceedings of the 34th Annual Scientific Meeting, Committee on Problems of Drug Dependence.* Washington, D. C., National Academy of Science, 1972.
Masuda, M. and Holmes, T. H.: The Social Readjustment Rating Scale: A cross-cultural study of Japanese and Americans. *J. Psychosom. Res.,* 2:227–237, 1967.
Neki, J. S.: Psychiatry in South-East Asia. *Br. J. Psychiatry,* 123:257–269, 1973.
Spielberger, C. D.: The nature and measurement of anxiety. In: *Cross-Cultural Anxiety.* C. D. Spielberger and R. Diaz-Guerro (Eds.), Washington, D.C.: Hemisphere Publishing Corporation, 1976.
Tan, E. S.: The symptomatology of anxiety in West Malaysia. *Aust. NZ J. Psychiatry,* 3:271–276, 1969.
Tsujioka, B. and Cattell, R. B.: A cross-cultural comparison of second-stratum questionnaire personality factor structures—anxiety and extraversion—in America and Japan. *Journal of Social Psychiatry,* 65:205–219, 1965.
Westermeyer, J.: Opium smoking in Laos: A survey of 40 addicts. *Am. J. Psychiatry,* 131:165–170, 1974.

PART III

Culture and Special Social Phenomena

CHAPTER 11

Culture, Religion, and Psychopathology

THE PURPOSES OF RELIGION

Because people ask questions, people formulate religion. Why does it thunder? What made me sick? How was Life created? And the ultimate question: What happens after I die? Religion, says anthropologist Keesing (1976), answers and explains.

Because human beings seek a sustaining, solacing force, they have religion. Religion reinforces human ability to cope with death, disaster and failures. "Religion," said Freud, "is . . . born of the need to make tolerable the helplessness of man." Because people live in groups which must observe moral and social rules to survive, they have religion, for religion validates and reinforces the social order.

To answer questions, provide strength and comfort, be the supreme authority behind religious reinforcement of social codes, and provide a focus for awe and fantasies, man had to conceptualize some great and vital power. It became necessary to create deity. Deity took many forms. It was an energizing, vital force; Pacific Island peoples called this *mana*. It was a god-head: To the Iroquois Indian, it was the "Great Spirit"; to Central African tribes, it was *Leza*, or "Cherisher," maker of the world. And with most primitive peoples, deity was also many gods and spirits, for in early beliefs, supernatural beings took animal, plant, and mineral form; they existed in sunlight and clouds and rainfall, and in every natural force. They also took the image of man.

Religious Concepts Are Formed

In one view, how deity is envisioned is shaped by culture and era. It has been thought that when some American Indians and Australian aborigines evolved their systems of totems, they were expressing kinship between man and animals. In present-day anthropological thought, the totem animals, each representing a family line, played out a human drama on a sacred-mystic stage. (One does not kill a member of one's family line if group existence is to continue; thus, if one's family totem is the turtle, one does not kill and eat a turtle.) Relationships between social groups were conceptualized as relationships between animals (Keesing, 1976). Certainly the ancestor gods of Africa, the American Indian culture, and the Pacific Islands are an expression of these cultures' high regard for the wisdom and authority of the family elders. Chinese ancestral worship extends filial duties beyond death.

Yet, in another view, the shaping of deity is seen as the projection of individual feelings and anxieties. To Ernest Jones, religious life expressed on a cosmic scale the "emotions, fears, and longings which arose in a child's relation to his parents" (LaBarre, 1970). Sigmund Freud (1955) saw one aspect of totemism as the symbolic dramatization of tribal guilt over parricide and incest. Derek Freeman notes that the Malayan Semang thunder god was a punishing father figure (Keesing, 1976). Christianity envisions God the Father, mighty judge of the righteous or sinful, and also makes Him approachable in the figure of Jesus, the Son. Anthropologist LaBarre suggests that "God" will change with each generation's experience with changing parental styles.

Religious concepts are thus formed either when certain fantasies, beliefs, or needs are naturally common to the group, or when a charismatic individual has his private vision, fantasies, and beliefs accepted by the group.

Religion Supplies Answers

Religion provides answers and explanations to disturbing questions: "Why am I sick, bereaved, a failure, in distress?" may be answered with the solacing and resigned, "It is God's will," "It is Karma," "This is the will of Allah." The questions may be answered with the guilt-tinged "because you have offended a god, nature spirit, ancestor ghost, disregarded a *tabu,* or broken a commandment." The answer to existence may be found in the Book of Genesis, or—long before Christianity—in the Persian Zoroaster account of a world created in six days, and of a man named Mayshya and a woman called Mashyoi, who were driven out of paradise because they disobeyed God.

The question "What happens after death?" and the answer religion gives, "There is life after death," are almost universal, yet the nature of this eternity is shaped by culture. Teutonic warriors once could look forward to Valhalla; Buddhist sects today differ in their descriptions of *Jodo* Land, Paradise, or the Pure Land. The heaven of Judaism, Christianity, and Islam, the Isle of the Blest of Chinese Taoism—all these are the eternity of bliss for the virtuous. Hindu faiths answer the ultimate query with yet more cycles of reincarnation and the ultimate, distant release of *nirvana.*

(Eternal reward is usually conceptualized as being in the sky; eternal punishment, beneath the earth and accompanied by fire. Yet cultures that have known and feared famine—Hawaii and India, for example—have also visualized the punished soul as being forever hungry.)

Religious concepts of life after death do more than answer and explain the riddle of the grave. In the doctrine of continuing existence of soul or spirit, religion sustains and comforts the bereaved. The prospect of eternal punishment for wrong-doing reinforces moral-ethical codes of society; the promise of eternal reward for virtue justifies the inequities of human fortune. Yet belief in hellfire for all time can reinforce guilts and anxieties. Undue emphasis on everlasting bliss can inhibit personal ambition and retard social progress. "It is God's will" may be alibi as well as solace.

Religion as a Social-Moral Force

"Religion," LaBarre (1970) wrote, "demands behaviors, loyalties, and commitment." With these demands, religion is a powerful social force. It is a kind of spiritual policeman who sees to it that society's rules of ethical-moral order are obeyed. In primitive societies it operated in religious taboos. The social uses of the taboo were many: They upheld the authority of chiefs, regulated food supplies, spelled out and enforced incest regulations and rules of warfare. Religion defined ethical-moral standards in the Ten Commandments of Christianity. The Koran of Islam and scholarly scriptures of Judaism include regulations governing marriage, divorce, food, and many aspects of daily life. Mohammed proclaimed that one must give alms in the name of Allah—and thereby insured succor for widows and orphans. He prohibited gambling and alcohol, both potentials of trouble in military camps of his people. Buddha taught the necessity of doing good deeds; Confucius outlined a complete code of conduct in his teaching of *Li,* the moral-religious way of life. Religion can also uphold social standards which in Western democratic thought seem undesirable. Hindu tenets strengthened and continued a preexisting caste system in India. The revival of Shintoism in Japan at around 1850 also revived belief in the divine origin of the emperor. Without this belief, would Japan have so obediently engaged in World War II? Would the Japanese soldier have fought with such fanatical bravery if he had grown up in a culture which questioned the decisions of an ordinary, mortal ruler?

Religion Can Fill Society's Lacks

Though religion often reinforces society's practices and prohibitions, it can also protest against established ways and attempt to fill gaps in the social structure. In fact, society's deficiencies often generate new religions. This is strikingly demonstrated in Korea where new religions have followed periods of social unrest since 1860. Kim (1973) counts approximately 240 new sects in existence today. All of these new religions contain elements of Confucian, Tao, Buddhist, and Christian doctrines. All believe that the world will shortly end and that the new world will be filled only with believers and will have no poverty, disease, or social classes. Thus, Korea will be the religious and political center of the world. Many of the new religions also incorporate sexual activities with their rituals and practice faith healing.

Kim sees the new religions as wish-fulfillments of the deprived. Most of the members are from lower socioeconomic groups and are illiterate. They are predominantly women; many are separated, widowed, or married to impotent men. Traditionally, Korea's culture has viewed sexual needs with shame; the new religions offer a sexual outlet. Modern medicine has still not advanced to any great extent, thus faith healing provides an apparent answer to health concerns. Traditional religions have failed in many ways, so new faiths have great appeal. Korea's burgeoning religious movements are an effort to supply what is lacking in the society.

Deficiencies in the social structure, plus personal grief and instability, helped bring about a small magico-religious cult in the province of Salerno, Italy. This began in the 1960s after an illiterate peasant woman became "possessed" by her dead nephew. Through him, she advised and "cured." The cult continues today as pilgrims come to seek relief from physical and emotional ills. Risso believes that the troubled clients go through an emotional state in which "real suffering is replaced by suffering on a ritual level where it can be undone." The area from which cult members come is economically deprived. Also, both conventional medical care and traditional religion have failed to meet the people's needs (Risso, 1973).

In Africa, new religions are now protesting against modern, white, economic and cultural inroads, and restating tribal feelings and beliefs. Nearly

5,000 new independent churches have been formed, most of them in areas where white oppression is greatest. One, the Bantu church, envisions a black Christ and a heaven which will close its gates to the privileged white people. To belief in the Christian God are added tribal elements, such as the ritual use of masks, drums, and drugs (Kiev, 1972).

New religions obviously arise when established beliefs no longer provide the spiritual and social benefits a congregation needs; when a group or a charismatic leader can no longer accept church tenets; or when a charismatic leader convinces others to follow his own, private, individual vision or theory. (Frequently all three conditions merge.) Martin Luther was a conscientious rebel; Guyana's Reverend Jones was (apparently) a paranoid schizophrenic who tapped the needs and desires of his followers. When the Japanese could no longer believe their emperor was divine, new Shinto sects without the dominant theme of emperor worship arose. In the United States, medical care is skilled, efficient, expensive, and, it is often claimed, impersonal. Here, thousands of conservative, middle-class persons have embraced faith healing in the last four years. Is religion attempting to fill some lack in the treatment system? The question is worth thought.

Religion: A Way to Transcend Self

To summarize thus far, religion fills many of man's needs. It answers and explains, strengthens and comforts, reinforces social-ethical codes, functions as wish-fulfillment, projects private and group feelings, supplies protective alibis, and provides a heavenly superhero—or heroes—on which man can focus his awe. Yet if religion did only these things, it would leave unsatisfied and unfilled yet another human need: man's urge to transcend his reasoning, practical self. If the pragmatic state is sanity, then, argues Keesing (1976), man is the "only animal that needs to be insane to survive." Religion lets man "lose himself" when he accepts on faith what he cannot accept on rational grounds; when, in varying degrees, he surrenders alert and conscious thought to the emotional stimuli of ritual, prayer, song, or chant; when he feels the "nothing-ness" of *nirvana* in its Buddhist meaning; when he loses a sense of reality in transcendental ecstacy.

Precisely because man must "turn off" some of his reasoning, questioning capacity to accept the inexplicable mystery of faith, religion can be a factor in either mental-emotional health or pathology. In this chapter, we are concerned with religious practices and religious bodies and with their effect on mental, emotional, and, sometimes, physical health.

THE TWO FACES OF RELIGION: HEALTH OR PATHOLOGY

Any religion may be put to normal or pathological use. Certainly, the line of normality is crossed when devotion becomes fanaticism, or when religious practices seriously disturb regular patterns of personal or community life or threaten private or public health or safety. Certainly, religion-influenced death is pathological religious behavior. Such deaths have occurred in faith healing which refuses life-saving medical treatment; in the religion-based refusal to allow blood transfusion, immunization against communicable disease, or abortion to save the mother's life; in the self-destruction of The People's Temple members. Certainly, religion is pathological when a leader uses it as a way to grow rich on the contributions of his followers; when salvation is peddled at a price. Certainly, religious conviction is put to harmful use when it joins politics: when Catholic is pitted against Protestant in Ireland; when Shi'ite fanaticism inflames passions in Iran.

To judge whether a particular religious ritual is healthful or pathological depends, among other things, on knowing what the ritual means and what effect it has on its devotees. Consider the following examples.

The Ghost Marriage

Ghost marriages were held in pre-communist China, and Jordan (1972) describes recent ceremonies in a village of Taiwan. In the Taiwan examples, the need for such a marriage becomes apparent when an illness strikes a family and a shaman finds the cause is that a ghost needs a living husband. Sometimes the ghost appears in a dream and sends what amounts to a "marry me" command. Until this husbandless ghost is wed, illness and disturbance will continue. Therefore, either a family male or an outsider lured with money must go through a wedding ceremony. For the ceremony, a "bride" may be made of cloth and paper and dressed in garments that resemble wedding garb and, in some details, symbolize a corpse. Once the ritual is held, the "ghost bride" becomes a member of her living husband's clan. Illness is no longer credited to an angry spirit; anxiety is eased; psychosomatic discomforts may indeed disappear. Among other reasons for ghost marriages are a believed prediction by a fortune teller that a man is fated to marry more than one wife (it's better to have one "ghost wife" than two live ones), or the urgings of a wife that her husband marry a powerful "ghost wife" so that he is watched and controlled.

A personal friend tells of a marriage that took place in her family in pre-communist China. In this case, a ghost bridegroom was needed.

When my aunt's fiance died, she was married to him by proxy. A rooster, symbolizing masculinity, took the groom's role. After the ceremony, my aunt went to live with her "husband's" family. She was a member of the family clan. My aunt remained a virgin for the rest of her life. Without the ceremony, she would have been a scorned spinster. With the marriage, she had security and status. She was in every respect a daughter-in-law in the household.

These macabre ceremonies stem from the traditional Chinese belief that a woman must not die unmarried. This rests on more than social contempt for the spinster; even infant girls who die are also in an unfortunate predicament, for until a woman has a husband, she has no chance of being worshipped after death. An ancestral tablet on the family alter will come to her only through her husband. (The ghost of an unmarried female, unworshipped, paid no ritual sacrifice, naturally becomes an angry ghost who can cause illness.) A ghost marriage entitles a living woman to status and freedom from want. Most importantly, it provides a woman, living or already dead, with a place in the spiritual realm of the ancestors.

Firewalking

In many places and through many years, men have demonstrated the art of walking on hot embers or rocks. Firewalking was done in ancient Rome; men in Greece tread glowing embers today. The practice continues in Singapore, Taiwan, India, Malaysia, Mauritius, South Africa, Trinidad and Spain. It is known in New Zealand, Japan, China, Tibet, parts of New Guinea, Fiji, Tahiti, and the Cook Islands. In religious context, firewalking can be done as purification or to worship, thank, or appeal to a god. By demonstrating mastery over heat and pain, it provides special status as the god's chosen one. Shorn of religious significance, it is also done to demonstrate the control of mind over body.

Some rural Taiwanese practice firewalking today when illness strikes the village, quarrels threaten the general peace, or an important community decision must be reached. Men of the village burn a huge pile of charcoal in the temple courtyard and spread the hot coals over a large area. Then eight to ten men, carrying traditional sedan chairs, each bearing a statue of the god, swing the chairs around the courtyard. Barefooted, the men then dash across the hot coals. Some are burned; others escape unharmed.

Indian firewalking may or may not be a religious ritual. As an offshoot Hindu sect practices firewalking in Fiji, it honors the mother-goddess Devi

(Lipton, 1972). The firewalking is preceded by prayer, partial fasting, bodily discomfort or flagellation, purifying baths—and a preparatory ritual that makes firewalking an anti-climax! To chant and drum beat, the devotees kneel before a priest who sticks sharp needles through cheeks, tongues and gullets. Neither bleeding nor pain is evidenced. After this, they walk over a pit of hot coals.

Only one select group of Fijians walk over hot rocks. They are the men of the Sauau tribe on the small island of Beqa. These men say they have the "gift" handed down from legendary times by an "eel god." Today, the Beqa firewalkers perform regularly for tourists, using the money earned to control coastal erosion of their island. In personal interviews, the men expressed a matter-of-fact view of their gift, but said they observed sexual abstinence and food taboos and prayed before a performance.

How many firewalkers escape unburned is not known; no adequate studies have been done. The pertinent topic is why the devotees practice their traditional ritual. For the Taiwanese, firewalking is an enabling rite. It increases the confident feeling that their god, pleased and honored with the ceremony, helps them. The Fijians put civic enterprise in ritual form; they are indeed helping to save their island from the sea. To them, firewalking is also a source of cultural pride; they are the sole Fijian tribe with the "gift." According to S. Cromwell Crawford, Professor of Religion at the University of Hawaii, the Indian firewalkers are demonstrating a stage of Hatha Yoga, that of mind-body control. This leads to control of instincts which are barriers to discovering the inner reaches of the mind.

God-tinged Altered Consciousness

Mankind has long known and sought spiritual experiences that transcend or obscure the fully alert and rational mind. Religious trance states, with or without possession, have spontaneously resulted from or been induced by chanting and candle flame, by drugs and drums, by solitary vigils and sheer group excitement. Kiev (1972) believed that the priestess oracle of ancient Delphi experienced trance by breathing carbon dioxide issuing from cracks in the rock; that the Sioux Indians used the stresses of heat and thirst; that the Sufi of Iraq held their breath as part of trance-induction; that the Egyptians brought about dissociation by sensory deprivation, fasting, and social isolation.

All of these means can also alter consciousness without any sense of spiritual exaltation. The non-religious man in a trance-like state may feel "I'm not quite here." The religious man may feel "the hand of God." Changing social conditions can change the content of visions. In Colombia, the subject matter of visions (and delusions) among patients was recorded for an eight-year period. Over the years, the supernatural content decreased and natural subjects increased. God and spirits took a back seat to police and government officials. What else had happened in those eight years? The transistor radio had come to Colombia! (Leon and Micklin, 1973.)

Dissociation within a religious context has never filed itself away in a dusty history book; it flourishes today. Bourguignon (1973) analyzed samples of 488 societies in all parts of the world and found that 437 (90%) had institutionalized (primarily sacred), culturally patterned forms of altered consciousness states, notably trance and/or possession-trance. She notes that trance without possession has certain characteristics: The subject may repeat messages from spirit or god, or give an account of a spirit's journey; he may have hallucinations or visions; he remembers and usually reports on the trance experience. In possession, the subject impersonates the speech and behavior of the spirit, does not hallucinate, and usually does not remember the possession episode. Possession usually takes place before an audience; trance alone may be before a group or may be a private experience.

Certain behaviors during religious states of altered consciousness seem to cross cultural borders. Dancing, shaking or shivering, shouting, seeing visions, becoming possessed, and "speaking in tongues" (glossolalia) are known in most parts of the world. What is seen in the vision, what is heard in the "message," and what spirit is thought to take possession are culturally, as well as individually, determined. Cultural appropriateness is among the factors that determine whether the entranced or possessed person is mentally healthy or disturbed. The Southern fundamentalist who "receives the Holy Ghost" during a revival is probably demonstrating normal religious behavior; if he were possessed by Buddha or an Indian rain god during his revival fervor, psychiatric investigation might be in order.

To the fervently religious person whose social and cultural background allows trance-induced behaviors, ecstatic states often carry great spiritual reassurance. "Speaking in tongues," seeing visions, or falling unconscious are considered evidence that one has been touched by a divine power. In the United States, one large evangelistic church has trained nurses on duty to care for the unconscious!

The fainting or "speaking" touch of the supernatural is usually felt during the height of group excitement; visions have long been associated with the solitary saint and hermit. Hallucinations and REM sleep dreams, which the subject may believe to be a vision, are frequently the impetus for founding a new religion. They are often deliberately induced. In the United States today, some holiness sects compel candidates for the ministry to fast until they dream or hallucinate; without dream or vision, they are considered unsuitable. Among the Shakers and the almost-identical Shouters of Trinidad, West Indies, visions are sought in a long period of "mourning." This is not grieving for the dead; it is mourning for one's sins. Henney (1973) studies this as done by the Shakers.

The "Mourning" Visions of Shakers

The decision to "go into the secret room" to mourn is voluntary, though the impetus comes from a "sign" from the Holy Ghost. If an individual goes through mourning successfully, he is given higher rank in the church's hierarchy. He deserves it; "mourning" is essentially a period of isolation that may last anywhere from six days to two weeks. After prayers, ritual washing of feet, and confession of their sins, the mourning candidates are blindfolded and placed on pallets where they must lie only on their right side or back for three days. They are not allowed to talk—only to pray and listen to the advice of the "mother" or "nurse" appointed to care for each mourner. After third-day rituals, marching in a circle about the Bible with a bell "to your feet," mourning in the secret room continues. Food is furnished, the "mother" provides toilet escort service, and the "pointer" (preacher) prays, advises, and questions. The entire ordeal is usually called "taking a spiritual journey" or "traveling." During the "travels," the mourner "sees" what his or her church duties will be. Seeing a dress means a woman will be a "mother" in church ritual; seeing a book designates preaching; a switch in hand indicates leadership. After the mourning is over, the individual recounts his or her visions to the assembled congregation.

Henney writes that mourners report a variety of visual and auditory phenomena. She notes the similarity of the Shaker's restricted and isolated practice with experiments in sensory deprivation, and suggests that these experiences probably ranged from daydreams to complex hallucinations. Though some mourners have "gone mad" and been hospitalized, others have willingly repeated the experience. Successful mourning brings enormous prestige within the church group; visions are highly valued. This provides strong motivation to hallucinate.

Glossolalia: "Proof of Salvation"

"Proof positive" that one is saved and chosen by God is invested in glossolalia. The devout Christian who "speaks in tongues" is convinced that the

Holy Spirit has entered him. Fundamentalist, Pentecostal Christian sects base this belief on Biblical text:

> And suddenly there came a sound from heaven, as of a rushing, mighty wind, and it filled all the house where they were sitting. And there appeared unto them cloven tongues like as of fire, and it sat upon each of them. They were all filled with the Holy Ghost and began to speak with other tongues as the Spirit gave them utterance (Acts 2:2, 3, 4).

In other faiths and other times, glossolalia was also thought direct evidence of a supernatural force. May (1956) summarized the rich history of ecstatic utterances and found that: Christian speaking in tongues was rooted in the ancient religions of Asia Minor. Virgil's *Aeneid* tells of a sibyl who used mystic speech during possession. In 853 B.C., four hundred prophets in the ancient kingdom of Palestine raved ecstatically. St. Paul was a glossolalist. The quiet Quakers made strange utterances during Oliver Cromwell's time. Joseph Smith told his Mormon disciples to rise and speak in tongues. In 196 A.D., a woman in China demonstrated xenoglossia (speaking a foreign language not consciously known). In present-day Japan, members of the Dancing Religion cult speak in both unintelligible syllables and foreign languages. Shamans, sorcerers, and healers from virtually every culture have, while entranced, spoken incomprehensible syllables.

May wrote that Lombard believed speaking in tongues was a form of regression in which infantile linguistic patterns come to the fore, and that Cutten believed that in glossolalia "primitive reactions which usually sleep in the subconscious find their way to the surface." Anthropologist Felicitas Goodman (1973) believes glossolalia is behavior learned while the individual is dissociated. In a study of a Mexican Apostolic congregation, she found that one charismatic minister taught his followers to superimpose glossolalia on the trance state. Within two months, 22 of the 24 in the minister's flock were speaking in tongues.

Pentecostal Practices Are Revived

Important as it is to the Christian wanting proof of salvation, glossolalia is only one manifestation of ecstatic, religion-linked states of dissociation. It is part of a total experience which, in the United States, traditionally has been incorporated in fundamentalist "holiness" sects. In North America, for one example, these sects once developed in periods of economic depression, notably in the 1907 Panic and the Great Depression of the 1930s (Boisen, 1939). Today, a revival of Pentecostal, evangelical belief has swept the United States and many parts of Europe. Pentecostal "holiness" religion includes, but is not limited to, the underprivileged, the under-educated, or the black. "Baptism in the spirit" is being embraced by the white, prosperous middle-class, and by Catholics as well as Protestants. In many cases, an important distinction is drawn: "Experiencing the Holy Spirit" does not necessarily mean ecstatic behavior and an altered state of consciousness. Yet, even in some traditionally formal Catholic and Episcopalian churches, glossolalia and healing by the "laying on of hands" occur. Faith healing is gaining widespread acceptance. Charismatic ministers become national celebrities. Thousands throng "ole time religion" revival meetings. Ordinarily reticent men and women sing and shout and wave their hands in religious fervor.

There is an evident reaching out for an intense religious experience. There is, perhaps, a protest against formal and intellectualized religious practice. As Dominican theologian Francis MacNutt (1978) states, "Philosophy cannot convert. It's the touch of Jesus Christ that converts."

Reasons for Evangelistic Movement

More than a protest against religion of the intellect is involved. The evangelistic movement seems also a reaction against many elements of our society. We feel the impact of technology—the threat of nuclear accident or World War III. We substitute impersonal encounters for leisurely friendships and supportive neighbors. We worry about money, a worry which affluence does not eliminate. We are under stress, and we seek ways to escape or release stress. Our forebears, in primitive, tribal life, got together, danced together, and conducted rituals together. Today some of us join the disco-fevered. Some of us shriek at rock concerts. Some of us sing, shout, pray, and weep at revivals and Pentecostal services. All are socially accepted behaviors. All, because they are group behaviors, provide a sense of community.

Evangelical fervor allows an unrecognized, never really suppressed, part of the human personality to come to the fore. Even the most coldly logical person has in his unconscious a reservoir of fantasy and dreamlike "magical" thinking. In the altered state of consciousness that often comes with religious excitement, this "child" in the adult mind emerges for a while. A total takeover would be disastrous; this brief appearance is therapeutic.

In many religious rituals, dissociation has accompanied or climaxed a period of chanting, drumming, or repetitive singing. Strong, insistent rhythm has been an integral part of ritual. According to Trainor (1981), Jilek and Prince cite the effect of drumming on the central nervous system and remind us of controlled EEG experiments in which auditory and photic driving produced auditory and visual imagery. Jilek, Prince and others (Trainor, 1981) speculate that with the stimulation of drumming, chanting, and ritual measures that are part of dissociative states, endorphin effects may allow firewalking or flagellation to be done without pain.

Fundamentalist Tenets Perverted: The Snake Handling Cult

Fundamentalist sects can obviously fill human needs; their services can be therapeutic. But when a pathological and charismatic leader puts Biblical passages to his own uses, harm often results. The emotion-charged nature of fundamentalist, evangelical services makes a congregation especially susceptible to suggestion; led by the wrong shepherd, the flock may easily become endangered sheep. Consider the following example investigated by LaBarre (1962).

In 1909, one George Hensley of rural Tennessee took literally the Biblical injunction, "They shall take up serpents; and if they [people] drink any deadly thing, it shall not hurt them; they shall lay hands on the sick, and they shall recover" (Mark XVI:18). Hensley then began his snake handling cult. In 1955 he died, a victim of snake bite.

In the intervening years, cults sprang up in eight rural Southeastern states. They attracted the South's "poor whites," most of them once farmers and now mill or factory workers. Sessions began with music (often guitar and tambourine), singing, preaching, and spontaneous praying. After that, members wept, shouted, went into trance states, and "spoke in tongues." Often the "preacher" was the first to pick up a snake; in some congregations, members competed to get to the "snake box" first. Some, in the author's words, "fondled" rattlesnakes or copperheads. Between 1945 and 1961, 20 members died from snakebite; one man drank strychnine and died.

In one congregation, a great deal of sexual touching took place between the preacher and almost-swooning women. The preacher "embraced them, one by one, and they toppled over like tenpins" (LaBarre, 1962). The sexual implications are clear. LaBarre speaks of snake handling as "symbolic masturbation" and says that the "ineffable experience" of one group of women is clearly "an induced, if sometimes unwitting, public orgasm."

The cult provided its members with more than the thrills of a "borrowed phallus"—sexual excitement without guilt; it also supplied the excitement of danger and the feeling of having supernatural power. Said one preacher, "We pick them [snakes] up under the power of God."

(Though the members undoubtedly did not know it, they were not doing anything really new. Snakes were handled ritually in ancient Greece.)

At first thought, the snake handling cults—except for the deaths—seem to have served a useful purpose. The "poor whites" of the congregations led narrow, repressed, and joyless lives. In the process of being transplanted from farm to factory life, they felt the stresses of acculturation. In the church, they found emotional release.

Yet, in LaBarre's opinion, snake handling did not solve any problems. Regarding the obvious sexual excitement, he believes snake handling expressed not mastery, but "*un*mastery," of sexuality on the phallic level. It was, he says, "indulgence rather than therapy." Instead of admitting sexuality and the phallus as a part of a confident body image, these were "projected, separate, and dangerous."

Culturally, snake handling also widened, rather than narrowed, the gap between the members and the community-factory setting they had entered. Acculturation to a new way of life was hindered and delayed by cult participation. Snake handling is now prohibited by law, but recent press reports tell of a still-existing congregation.

Twenty-one persons died during the 16-year existence of the snake handling cult. Almost a thousand died in a more recent religion-linked tragedy. We refer, of course, to The People's Temple.

RELIGION BECOMES PATHOLOGY

The simple facts of the Guyana-based cult deaths are recent history. Late in 1978, nearly 900 members of The People's Temple swallowed cyanide—some voluntarily, some by force—and died. These people had followed their leader, The Reverend Jim Jones, from California to establish a new life in the jungles of South America. To Jones they had given their property, their money, their U.S. passports—and the burdens or satisfactions of taking responsibility for their own sustenance, welfare, and decision-making. They had become a cult, or, in the social scientists' term, a sect—a fundamentalist Christian sect. Except for its tragic end, The People's Temple had much in common with other fundamentalist sects. Weber (1964) pointed out that such sects are characterized by an authoritarian social structure, membership by voluntary choice, a kinship-like organization, ritualism with the testing of faith and divine power, a dualistic philosophy with ideas of absolute truth, and leaders with compelling personalities.

Certainly, in the person of Jim Jones, The People's Temple had a leader with charisma and authority. Jones fulfilled other fundamentalist requirements: He had received a "call" in a self-reported vision; he had demonstrated "healing." At one time, he "healed" by drawing forth "cancers" which turned out to be bloody chicken gizzards. Jones "tested" his followers with a kind of death rehearsal by ordering them to drink what he said was poison. He had also lectured his flock many times on the beauty and dignity of dying (*Time,* 1978).

This concept of death is in keeping with fundamentalist ideas of life as "suffering" or a "burden," and of death as a way to become "free at last" and to "lay the burden down."

Aside from his supernatural "gift" (healing), Jones, like many other fundamentalist leaders, required that his followers call him "father." Symbolically, this made church members brothers and sisters, and identified Jones with God. "Siblingship" of church members and the physical relocation of the group to Guyana emphasized the group's isolation from others not in the "family" and made the group more vulnerable to the whims and will of the father/leader.

Certainly, the fundamentalist tradition was not new or strange to the members of Jones' Temple. In fact, the Jones sect might not have been atypical or sick, except for one key ingredient: the psychopathology of its leader. Jones' disorder was probably paranoid schizophrenia. But the key point is that his illness seems to have utilized a preexisting ideology—one of separatism and withdrawal from the world, of "family," and of release from suffering. Out of his own delusional fears and fantasies of destruction and retaliation, Jones carried this ideology and its adherents to their cataclysmic conclusion.

The snake handling cult and the People's Temple illustrate religions that make "cult" a pejorative term. Certainly, pathological behavior is often found in cults and sects that are outside the mainstream of accepted religions. Conversely, the most respected of established faiths may include doctrines which affect mental health. The Catholic prohibition on birth control is a case in point. For years, Catholic women went through unwanted pregnancies or suffered intense guilt if they used forbidden contraceptives. For years, Catholic couples attempted to live together without intercourse, with resulting tensions and marital stress. In the 1960s, with a more permissive stance expected from the Vatican, Catholics began practicing contraception with greater ease of conscience. Most priests and bishops in the United States allowed freedom of choice; an estimated 95% of Catholics in the child-bearing years used birth control (Greeley, 1979). Then, in 1979, Pope John Paul II made his position public: The church would not rescind its earlier edicts against contraception. The 1979 pronouncement may well bring about renewed guilts and conflicts and the tragedies that stem from having an unwanted child.

The Mormon church is admired for its social conscience and its emphasis on responsible parenthood and a harmonious and stable family life. Yet its implacable stand against masturbation has caused adolescent guilt and anxiety, its rigid denunciation of homosexuality has undoubtedly been traumatic to many, and its depreciation of women and blacks is socially if not psychologically harmful.

Clearly, religion can reinforce, if not cause, emotional and mental disorders. It may contribute to anxieties, help form guilts, shape delusions and dreams, and instigate conflicts. The manifestations of mental illness may sometimes be influenced by religion. Psychiatrist Iago Galdston (1971) speculates that the frequency of catatonic stupors in India and other Asiatic countries may be due to Hindu and Buddhist teaching that emotional withdrawal is an acceptable way to react to difficulties. Yet the practices of religion have always included what is therapeutic.

RELIGION AS THERAPY

The process of grief is aided by the rituals of many faiths. The music and prayer of Christian faiths not only console, but also help bring about the open expression of loss. The shaman of Korea, who ritually sends the spirit "across the bridge" to heaven, also enacts and is joined by the bereaved in a psychological detachment from the dead. A physical change in life is healthfully recognized in the (post-World-War-II) Shinto blessing on the climacteric. Interpersonal relationships and mental ills are the concern of the *hoza* (counseling sessions) that are an important part of the practices of Buddhism's *Rissho Kosei-Kai* sect.

Confession, an Ancient Practice

Religion employed certain therapeutic practices long before Freud incorporated them into psychoanalysis. Confession as catharsis is a conspicuous example. Some 500 years before Christ, Buddhist monks met together and "those who had committed offenses were obliged to confess them and submit to the prescribed penance." So state the sacred scriptures of Buddhism (Oldenberg, 1969). LaBarre (1964) writes that the Indians of Mexico went to confession long before they had any knowledge of the Christian faith; and that the Saulteaux (an Algonquin tribe) believed sins, especially sexual ones, caused illnesses, and employed public confession as the cure. In the present day, members of various fundamentalist sects stand up and confess their wrong-doing. The Roman Catholic Church continues its practice of private confession. To quote LaBarre (1964) again, "A . . . potent way to liquidate guilt and anxiety is to confess ritually to supernatural parent-surrogates or ancestors, via real human beings who are religiously sanctioned or otherwise socially credited for this function.'' The effectiveness of confession is influenced by the skill, patience, and concern of priest or psychiatrist. Neither the mechanical two-minute recital of sins nor the surface-skimming voicing of anxieties can be considered catharsis.

Church and Psychiatry

For some years, minister and psychiatrist have joined hands—but the handshake is sometimes perfunctory. Joint seminars have increased cooperation between the two professions. Courses in pastoral counseling include a background in aspects of psychiatry. It is possible that today's clergy know more about psychiatry than psychiatrists do about religious beliefs. Yet, some knowledge of a patient's belief is vital. This is particularly true when the patient's faith is that of another culture, is generally criticized, or is that of a minority group. There is conveyed a certain respect for a belief and its practitioner by knowing something about it. Even evidence of some slight knowledge shown by the therapist helps the patient feel that he can talk about religious cultural practices without exposing them—and himself—to skepticism, to the charge of being ''superstitious,'' or even to ridicule. Though no therapist would exhibit these responses, the patient has previously met with them in social encounters.

No busy clinician can devote himself to studying many religions. However, a helpful librarian, minister, or the department of religion at the local university can often provide some briefing on a given faith. Knowing a patient's religion and the specific congregation he belongs to can lead to treatment resources. A psychiatrist from a public clinic commented to us, ''Here, we offer short-term therapy. The need is to move the patient on out to other support systems. The family is too often non-supportive and destructive. Religion and church activities can provide a vital support system, psychologically and socially.''

Priest, rabbi, or minister sometimes provide immediate and practical help. Reports another psychiatrist, ''When the schizophrenic flatly refuses medication because 'God will get me well,' I call on a minister of his faith to explain that God wants him to take his medicine and accept treatment. I've become acquainted with a whole list of clergymen of different faiths. I've found that all, except the real fanatics, are cooperative and genuinely helpful.''

Cooperation rather than chasm between clinician and clergy is one thing.

Incorporation of religious principles or practices in therapy is quite another. Can—and should—this be done?

"Psychological problems should be worked out on psychological lines. Religion should not enter in this," is one view.

In another view, prayer can be a part of therapy if the therapist feels comfortable with it. At the Queen Lili'uokalani Children's Center in Hawaii, psychiatric social workers sometimes pray with their deeply religious Hawaiian clients. Family therapy often begins with family prayers. The Christian God, sometimes the Hawaiian *'aumakua* (ancestor gods), and occasionally both, are asked to "help us examine how we have hurt each other and how we can *kala* (release with forgiveness) the bonds of ill-feeling that bind us." From a religious and cultural standpoint, the practice is in accord with Hawaii's traditional *ho'oponopono* (setting right) therapy that families once practiced.

At least one psychiatrist believes the therapist must be more than comfortable to make use of prayer. "He must believe," says Irene Solzbacher, M.D. (1981). Dr. Solzbacher does believe; she is both a Catholic nun and a psychiatrist. In her rural practice, she uses standard medication and orthodox psychotherapy, but combines this with prayer if religion has deep meaning to the patient. In such cases, she often teaches the patient a prayer asking for inner healing.

"In this," she explains, "the patient asks Christ or God (depending on religious belief) to take him back to the times he was hurt, to the times when traumas occurred. To be with the patient as he reexperiences trauma so that this time He is with him, caring and loving. Giving the love that, perhaps, the mother or father was not able to give.

"In a sense, I teach patients to use God as a therapist. I teach them to examine a situation they overreacted to and reexperience it with Christ's compassion beside them and supporting them. As therapy advances, they pray to be given love and compassion so they may forgive the persons who inflicted the traumas. It's one thing to become aware of why you are so angry, of who and even why someone mistreated you. But I don't believe it's sufficient merely to realize and reexperience and find the causes that made someone—a parent, so often—inflict the hurts. Until one can forgive, the wounds aren't really healed."

The prayerful use of imagination is encouraged. Christ, or the Virgin Mary, in some instances, becomes a parental figure. Dr. Solzbacher continues, "When someone has had a completely devastating childhood, has received little or no emotional nurturance, there's really no way of undoing this, as far as I know. And yet I find some of these totally devastated persons can go back in imagination and let Christ or Mary do for them what their parents did not do. In the imagination, the patient is nurtured, held, cuddled."

Dr. Solzbacher was asked how this affected the development of transference, a key therapeutic vehicle in psychodynamic psychotherapy. She answered, "I find it minimizes it. I don't want too much transference to take place, especially with a patient who is schizophrenic or one who is already extremely dependent. It's very hard then to get the patient *un*-dependent. When, to the patient, I become almost like the parent, then I must help him to grow up. But in this method, I shift the patient's dependence onto God."

Dr. Solzbacher finds that teaching the patient to pray allows therapy to proceed faster. The fear of going back into the past is diminished. However, she again emphasizes her point that using religion as a part of therapy should be done only when both therapist and patient believe in a supernatural presence and find prayer a natural and comfortable spiritual-emotional resource.

REFERENCES

Boisen, A. T.: Economic distress and religious experience: A study of the holy rollers. *Psychiatry,* 2:185–194, 1939.

Bourguignon, E. (Ed.): *Religion, Altered States of Consciousness and Social Change.* Columbus: Ohio State University Press, 1973.

Cutten, G. B.: *Speaking with Tongues.* New Haven: Yale University Press, 1927.

Freud, S.: Totem and taboo. In: *The Standard Edition of the Complete Psychological Works of Sigmund Freud,* Vol. XIII. J. Strachey (Ed.), London: Hogarth, 1955.

Galdston, I. (Ed.): *The Interface Between Psychiatry and Anthropology.* New York: Brunner/Mazel, 1971.

Goodman, F. D.: Apostolics of Yucatan: A case study of a religious movement. In: *Religion, Altered States of Consciousness and Social Change.* E. Bourguignon (Ed.), Columbus: Ohio State University Press, 1973.

Greeley, A. M.: A priest examines his church. *Honolulu Star-Bulletin,* 19 Sept., 1979.

Henney, J. H.: The Shakers of St. Vincent: A stable religion. In: *Religion, Altered States of Consciousness and Social Change.* E. Bourguignon (Ed.), Columbus: Ohio State University Press, 1973.

Jordan, D.: *Gods, Ghosts, and Ancestors: Folk Religion in a Taiwanese Village.* Berkeley: University of California Press, 1972.

Keesing, R. M.: *Cultural Anthropology, A Contemporary Perspective.* New York: Holt, Rinehart and Winston, 1976.

Kiev, A.: *Transcultural Psychiatry.* New York: The Free Press, 1972.

Kim, K. I.: New religions in Korea: The sociocultural consideration. *Transcultural Psychiatric Research Review,* 10:30, 1973.

LaBarre, W. A.: *They Shall Take Up Serpents: Psychology of the Southern Snake-Handling Cult.* Minneapolis: University of Minnesota, 1962.

LaBarre, W. A.: Confessions as cathartic therapy in American Indian tribes. In: *Magic, Faith and Healing.* A. Kiev (Ed.), New York: The Free Press, 1964.

LaBarre, W. A.: *The Ghost Dance: Origins of Religion.* Garden City, New York: Doubleday, 1970.

Leon, C. A. and Micklin, M.: Community opinions concerning mental illness and its treatment in Cali, Colombia. *Transcultural Psychiatric Research Review,* 10:169–171, 1973.

Lipton, S.: *Fiji, Love You, Full Speed.* Wellington, New Zealand: South Seas, 1972.
Lombard, E.: De la glossolalie chez les premiers chrétiens et des phenoménes similaries. Lausanne, Bridel.
MacNutt, F.: Catholic charismatics: An evangelistic thrust. *Christian Today,* 22 September, 1978.
May, L. C.: A survey of glossolalia and related phenomena in non-Christian religions. *American Anthropologist,* 58: 75–96, 1956.
Oldenberg, H. (Ed.): *The Vinaya Pitakam.* One of the Principal Buddhist Holy Scriptures in the Pali Language. Vol. 1, page XV, London: Luzac and Company, 1969.
Risso, M.: Misery, magic and psychotherapy, a magico-religious community of Mediterranean Italy. *Transcultural Psychiatric Research Review,* 10:82, 1973.
Solzbacher, I.: Personal communication, 1981.
Time: Messiah From The Midwest, pp. 22 & 27; Nightmare in Jonestown, pp. 19–21; 4 Dec., 1978.
Trainor, D.: Shamans and endorphins. *Psychiatric News,* 2 Jan., 1981, pp. 28–29.
Weber, M.: *The Sociology of Religion.* Boston: Beacon Press, 1964.

CHAPTER 12

The Cults of Youth—Hidden Subcultures in Our Society

Though the People's Temple tragedy described in the previous chapter is now a horror of the past, it continues to ring alarm bells in the public consciousness. It stands as the death-imprinted proof that a charismatic cult leader can bring his followers to mental and physical destruction. Today, many concerned parents ask: Will the cult my child has joined ultimately destroy him or her?

There are many such anxious parents. Estimates of U.S. cult membership in the 1980s range from three to seven million. The "Moonies" alone have approximately 37,000 members in the United States (Newsweek, 1978). Cults exist in Europe, Asia, Canada, Australia, Central and South America.

IDENTIFYING THE CULTS

To arrive at any judgment on cult life, we must first know what these cults are. This is often difficult, for the same basic cult may change its name many times. However, some of the well-known cults at the present are listed below.

- *The Unification Church of the Reverend Sun Myung Moon, the "Moonies."* The cult has also been known as One World Crusade, the Council for Unified Research and Education, the Creative Community Project, New Hope Singers International, International Re-Education Foundation, High School International Family Association, Holy Spirit Association for the

Unification of World Christianity, International Cultural Foundation, International Federation for Victory Over Communism, World Freedom Institute, The Little Angels of Korea, Professor's Academy for World Peace, Project Unity, Educational Redevelopment, Collegiate Association for the Research of Principles, American Youth for a Just Peace, and New Ideal City Ranch. World membership has been estimated from 300,000 to 500,000 (Sparks, 1977). As of 1975, this included 40 countries (Delgado, 1977).

- *The International Society for Krishna Consciousness (ISKCON).* Better known as the Hare Krishnas, this cult has, as of 1980, 100 temples and 19 farming communities in existence around the world (ISKCON Report, 1980).
- *The Divine Light Mission,* a cult of Hindu-influenced beliefs. Though it maintains centers or "ashrams," members do not need to live in communal homes.
- *The Children of God (COG).* This is also called the Christian Faith Association, Contact Jesus, United Family, and other aliases. Following court actions against the cult in the United States, COG shifted its proselytizing to Europe. In 1975, its membership extended over 65 countries (Delgado, 1977).
- There are also many less publicized cults. They include: The Church of the Armageddon, also called "Love Israel Family," and "Love Family"; the Alamo Christian Foundation; the Way; the Source; Ananda Marga in 84 U.S. and Canadian cities; the Pilgrims; the 3HO (Healthy, Happy, Holy Organization) with more than 100 ashrams and teaching centers; the Sri Chinmoy; the Migrant Followers of Yes; the Sullivanians; the Ananda Cooperative Farm; the Lama Foundation; the Waialua University of Contemplative Arts; and the Aquarians. New ones develop, while others die out; such is the nature of their existence and their underlying dynamics.
- *Scientology.* Considered a cult by some, an established church by others (the organization has been denied religion's tax-exempt status by the Internal Revenue Service), Scientology has an estimated 600,000 members in the U.S. It combines Christian and Eastern theology with occultism and approaches to mental health which include the use of a device called an "E-meter" (Korns, 1979).
- *The Neo-Pagans.* These are small, often widely diverse groups who conduct esoteric rituals based on practices of ancient Greece, Egypt, Rome, and certain American Indian tribes. They include scattered covens of "witches" who practice the rites of European folklore. The 1979 Neo-Pagan membership was estimated at 40,000 (*Time*, 1979). Included are men and women who live otherwise ordinary lives and hold ordinary jobs. There is even a feminist cult, The Craft, based on worship of a goddess and belief in witchcraft. One all-women witchcraft group is called The Susan B. Anthony Coven!

WHO JOINS THE CULTS—AND WHY?

With the exception of the Scientologists and Neo-Pagans, the members of religious cults are usually under 25. The median age for 237 Moonies was 24.7 (Galanter et al., 1979). The median age of 106 members of major cults interviewed in one study was 21.5 (Levine and Salter, 1976). California investigators found that for one hundred members of five major groups, the average age was 23 (Singer, 1979).

Members have in common a middle-to-upper-class background. Most have finished high school; many have dropped out of college. They mistrust science and orthodox medicine, find formal education of little value, and consider themselves outside the world of careers, progress, and ambition. Many seek cult life to get away from drugs. (Coffee houses and snack bars near universities often display leaflets that invite students to attend meetings and learn how chanting and meditation can replace drugs. Some of these are cult recruitment overtures.) Singer (1979), who interviewed 300 current or former cult members, found that many had been "struggling with issues of sexuality, dating, and marriage." Cults that restrict sexual contacts lessen these anxieties.

All these young cultists seem to share the special vulnerability of adolescence and have prolonged struggles over heterosexuality, achievement of independence, and vocational choice. Cult members in their twenties are prone to almost the same anguished seeking for identity that a teenager feels.

To the cults go both the merely purposeless, discouraged, or dissatisfied young and the mentally ill. John G. Clark (1979a), a psychiatrist at Harvard Medical School, has studied cults for a number of years. He found that of the cult members he studied 60% had preexisting chronic emotional or personality problems of a pathological nature and 40% were normal young people facing ordinary crises of adolescence and separation from home. Of 237 Moonies studied, 39% felt they had previous serious emotional problems, 30% had had professional help, and 6% had been hospitalized. Singer (1979), on the other hand, believes that approximately 75% of those joining cults are essentially normal.

One of the few reports based on a psychiatrist's knowledge of a particular group of cultists comes from Alexander Deutsch. Over a three-month period, he observed and interviewed 14 followers of an American who had become a guru of Hindu-influenced belief. His diagnostic impression was that they represented a spectrum of previous psychiatric illness ranging from primary disorders to psychosis. All had "dropped out" of the competitive school or career world before meeting the guru. Many had already adopted some atypical or restrictive eating habits. All said they had been unhappy for several years and felt "out of step" with their peers. Relationships with parents had been unsatisfactory, and half of the member's mothers and one father had had serious mental disturbances (Deutsch, 1975).

The proportion of previously mentally ill in Deutsch's study is unusually high. This may be an example of a mentally ill leader's attraction for the already unstable. This particular "guru" sat all day on a park bench and never spoke. His teaching was conducted in sign language which devotees translated, and his own background included hospitalization for a psychiatric disorder and a period of apparent mutism and paralysis when he was 18.

The existing mental disorder and personal needs of a leader can shape the founding of a new cult. In Boston, one psychiatrist treated a former male prostitute who founded a cult using meditation to "receive messages from outer space." To do this, the cult demanded that one live a "life that is pure and clean and celibate."

The cults also attract the lonely but mentally normal young. Common reasons given for joining are "feeling rejected, sad, and not belonging anywhere" (Stoner and Parke, 1977). Singer (1979) found that many joined during periods of depression and doubt, though some "just drifted in." Judah, a professor of religion who interviewed members of two cults, writes that almost two-thirds of the Moonies he questioned said they joined in hopes of finding "a true religious experience" not found in their parents' faith, and that three-fourths of the Hare Krishnas interviewed gave much the same reasons (Judah, 1978). Some members of the clergy believe many young people join cults because organized religion now requires no real commitment. Conversion to cults may stem from rage against parents and the religion they represent (Deutsch, 1975).

For some young people, the search for a hero to worship undoubtedly shapes the decision to join. The Divine Light cult with its teenage guru used rock bands in many of its early public meetings. To transfer worship for Elvis or the Beatles to the Maharaj-ji may have been easy for the younger converts.

Many vaguely anxious and unhappy young persons join cults simply because they have been skillfully recruited during a vulnerable period. In fairness, we point out that not all of the previously listed cults actively proselytize and recruit. We know of branches of Ananda Marga which have refused membership to those considered too young or unstable. Some cults allow members to live in an ashram only after a trial period. The most sophisticated recruiting methods are used by cults which insist on communal center or temple life and strive for total control of members.

In these cults, recruitment is aimed primarily at the college student or the dropout trying to find himself. The worried are ideal targets. Children of God recruiters at college campuses go into high gear when students are most anxious—at examination time. Moonie recruiters with teams on 150 campuses in 1975 were told to "watch for the lonely" (Stoner and Parke, 1977). Children of God recruiters invade the waiting rooms of university counseling centers to find already troubled youths. Moonie teams concentrate on freshmen, confronting separation from home, and seniors, about to confront independence (Delgado, 1977).

The techniques of various cults differ. Children of God recruiters use a fear-inspiring approach; they predict approaching doom and use direct "eyeball-to-eyeball" confrontations. Their recruiters are also told to use sex appeal—to mention the cult's sexually permissive ways if that seems to entice a prospect (Stoner and Parke, 1977). An opposite approach is used for the sexually timid. The emphasis is on spiritual warnings and "brotherly-sisterly love" (Enroth, 1977).

The Moonies and Hare Krishnas approach softly. Moonies overwhelm a prospective member with flattery and personal attention; they call this "love bombing." Recruitment often begins with dinner at a communal home or temple and advances to longer visits and weekend or weeklong "workshops" or "retreats." These are almost non-stop sessions of intense personal attention, lectures, group singing, chanting and dancing, and very little sleep. The Hare Krishna guest hears and takes part in hours of uninterrupted chanting. The Children of God and the Moonies often recruit through deception; the cult may not be identified until the prospect is ready to join. The Hare Krishnas, except for a few non-conforming temples, wear Indian garb and are completely identifiable; often their recruits are already attracted to the chanting, costume, and mystique of India. During recruitment visits to a center, little opportunity is allowed for logical thought. Questions are not answered. Lectures use hypnotic metaphors and exalted ideas. The recruit is never left alone. Little by little he is cut off from his own world and attached to the tentacles of the group (Singer, 1979; Stoner and Parke, 1977; Edwards, 1979; *Newsweek*, 1978).

Though the recruiting methods may be varied, those of the large cults are carefully planned and well taught. They bespeak a knowledge of psychology and the expertise of an advertising agency. Deception is often employed; fear of eternal doom is emphasized; sexual urges or conflicts are sometimes played upon; flattering and constant attention are always used.

LIFE IN THE CULTS

The flattery and attention soon cease once the new recruit joins. "Before I joined, I was the object of all their attentions. . . . The day after I moved into the group, I found myself cleaning their toilets," reports one young man.

"But I didn't mind. I had hypnotized myself with their mantra . . . Hare Krishna" (Stoner and Parke, 1977).

The old, individual self that would not have cleaned toilets was being shed; identity with the group was being formed. To help the process along, some cults have members take new names. The Hare Krishnas, Church of the Armageddon, Eternal Now (also called The Source and the Brotherhood of Aquarians) are examples. The mind is bombarded; the body exhausted. Newly recruited Children of God must study the Bible 12 hours a day, earn their meals and rest by memorizing Bible verses. In one Moonie commune, new members heard the same series of lectures every day for six weeks (Stoner and Parke, 1977). In one large Hare Krishna temple, Prabhupada's (the founder) lectures were played 24 hours a day (Daner, 1974). Ties with family are discouraged or arbitrarily cut off. A former member of The Love Family (Church of the Armageddon) recalls that "the first thing we were told to do was to stop writing letters to our parents" (Enroth, 1977). In the Alamo Christian Foundation, parental concern was explained as overtures of the devil. Delgado (1977) cites the extreme statement of a cult member that, "If my family proved to be a threat to the Messiah, I would murder them."

Members of the closed, community-life cults live a totally structured life. Some Hare Krishna schedules break down duties into 15-minute segments. The Hare Krishnas dictate the most intimate details of hygiene: devotees are not allowed to use toilet paper; they shower after defecation (Daner, 1974). Children of God are told exactly how often and in what method they should brush their teeth. In some extremist cults members must ask to go to the bathroom. There is little or no privacy. "They told us that when you are by yourself, you tend to think . . . we—cult leaders—are your mind," a former member of the Church of Armageddon reported (Enroth, 1977). There is an effort—all too often successful—to reduce members to a childlike state. One Children of God prayer goes, "Dear Lord Jesus, please forgive me for being bad and naughty and deserving a spanking" (Sparks, 1977). "The group used to reward me with candy and sugar when I was good," a former cult member reports (Singer, 1979).

Hours are spent in directed group singing, chanting, and talks on the theme of "how happy we are to be here—but if you leave, you will be damned." The cult mission is described as an idealistic one: to love God or chosen deity (or, too often, the cult leader) with passion; to improve, if not save the world; to live in and demonstrate peace.

Most cult members work long hours, selling candy, peanuts, literature or flowers, or "witnessing" and handing out tracts. Single males at the Honolulu Hare Krishna Temple typically rise at 3:30 and go to bed at 11:30 (Brooks,

1979). Moonie working days of 18 hours are described (Delgado, 1977). Successful members rise to supervisory or executive posts within the cult and its manufacturing and publishing enterprises and public relations staff. The very fortunate may live on a pleasant communal farm, as do some Hare Krishnas, or, in the case of Moonie men, go on to seminary training in comfortable surroundings. Living conditions vary by cult and within a cult's centers or temples. While a former member of The Love Family (Church of the Armageddon) described eating "nice vegetables" and enjoying pleasant "family gatherings" (Enroth, 1977), the same cult was subject to criminal investigation for two deaths caused by inhaling toluene (Delgado, 1977). The cult then stopped the practice and used hyperventilation and electric shocks for experiencing body sensations (Enroth, 1977). Though some cult members, soliciting on the streets, look well nourished and rested, others demonstrate physiological arrest and dysfunction. Clark (1979a,b) wrote that young women in cults often stop menstruating for long periods and that men's beard growth may be substantially slowed.

Sexual Mores Vary

Three large cults hold different views on sexual matters. In general, celibacy is the ideal in cults modeled more or less on Hindu thought. Married couples in Hare Krishna are allowed intercourse only when the woman is ovulating; in some temples, the president keeps track of fertile periods. Males are told to wear a kind of loin cloth even in the shower, lest the sight of their own genitals excite them (Brooks, 1979). Most Hare Krishna couples who are allowed intercourse are supposed to chant first for purification and then maintain a rather unemotional detachment during the act (Daner, 1974). The Moonies also deemphasize sex, disapprove of casual unions, but conduct arranged marriages, often without regard to an individual's choice of partner.

On the other hand, the Children of God leadership condones unusual sexual expression. According to a report by New York Attorney General Louis Lefkowitz (1974), the COG leader, Berg, has taken a "positive position on incest and youthful intercourse, has condoned polygamy, and has himself consummated an extramarital sexual union in the presence of his own wife, children, and cult members." Rape of a 14-year-old girl has been reported, and cult literature contains pornographic material. At one extreme, a California group's slogan is, "If you haven't fucked your kid by eight, it's too late."

A middle ground is sought by various small, non-Indian cults who set their own rules. At The Farm in Tennessee, marriage is advocated, married couples discuss their sexual life freely with each other, couples live in communal tents, and some members engage in a two-couple "trade-off" system of intercourse (Greenfield, 1975).

Cults Exploit Guilts

Many cults have lists of sins and offenses members must avoid. The Alamo Christian Foundation lists more than 70 "group offenses." These include "nodding during services." Alamo Christian members are encouraged to watch each other's behavior (Enroth, 1977). In cults, Stoner and Parke (1977) believe, there is an emphasis on unattainable perfection and "purity" that adds to the burden of guilt and shame individuals already carry. The Hare Krishnas use rituals of degradation that reinforce the idea that one is an "impure, fallen soul" (Daner, 1974). A member of a smaller cult relates that his guru presents himself as a scapegoat-savior who is sick from "taking the poisons" out of his followers' souls. Members then "cry like babies" (Greenfield, 1975). In general, writes Delgado, cult life exploits guilts to bring about compliance, control converts, and facilitate the break with the past.

The patterns and purposes of cult life show great variety. At one extreme are the closed cults in which established society is disregarded and/or excluded; at the other are cults in which the break with society is minimum. Below we look at examples of both.

The Restrictive, Extreme Cults

The Children of God, which has transported many of its American members out of the United States, is certainly one of the largest cults which physically and psychologically separate people from home ties and normal existence. There are many smaller ones; some appear in first one city or state and then in another under changing names. One was subject to legal action on two separate occasions for keeping the unreported, unembalmed bodies of dead members in the cult's house for three days. Though members knew their leader had previously killed, they were convinced he was a "savior." This is chillingly reminiscent of the Charles Manson Family, whose members equated Manson with Jesus Christ.

Some cults offer mental health "help" rather than salvation. One, notable for its leaders' skilled psychological assessment, ostensibly operates as a system of therapy." It uses memories of painful, early childhood experiences as a means to break off family relationships. The development of many new superficial relationships is then insisted on and the group becomes a substitute for family ties. Strong, lasting relationships between individuals are discouraged; members are encouraged to have lunch, dinner, evening, and late night "dates," each with a different person, and to have many sexual partners, whether homo- or heterosexual. The group does not use chanting or meditation. Some members hold outside jobs, but most live communal style. Men and women live in separate quarters until a leader decides a couple can live together. The group has bought a hotel, has its own theatre which produces plays written by members, and carries on a round of activities which keep members up until two or three in the morning. Only organic food is eaten. The group has a bus ready for evacuation in case of nuclear or other environmental emergency. After the 1979 accident at the Three Mile Island nuclear plant in Pennsylvania, many members fled from the Northeast to Florida. The ex-member interviewed believes that even though members are not restricted to 24-hour existence with the group, control over their minds has become so strong in the last two years that he now considers the cult both a powerful and damaging force.

The Less-Restrictive, Moderate Cults

In favorable contrast are certain cults—or centers within them—which allow a choice between communal or independent living, do not flout the law, and maintain less control over their members' lives. In fact, whether to designate some of these as "cults" or merely shared-belief groups is difficult. There are ashrams within various Hindu or Sikh-inspired beliefs which allow either communal or independent living and encourage or even insist that members have jobs in the outside community. An ex-Ananda Marga and a former 3HO (Healthy, Happy, Holy Organization) member report less restrictive experiences, though both describe the organizations as cults. It seems reasonable that the potential damage of any group increases with secrecy of ritual, withdrawal from outside social and employment contacts, and separation of members from their families. The danger is that with the wrong, but charismatic, leader, the harmless shared-belief group may gradually become the closed-in, controlled, and destructive cult.

WHY PEOPLE STAY IN CULTS

The concerns of parents and psychiatry are most specifically directed at the cults which totally remove their members from the mainstream of society: the Hare Krishnas, Moonies, Children of God, Church of the Armageddon, Alamo Christian Foundation, and similar organizations. The question that begs for answers is: Why? Faced with pre-dawn awakening, rigorous work, submission to total authority, and often inadequate food, why do young people remain in the cults? Among the reasons are: the charisma of the leaders; symptom removal (relief from conflict over authority, sexual fears and conflicts, and drug use); manipulation of guilt; individual needs for a structured existence; coercion and threats that prevent leaving; and a long-established recurring state of dissociation with diminution of cognitive powers.

Charisma of Cult Leaders

Both financial records and the statements of cult members testify to the awesome, charismatic power of various cult leaders. When we consider that Moon's income for one year (1975) was $60 million (Delgado, 1977), it becomes obvious that cult leaders are masters of manipulating human beings and their purse strings. Absent or present in a cult setting, living or dead (as in the case of the Hare Krishna founder), the magnetic power of the leader is communicated and perpetuated by top-echelon assistants and by print, photograph, and recording. Cult members who actually see their leader are already primed with the mystique that surrounds him. One former Moonie recalls that "We were told that when he—Moon—visited the zoo, all the animals came to him . . . all the fish swam to him." (Earlier, some followers of murderer Charles Manson had said nearly the same thing about their leader [Bugliosi and Gentry, 1974].) The actual meeting may be ecstatic: "When Moon entered a room you felt blown against the wall" (Enroth, 1977). When his Hindu-style guru touched him, another young cultist "started shaking and I said 'I'm gonna bust right open. I'm afraid I'm gonna die.' " "I surrendered," and "I started crying," are reported (Greenfield, 1975). Though God or an Indian deity may ostensibly be worshipped, "Thou art the Father . . . I am the son" is often recited as devotees view a leader or guru's picture. If this is a case of adolescent personalities finding a father-like figure, there is a notable difference from an ordinary "family picture." Absent is criticism. The cult leader remains venerated if not openly worshipped, no matter what he does.

Deutsch (1980) did a follow-up study of devotees who remained faithful to Baba the "park-bench guru" described in his 1975 paper. The guru, always eccentric, had become progressively more inconsistent, domineering, and cruel. He had publicly subjected some of the women to sexual abuse and suddenly changed the cult's Indian orientation to that of fundamentalist Christianity. To reach any decision, Baba had begun to spin like a top and interpret where his nose pointed at the end of a spin as a "sign from God" telling him where to go or what to do. The followers who remained loyal told themselves that though Baba was crazy, this was "divine madness." Baba's actions were explained as ways of "teaching us a lesson" (the sexually abused woman had been holding too tightly to her chastity; his wasteful spending was to teach people they should let go of money). Denial, rationalization, and turning anger towards Baba against oneself were all employed. One devotee, hit 20 times by Baba, handled his anger by viewing the abuse as a "message of love" from his guru. Perhaps those attracted to cults are still at the early adolescent level of "splitting" people into all-good or all-bad and are unable to integrate good and bad in a single person. The sheltered cult life (these members had followed Baba to a communal home) can perpetuate developmental arrest at this level.

The devotion to a leader, the happy compliant role of the follower, can have tragic consequences. We recall with a shudder the report of Prosecuting Attorney Vincent Bugliosi when, nearly a decade ago, he first met members of the infamous Charles Manson family. These young people, responsible for or associated with murders, "seemed to radiate contentment. . . . For them all the questions had been answered. There was no need to search anymore, because they had found the truth. And their truth was 'Charlie [Manson] is Love' " (Bugliosi and Gentry, 1974).

The Structured Life and Symptom Relief

Some young people remain in cults because cult life fills a preexisting need for a structured existence under an accepted authority figure. Thus, a dependent level of personality development can be maintained. When growing up with its questions about career, sexuality, and self are confusing, when decision-making frightens, the positive order, the regimen that is not to be questioned, brings a sense of security. If one cannot control one's impulses, controls are provided. The same troubled adolescent who joins a cult partially in anger or protest against his parents still has the need to be told what to do. This the cult fulfills. Once the cult member fully believes the creed and follows the regimen of his cult, certain personal conflicts are often resolved. Sexual activity or abstinence, a cause of much adolescent anxiety, is directed by the cult. Academic or career misgivings are quieted. As Deutsch (1975) wrote in his survey of the literature, the mystical state and conversion with mysticism may be a way of protecting oneself against loneliness, resolving conflicts, and even a preventive of suicide. Certainly, many cultists have ended their drug use (though some cults, notably the Church of the Armageddon, use drugs). Chanting and ecstatic states seem to serve as drug substitutes.

Gattozzi et al. (1974) reported that transcendental meditation (not necessarily in cults) has lessened or ended drug abuse. However, symptom relief is not the same as cure. Symptom relief, as cultists reported it in answering questionnaires (Galanter et al., 1979), could reflect the unreality of escape and near euphoria; it may be only a pause in the action as one symptom exits the psychic stage and another prepares its entrance.

Fears, Guilts, and Coercion

Not all cult members remain satisfied with a structured life; not all accept a leader's decrees without question. Many of these young people remain in their cult because of internalized guilts and fears and actual, external threats and coercion. Members of some cults are often convinced they will be eternally damned if they leave. A pervasive sense of guilt and low self-worth does not lead to such an independent action as forsaking the cult. Guilts are well exploited. Former Moonies report feeling "like Judas after a reprimand," and suffering guilt for "falling asleep during a prayer" (Enroth, 1977). Efforts to leave a cult often bring peer pressure and coercion. Threats to members attempting to leave and harrassment of ex-members have been documented. For example, the Lefkowitz Report (Delgado, 1977) stated that former cult members said they were told they would be killed or sent to mental institutions if they left the cult. Charles H. Edwards, M.D. (1976), who literally kidnapped his son from the Moonies, claimed that he received harrassing phone calls from the cult 24 hours a day, with threats so serious that he hired bodyguards. One young man told his psychiatrist that when he was thinking of leaving a cult, members told him that "people get hurt that way" and "people who leave have accidents." "I think his fear was exaggerated, but I also think it had the kernel of truth," says the psychiatrist.

Reduced Cognitive Powers; Long Continued Dissociation

Perhaps the dominant reason young people remain in cults is that, just as their emotional life is acutely constricted, so their ability to think rationally is also sharply diminished. Evidence of reduced cognitive ability is summarized by Delgado (1977), whose study showed that cult life gradually reduced decision-making capability so that cult members' behavior regressed to resemble that of young children. A former member of the Divine Light Mission reported that some of his fellow cultists literally lost the ability to read, and that he, himself, could no longer add or subtract and had become incapable of questioning anything (Enroth, 1977). Dr. Edwards noted that while his son was in the Moonies, his letters indicated that this 21-year-old Yale graduate had "somehow reverted to the sixth grade." Later, his son described two young Moonies playing "patty-cake" and told of his own gradual enjoyment of the "role of little child that they—Moonies—had given me" (Edwards, 1979). A young cultist who had been considered gifted in high school and had won a scholarship wrote such phrases as, "We like animals. We are not afraid of animals . . . we all get better together." Her parents said the letter resembled those she had written at age nine (Delgado, 1977). This is the so-called "brainwashing" phenomenon.

This lessening or loss of clear thinking and rational judgment seems due to many factors of cult life. "Mental nourishment" is that of stereotyped clichés. With existence centered in the cult "family" and the outside world rejected, reality-testing is impaired. Long continued, daily periods of chanting, dancing and leaping, and meditation can bring about semi-continuous states of dissociation. Hare Krishnas are obligated to repeat their mantra 1,788 times a day, though some members chant it as many as three, four, or even ten thousand times in 24 hours. Older swamis may "ignore normal conversational etiquette and . . . insert a mantra or two in any pause or gap in dialogue" (Brooks, 1979). Daner (1974) tells of a young girl who, when frightened, chanted continuously for two hours. In one large Hare Krishna temple, chanting, drums, cymbals, and harmonium organ are amplified to create a "crescendo of sensory bombardment" (Henderson, 1975). "I was blissed out all the time" is how one ex-cultist describes his life. Fatigue and sleep deprivation further dissociation. A former Moonie reports that "Many times when we stayed up late we would see all kinds of things." An ex-participant in The Way International sums up the total effect of cult life on him in the words, "I lost my free will; I was a robot" (Sparks, 1977).

As Clark expressed it in his "Manipulation of Madness" (1979b), the central phenomenon of modern cults is "that of massive dissociation, its systematic maintenance, and pathological consequences."

THOSE WHO DO COME OUT OF THE CULTS

Fortunately, some young people do leave their cults—some by parental rescue, including "kidnapping" and deprogramming; some through their own disillusionment and disbelief. Parental kidnapping followed by deprogramming as described by Patrick and Dulack (1976) is fraught with legal hazards.

What Are the Mental-Emotional States of Ex-Cultists?

In general, the answers rest on the following factors: the preexisting stability or instability of the cultist; the length of time spent in the cult; and the degree of control the cult maintained over its members. Two quite opposite examples illustrate these points. Ungerleider and Wellisch (1979) evaluated two young people who had been "kidnapped" from their cult. They found both unimpaired, above average in intelligence, and with superior comprehension and judgment. However, we note that their cult welcomed the visits of parents, allowed members to visit home, offered varied and satisfying occupations, and maintained daily trips and contact with the surrounding town. The two young people obviously belonged to a cult which only minimally controlled their members' lives: We wonder why "kidnapping" was necessary. At the other extreme, we recall the infamous Charles Manson "Family" of a decade ago in which members with existing pathology became so controlled by Manson that they committed murder at his command.

According to Clark (1977), for even the essentially stable person, continuing cult membership brings about an increased acceptance of mind control and diminishes normal thought processes. Intelligence Quotient is lowered, reality-testing is difficult, and judgment is poor. The young person with even moderate preexisting psychological disability is apt to have his emotional, cognitive, and social maturation to adulthood retarded considerably, and even permanently. Irreversible damage, both to the previously stable and the already mentally disturbed person, is apt to come after four to seven years in cult life. These unfortunates, Clark wrote, can be compared to the "hospital back ward" schizophrenics of past years who, untreated and unchallenged, simply deteriorated. Long-term effects of cult-induced mental states do not respond well to antipsychotic drugs, though the acute psychosis of a cult victim may. However, "talking him down" is probably more effective than drugs.

Psychologist Margaret Singer (1979) has interviewed approximately 300 young persons who have left the cults and, with her colleague Jesse Miller, has conducted discussion groups with one hundred. She outlines some of the problems ex-cultists experience. Among these are loneliness, difficulty in making new friends, and the feeling that the non-cult world is devoid of understanding. Some former members whose cults had prohibited sexual intercourse go on "binges" of dates and sexual encounters that leave them shamed and guilty; others, inhibited or "feeling guilty if I think of asking a girl out," avoid social contacts with the opposite sex. Cessation of structured cult life leaves some almost unable to make simple decisions or organize their days. One young woman could not decide whether to make her bed, clean her apartment, cook, or sleep. The effortless decision, to sleep, won. Dropping out is easy; dropping back in is much harder.

One conspicuous cult effect is that of "floating": a return to the trance-like state of cult existence. Depression, stress and conflict, or significant words or ideas are the triggers. During such "floating," some ex-cultists seem to hear the cult leader; in at least one case, the voice seemed to say, "You'll come back. You are one with us." Singer and Miller have observed members going into this "flash-back" trance, especially when an ex-member uses the abstract jargon of a cult. Control consists of discussing concrete topics in precise language and speaking directly to the listener. Otherwise, the trance-like state can become a kind of contagion within the group. It is important to assure the "floater" that he or she is not going crazy and that the experiences will eventually diminish. Episodes that continue for as long as two years are more apt to be found in young people who had severe depression, were extremely indecisive, and had other pathological signs before they became cult members.

Among the fears of ex-cultists is the feeling the cult may retaliate or somehow lure or force them back into membership. Some former cultists still have residual beliefs in cult doctrine and fear they may be eternally damned for leaving. Along with the fears is the embarrassing sense that one is a kind of emotional time bomb to family and friends, who are constantly watching for behavior and moods that may signal the return to cult life.

Also experienced is difficulty in expressing thoughts and thinking efficiently. Many former cultists of graduate student status take simple jobs until they regain their former cognitive levels. An extreme of emotional regression with uncritical passivity and obedience is common; many take simple remarks as commands and immediately obey. In group discussions, the "listen don't question, obey" injunctions of various cults and their effects on people are brought out.

Among cult members are many genuinely idealistic young people, convinced their cult had high purpose for social uplift. As ex-cultists some of these persons continue to want to "do good." They are, in fact, vulnerable to altruistic appeals of other, perhaps undesirable, groups. Singer advises caution against joining an "uplift" movement and suggests that energies be directed to work, school activities, or purely social experiences.

In Singer's view, it is necessary to know something about a particular cult's program to understand what an ex-member is trying to describe. In therapy, the cult experience must not be bypassed in order to focus on long-term personality attributes. However, because cultists do undergo pervasive changes of personality and intellect, the therapist must depend on other sources of information on pre-cult functioning and the changes observed while the patient was in the cult. Parents, friends, or spouses are needed so a complete history and evaluation can be made. Singer suggests that at least two persons should be interviewed.

CONCLUSION

Clearly, the cults we have discussed are one of the dangers to mental health that young people face in the 20th century. While it is true that cult life may provide a needed shelter for certain schizophrenic youths, for most young people, joining a cult is a tragedy. Cult existence arrests normal maturation, encourages or induces regression, substitutes escape rather than the confrontation of problems, and further alienates the young person from the normal world of school, employment, family, and civic involvement. Unfortunately, too little is known about why people join cults and how to treat those who leave them. A great need exists for dissemination of information among psychiatrists. The teaching and counsel of clinicians with a number of ex-cultist patients must be shared in professional meetings and seminars. The more we know about cultists, the greater are our chances to treat successfully the mental-emotional damage of cult life.

The ultimate goal is, of course, to prevent young people from joining cults. Perhaps this can be accomplished by finding and filling the gaps both in personal lives and society that cause young people to accept cult life. Some of these seem to be too much or too little parental authority and the absence of other close family ties, the lack in our affluent society of a demonstrated need to complete an education or get a job, the lack of religions that demand commitment, and perhaps insufficient appeals to youthful altruism, so that the adolescent seeking cause and affiliation finds it in a cult rather than in social service.

The "cure for cultism" may come in correcting the cultural factors that brought about the burgeoning of cults. This will not come about overnight. It may never come about unless psychiatrists, educators, clergy, and parents become fully aware of the phenomena of cults, recognize them as the warning signal they are, and pool their information for the better interpretation of this signal.

REFERENCES

Brooks, C. R.: *The Path to Krishna: Situations in the Development of American Hare Krishna Devotees.* Unpublished Master's Thesis (Anthropology). Honolulu, Hawaii: University of Hawaii Library, 1979.

Bugliosi, V. and Gentry, C.: *Helter-Skelter, The True Story of the Manson Murders*. New York: W. W. Norton & Company, 1974.
Clark, J. G., Jr.: Destructive cults: Defined and held accountable. Presented to National Guard Reserve Chaplains, Minneapolis, Minnesota. 1977.
Clark, J. G., Jr.: Cults. *J.A.M.A.*, 242: 279–281, 1979(a).
Clark, J. G., Jr.: The manipulation of madness. Presented to Deutsche Gesellschaft fur Kinder und Jugendpsychiatric und Bundeskonferenz fur Enzielhungsberatung, Hannover, W. Germany, Feb. 1979(b).
Daner, F. J.: *The American Children of Krishna*. New York: Holt, Rinehart and Winston, 1974.
Delgado, R.: Religious totalism: Gentle and ungentle persuasion under the First Amendment. *Southern California Law Review*, 51:1–98, 1977.
Deutsch, A.: Observations on a sidewalk ashram. *Arch. Gen. Psychiatry*, 32:166–175, 1975.
Deutsch, A.: Tenacity of attachment to a cult leader: A psychiatric perspective. *Am. J. Psychiatry*, 137:1569–1573, 1980.
Edwards, C. H.: How I rescued my son from the Moonies. *Medical Economics*, 53:72–80, 1976.
Edwards, C. H.: *Crazy for God*. Englewood Cliffs, New Jersey: Prentice-Hall, 1979.
Enroth, R. M.: *Youth, Brainwashing, and the Extremist Cults*. Grand Rapids, Michigan: Zondervan Publishing House, 1977.
Galanter, M., Rabkin, R., Rabkin, J., and Deutsch, A.: The Moonies: A psychological study of conversion and membership in a contemporary religious sect. *Am. J. Psychiatry*, 136:165–170, 1979.
Gattozzi, A., Luce, G., Wallace, R. K., and Benson, H.: A meditation technique to cure drug abuse. In: *Alternative Pursuits for America's Third Century: A Resource Book on Drug Abuse*. Rockville, Maryland: National Institute on Drug Abuse, 1974.
Greenfield, R.: *The Spiritual Supermarket*. New York: Saturday Review Press, 1975.
Henderson, C. W.: *Awakening: Ways to Psycho-Spiritual Growth*. Englewood Cliffs, New Jersey: Prentice-Hall, 1975.
ISKCON Report, Feb. 1980. Los Angeles, California: Int. Soc. for Krishna Consciousness.
Judah, J. S.: New religions and religious liberty. In: *Understanding the New Religions*. J. Needleman and G. Baker (Eds.), New York: The Seabury Press, 1978.
Korns, W. B.: The growth of religious cults. *Honolulu Star-Bulletin*, May 16, 1979, p. A-16.
Levine, S. V. and Salter, N. E.: Youth and contemporary religious movements: Psychosocial findings. *Can. Psychiatr. Assoc. J.*, 21:411–420, 1976.
Newsweek. The World of Cults. 4 Dec., 1978.
New York Attorney General, *Final Report on the Activities of the Children of God*, 1974.
Patrick, T. and Dulack, T.: *Let Our Children Go!* New York: E. P. Dutton, 1976.
Singer, M. T.: Coming out of the cults. *Psychology Today*, 12:72–82, 1979.
Sparks, J.: *The Mindbenders*. Nashville, Tennessee: Thomas Nelson Inc., 1977.
Stoner, C. and Parke, J. A.: *All God's Children*. Radner, Pennsylvania: Chilton Book Company, 1977.
Time. Preaching Pan, Isis, and "Om." 6 August, 1979, 82.
Ungerleider, T. J. and Wellisch, D. K.: Psychiatrists' involvement in cultism, thought control and deprogramming. *Psychiatric Opinion*, 16:10–15, 1979.

CHAPTER 13

Intermarriage

Survey the vital statistics of any large U.S. city and you will read that Wong has married Jones, Gomez has wed Johnson, and Santiago has recited nuptial vows with Nhu; that marriage licenses have been issued to such pairs as Liu-Cunningham, Fitafala-Badang, Murphy-Ichimura, Watkins-Iglasia, and Kim-Olafson.

Each year the unions arouse less notice. Each year family and social disapproval of interracial, inter-ethnic marriages softens to some extent. Many couples of differing race or culture will have successful marriages. Others, however, will suffer extraordinary marital stresses and encounter more than the usual adjustment difficulties. The factors that make for happiness or misery, success or failure, in the intercultural marriage occupy our attention in this chapter.

ASSESSING THE INTERCULTURAL MARRIAGE

It is impossible to ignore still-existing social prejudices and pressures and their effect on intercultural couples. In general, marriage adjustments are easier when both partners come from similar racial backgrounds. The black-white union still faces social disapproval, and negative attitudes of others can put this marriage under severe strains. The mates who are fairly much alike in all the aspects of culture—race, ethnicity, education, religion, and socioeconomic status—face fewer areas that call for adjustments.

Yet some marriages of opposite race and ethnicity succeed; some of similar cultures fail. Often more personal factors are the causes. Obviously, the flexible personality is more apt to succeed in an intercultural (or any) marriage. The realist who can evaluate his, and his partner's, cultural background for similarities, differences, and areas that will call for patience and understanding stands a better chance of success. And, to a great extent, the fate of the marriage rests on the reasons each partner had for choosing a mate.

MOTIVATIONS FOR INTERCULTURAL MARRIAGE

As therapists, we ordinarily do not see interracial or intercultural couples until they are already married (or living together) and beset by adjustment Corps marriages), they include: the need to be different; the achievement of tion long before: Why did you marry this person?

The reasons for marrying outside one's race or culture are many. Leaving out sheer proximity and availability (as in many overseas military or Peace Corps marriages), they include: the need to be different; the achievement of economic and social gain by marrying into a dominant and accepted culture or, conversely, the search for acceptance by marrying into the "inferior" culture; the desire to demonstrate or prove idealistic concepts and the quite opposite wish to humiliate or defy another culture by marrying into it; the fulfillment of fantasy and the resolution of, or flight from, incestuous fears.

And the reason not to be overlooked (and seldom explained): genuine love.

Usually, several of these motivations overlap. Let us consider some of them.

The Need to Be Different

Being "different" may be a characteristic of the flexible, adventurous, often highly intelligent person, or it may identify the exhibitionist. Some persons seek the enlarged horizon; they are interested in new ideas, new people, new places. They are more apt to marry into another culture than their tradition-minded counterparts. However, the attention-seeker who marries outside of his or her race is apt to do so for different reasons. His motivation is more "Hey, everybody, look what I've done now!"

Intercultural marriage may satisfy other needs to be different. Sometimes the need is to emphasize contrasts with one's own family. Rebellion against parents is dramatically demonstrated by marrying someone who does not look like, speak like, or share the attitudes and values of one's parents. Parental insistence that a youth wed a Jewish girl may send him hunting for a Gentile mate; the Catholic girl urged too often to "make a good Catholic marriage" may find her mate from an exclusively Protestant or agnostic group of young men.

Marrying "Up" or "Down"

Whether we like it or not, society ranks races and ethnic groups as superior or inferior to each other. Thus, marrying into a different group is often thought of as marrying "up" or "down." The "superior" race or culture may be the economically dominant one; marrying "up" into this group may be motivated by a need for financial security. Marrying "down" may come about from love, identification with and the desire to help the "underdog," or the wish to demonstrate ideals of racial equality and the brotherhood of man. Yet, more deeply personal feelings are often operative. A sense of inferiority ("nobody from my own racial/ethnic/cultural group could possibly love me") may result in marrying "down."

The social judgments that one marries "up or down" are, of course, based on many more factors than race. The sheer length of residence in a certain place may mark one ethnic group as "superior to the recently arrived immigrant group. Economic status, educational or artistic attainments, past or present political dominance, religion—these, too, determine what each community considers the inferior or superior racial-ethnic-cultural group.

Marriage to Express Hostility

The intercultural marriage may represent defiance or hostile aggression against society. A black man may express his hostility to whites by marrying a white woman, thus, at least in some parts of the United States, humiliating whites in general. To this marriage, the white mate may often bring complementary feelings of personal inferiority, or anger and rebellion against her own parents and her white culture.

Especially when the racial variation is marked and the social disapproval extreme, the interracial marriage may be a sadomasochistic one. The white man may marry a black "slave" whom he can control and hurt; the black man may marry a white "slave" whom he can humiliate, secure in the knowledge that, by the marriage, his wife has already alienated herself from family and friends. Motivations in the black-white union are not necessarily so negative. Some marriages, as for example those in liberal intellectual circles, are apt to be based on mutual perception of each other as individuals, rather than as representatives of race.

Making a Fantasy "Come True"

For many years, Western men heard about the "Japanese doll" who figuratively, if not literally, bows down to her husband, who obeys him without question, is demure, retiring, and ladylike—but also wondrously skilled in the arts of sex. Since pre-Civil War years, the United States has heard of the sexual prowess of the black man. Since tourism discovered Hawaii, somewhat the same attribute has been given the Hawaiian beach boy. The Scandinavian miss is sexually permissive; the Latin male, romantic; the Korean girl, passionate.

Stereotypes, all.

Not all stereotypes are sexual. Oriental people are wise. Scots, thrifty. Latins, fiery. French, polished and elegant.

Some stereotypes are based on truth. Some were once based on truth. Some were never true. This is not the point. The point is that intercultural unions sometimes represent marriage to fulfill a stereotyped fantasy.

Flight from Incest Fears

In psychoanalytic reasoning, choosing a mate from a completely different racial-cultural group may be a way of fleeing from fears of incestuous wishes. A Jewish man who has remained extremely close to his mother might marry a Vietnamese Catholic girl; he has thus found a mate who has the least possible resemblance to the mother. Fears of incestuous impulses toward an opposite sex sibling may similarly be an impetus for an interracial, intercultural marriage. Intensely negative feelings toward a parent or sibling of the opposite sex may also influence choice of a different-as-possible mate.

PROBLEMS IN INTERCULTURAL MARRIAGE

Many of the motivations just listed foreshadow problems that will later mar these unions. Some reasons to wed—interculturally or not—are in themselves neurotic. Marriages to "prove something," to "spite someone," such as parents, to punish or humiliate a person or ethnic-racial group—these bear the fertile seeds of pathology. Marriages from other, less than perfect, motivations can—with luck—succeed. It is possible to marry "up" for financial-social gain and love the partner who improved one's lot. The marriage for fantasy fulfillment may yet succeed if the fantasy can be adjusted to reality, or if the fantasy-object happens to fit the preconceived mold. Yet, in general, the more the marriage is based on each partner's realistic perception of the other, the greater the chances of a truly successful marriage. To "know" one another is not necessarily limited to its Biblical-sexual meaning.

However, the intercultural union is apt to have some particular sources of problems. One of these is communication—not only the obvious barrier of different languages, but also the subtleties of message sending-receiving. The complaint of one Caucasian-American wife was that her Japanese husband failed to thank her for a gift. The husband, she learned, followed the traditional pattern in which verbal thanks are given in fairly formal, outside-the-home situations, but are not expected between members of the family. In several Chinese-Caucasian marriages, the non-specific, non-confrontive style of Chinese communication caused problems. "We never quarrel," said one wife, "but we also never have a frank discussion—about finances or sex, or what he likes or does not like about my cooking, or how I dress, or whether he really wants to take a vacation trip or not. Through the years, I've just learned to sense what other couples learn by discussing." Another Caucasian wife complained that, when her Japanese husband went back to Japan for a family visit, he never wrote that he loved her and missed her. During counseling, the man explained that he had sent this message in every letter. We went over the letters and found numerous, almost poetic references to moonlight and scenic beauty and whispering pines and a certain vague mood of wistfulness. To this educated, tradition-minded Japanese, the unspoken message "but you are not here with me, beloved" was clear. He also explained that to put his feelings into definite words would "spoil things."

Problems in the intercultural marriage may arise from differing religious and moral convictions, or merely from variations in manners and style of living. Caucasian-American Fay Calkins (1962), who married a Samoan, tells of conflicting concepts of property in her book, *My Samoan Chief.* The couple's car was, in Calkins' view, their personal property. To the many Samoan relatives, the car—as indeed all property—belonged to the whole extended family. The Filipino culture (like the Spanish) demands virtue of wives, but is tolerant of husbands' infidelities. Here is fertile ground for conflict in the Filipino-non-Filipino union. A personal friend, an English woman married to an ultra-conservative Mexican, is both wryly amused and irritated at the social role thrust upon her. Even in modern Mexico City, her husband expects her to "stay with the women" and "make woman talk" at parties. In some Middle East cultures, women are expected to be silent or absent themselves when male guests arrive—a situation that might infuriate a Western wife or embarrass a Western husband. The ritual, often expensive, gift-giving of Japan might well disturb a thrifty Vermont spouse. Some cultures believe only the husband should issue invitations; others insist the wife is the one to ask friends to dinner.

Money, as in any marriage, can cause conflicts for the intercultural couple. One culture may advocate the accumulation of wealth; another may place financial solvency second to enjoying life. One may consider all earnings are to be pooled in a joint bank account; another may feel only the male household head should handle finances. In the culture of middle-class France, for one example, women are expected to spend substantial amounts for the hairdresser, beauty treatments, and clothing; the expenditures might horrify a Dutch husband.

Problems When the Children Come

Many intercultural couples have few real adjustment difficulties until the first child is expected. Then, for both parents, dormant culturally based conflicts often surface. The pregnant woman's resurgent emotional ties to her own mother can bring about a renewal of old childhood feelings, including racial and ethnic prejudices. If the marriage partners are of different races, anxiety and tensions center around the coming baby's appearance. Will he be black or white? Will her eyes be round and blue, or black and somewhat slanted? How will my family feel if he is not my color? And, the more painful thought, how will *I* feel about my baby if he is black and I am white (or vice-versa)? These troubling concerns may arise even when a couple has previously discussed the issue of having a racially mixed child. The reality of approaching parenthood brings fears, doubts, and hidden prejudices into sharp and painful focus.

With the baby's birth, cultural differences in child-rearing often arise. For example, in the Japanese culture, women give almost exclusive attention to the new baby. Anthropologist William Caudill and his colleagues (1969, 1973) note that the Japanese mother views her child more (or longer) as an extension of herself; ego boundaries are blurred. The infant has less need to tell his mother what he wants vocally. There is greater emphasis on physical communication. The Japanese mother rocks, lulls, and soothes her infant more often and sleeps with him or her. The non-Japanese husband may feel totally excluded.

The Chinese father who follows tradition believes children should be obedient, respectful, and study hard; the mother whose culture embraces the American ideal of individuality and assertiveness may want the children to attend a relatively "permissive" school and "be creative." She may consider mischief and speaking out to teachers as "self-expression"; the father may be shamed and embarrassed.

The Okinawan mother believes in liberal praise and little physical punishment. She discourages aggression and encourages socialization and integration with the group; the Anglo-Saxon husband may believe, especially if the baby is a boy, that she is encouraging the child to be "soft," "sissy," or unable to "stand on his own two feet."

The mother from Micronesia may casually bare her breasts to feed her infant in public, thereby embarrassing her Anglo-Saxon husband. Whether or not the baby should sleep in the parent's bed, the duration of close mother-baby ties, the importance attached to early toilet training—these are among the differences that can spark husband-wife conflicts. Relatives often add to the stresses, as grandparents on each side insist the child should be brought up *their* way, in *their* religion, or as in-laws accept the child as "one of us" or reject him because he is "different."

The Mixed-Race Child

Yet the ultimate stresses descend on the child. All the memories, attitudes, and feelings recalled and revived during the pregnancy are then acted out on the child, like a movie superimposed on another drama already on the screen. As the child grows, he may have more than the usual problems of achieving identification, of knowing who he is. This is particularly true in the interracial marriage where physical appearances are markedly different. Stevenson and Stewart (1958) found that both white and black children preferred the physical characteristics of white children and have more negative attitudes to black ones. The children's identification with parents centered on certain over-valued and ill-understood body parts, capacities, and physical charactertistics. There has been a shift in more recent years to a more positive self-esteem reflected among black children in their drawings (Fish and Larr, 1972). But questions still remain. Thus, in the racially mixed marriage, does the girl identify with her mother and the boy with his father or does white identify with white and black with black? Or does black identify or seek identification with white? How much does physical similarity influence identification?

From preschool on, the racially mixed child is exposed to society's perception of him. This may not agree with his own self-image drawn from his parents. Society usually sees the child of a black-white union as black. In some black groups, the lighter skin is valued; yet, as black society builds racial-ethnic pride, it increasingly rejects the mixed child. (The Asian-black children born of overseas servicemen fathers have often found acceptance only in an adoptive family with adoptive siblings of many races.) In the interracial family when blood-kin siblings are different shades of color or physiognomy, parental favoritism and sibling rivalry may be marked. The child's own process and sense of identification may be increasingly confused. One such child expressed it: "I do not belong anywhere. Nobody wants me anywhere."

The following quotation from Piskacek and Golub (1973) describes, perhaps at its negative extreme, the predicament of the interracial child:

> An organism cannot tolerate a permanent state of tension. If there is no resolution and integration, there is maladjustment. . . . An inter-racial child . . . is truly representative of a class of one. He cannot be supported by the defenses that a culture provides. He cannot profit from the experience of his parents and share their defenses, since they are a product of a different . . . background and will never be able to experience his position. . . . The child may choose to identify with one race as a defense against the identity confusion, which might paradoxically lead to an actual loss of identity. Another solution is negative identification, with rejection of one part of identity. . . . There is also a standstill solution leading to alienation and depersonalization, resulting in final distortion of personality.

Preventing Emotional Damage to the Interracial Child

Does each interracial child indeed suffer severe emotional damage? Or can he feel less a "representative of a class of one"?

Certain circumstances in themselves lessen identity confusion. The interracial child who lives in a racially cosmopolitan setting where differences of color and physical appearance exist in all shades and gradation may suffer less trauma. He does not perceive himself as so markedly different and he does not experience as much curiosity or ridicule from school or playmates. More importantly, his parents may not attach to him as heavy a burden of doubts and conflicts as they would in a less accepting environment.

Where a child lives and how different he looks from his social group will, of course, affect his present and future adjustment. The black-white child faces difficulties nearly everywhere; the Asian-Caucasian child in Hawaii may suffer not at all; the mixed-race child in Korea is a social outcast.

Before he is conscious of color, before he encounters school or society, the racially mixed child is exposed to the emotional climate that affects his sense of identity. He knows if his parents are polarized. He may not really know what his parents look like; he does sense what they feel. During his first two years, the child perceives himself, not as an individual, but more as a part of both parents. When parents depreciate each other, he, too, is depreciated. Or, as Comer and Poussaint (1975) express it, "A child's first idea of himself as a person depends upon the responses of others." When parents are loving to each other and the child, when they agree rather than make a tug-of-war over child-rearing methods, the child senses love and harmony. Thus, the child's own identity becomes secure.

As the child becomes aware of differences in color—usually by age three—parents should begin to discuss these differences: that Daddy is white (or brown, or black, or yellow) and Mommy is black (or white, or brown, or yellow) and both are nice. Then, when the child enters preschool, he is better equipped to deal with childish, prejudicial attacks.

COUNSELING AND THERAPY WITH THE INTERCULTURAL COUPLE

Ideally, counseling should be preventive; it should take place before marriage. Therapy to help the racially mixed child should begin during his mother's pregnancy.

Unfortunately, not many intercultural couples do seek counseling before they marry. When they do, the motivations outlined earlier need to be explored. The flexibility of both partners needs to be assessed. Both prospective mates must be helped to look realistically at their cultural preconceptions and stereotypes and the social attitudes they may encounter later.

"Pre-testing" of each other's cultural-ethnic setting is to be encouraged. One young Caucasian woman who was considering marriage to a black changed her mind after counseling. After a few sessions, she decided to "try out" living in a black culture by moving into New York's Harlem for a few weeks. There, she faced her own lack of flexibility and pioneering spirit and broke the engagement. As she developed insight, she realized that her motivation for the marriage was really to demonstrate a protest against discrimination. She then began to look for other ways to work for racial equality.

Such pre-testing of later realities is not always possible. However, specific information on what life will be like in another's culture usually can be gained. The couple needs to find out and discuss quite specific matters. For example, the young woman who is planning to live with her husband in India or Pakistan must know and consider in advance the position of women in her new homeland. What will the city or village where they will live be like? Will the couple live by themselves or as part of an extended family? Have the prospective relatives expressed their attitudes to the coming marriage? Has the prospective bride ever lived in an entirely new setting? How did she adjust to a new climate, language, and customs?

The counselor should encourage the couple to associate as much as possible with each other's family and friends. One of the criteria for success or failure in any marriage is whether the union removes or erects barriers between the couple and other persons. The intercultural couple needs to face the reality of social and family attitudes well ahead of marriage.

The counselor must assess whether the clients, both as individuals and as a couple, have the mental capacity and ego strengths to handle the problems of intercultural marriage. Individual strengths can be assessed by gaining information on past adjustments, education and work history, interpersonal relationships, and coping mechanisms. To assess the relationship as a couple, inquiries may center around how the two handle differences. Do they compromise—or does one always give in? How often and how intensely do they quarrel? Does a quarrel result in better understanding or does it block off certain issues behind a wall of silence? Do the two respect each other's moral standards, habits, occupations, goals, ideals, and judgments?

Judson and Mary Landis (1973) note some danger signals during courtship that serve as warning against forming a permanent relationship. They are: repeated quarreling with a discernible pattern, repeated break-ups, a strong wish to change the other, moodiness and depression, and a feeling of regression rather than of growing more adult. All these can well be applied to the intercultural marriage.

Equally a warning signal may be an extreme defense of the partner's race, religion, or culture. This may be a reaction formation to cover up deep-seated prejudices. One way the individual can become conscious of this is to note his response to certain occurrences. For example, if David, the Jewish partner, does something socially rude, and Mary, Anglo-Protestant, immediately thinks "Jewish," then prejudice exists. If Jeanne, the Caucasian, offends Kimo, the Hawaiian, and Kimo immediately thinks "dumb *haole*" (Caucasian), then prejudice exists. The conscious intellect tries to be without prejudice; the emotions fail in the attempt.

Counseling After the Marriage

Usually, the intercultural couple appears in the therapist's office after the marriage and after conflicts have become serious. These couples present many difficulties to the psychiatrist. One of the primary challenges is to sort out which of the couple's problems is due to, or complicated by, cultural factors. This determination is more accurate when a cultural and family history is obtained from each partner. This involves questions regarding the type of family each partner came from, the models the parents set, the roles of the father and mother, communication styles within the family, family attitudes towards religion, family and cultural values placed on marriage, work, future; how emotions and affection are displayed, and family attitudes toward the marriage.

There should be an early discussion with each partner on personal and family cultural attitudes about seeing a therapist. In more than one case, the highly reticent Asian partner has made couple therapy useless; individual counseling with the verbal and communicative non-Asian partner has been the only possible therapy.

Though any cross-cultural therapy puts particular demands on the psychiartist, working with the intercultural couple has its particular hazard. The therapist is apt to unconsciously identify with the spouse of his or her own background, or, in an effort to avoid this, may unduly support the spouse of the different culture. Full awareness of his or her own value system can help the therapist walk this tightrope more successfully. The therapeutic team with representatives of both cultures may be the ideal solution; it is not always possible.

Not the least of the snares and pitfalls the therapist faces is seeing cultural implications where they do not exist. Does the Portuguese wife quarrel explosively with her husband because she is the almost stereotyped "hot-tempered Portuguese woman"? Or does the periodic nature of the quarrels suggest pre-menstrual tension? Are mealtimes constantly fraught with hostility because of Samoan *vs.* Irish culturally formed food preferences—or because the young wife is now noticing that her husband's table manners are terrible?

WAYS OF ADJUSTMENT

Intercultural couples do not inevitably head for the divorce court or live out their lives together in mutual disharmony. Many who have initial conflicts work out their ways of adjustment; some do this successfully, others attain what is more accurately termed a maladjustment. These ways of adjustment present certain fairly identifiable patterns. We could label these the "one-way," the "alternating," the "mid-point" compromises, and the "creative adjustment."

In the one-way (or asymmetric) adjustment, one partner gives up his/her own cultural behavior and takes on that of the other. Frequently, proximity to relatives of the dominant culture, relocation to the country of the dominant culture, or previous liking or fascination with the partner's culture helps determine this adjustment. In some cases, one partner already dislikes and feels separated from his or her own background. Sometimes certain aspects of the dominant culture demand the one-way solution: One partner must adopt the other's language and religion. Total capitulation to the partner's culture can indicate a pathological relationship between a dominant and a submissive partner.

The alternating adjustment, as the word suggests, comes about when wife and husband adopt each other's cultural ways on a trade-about basis. The Jewish partner takes an active part in Christmas festivities; the Christian partner joins in observances of the High Holy Days. The white partner eats soul food; the black enjoys lean broiled meat; the Javanese attunes his ear to Beethoven; the American symphony-goer discovers the nuances of the gamelan orchestra. The alternating adjustment is more apt to succeed in intellectual and social matters and in style of living, than in deeply felt religious convictions. Even in today's ecumenical spirit, there are Catholics who cannot in good conscience attend Mass one Sunday and their partner's services the next, and Jews who feel they disavow their religious heritage when they attend Christian churches.

The mid-point compromise is applicable to specific issues. If an Oriental husband feels he must give $200 a month to his parents, and the thrifty French wife argues that this strains the household budget, the compromise solution may be to give $100 a month. If the Caucasian bride wants a wedding reception with dainty sandwiches and champagne, and the Polynesian husband says this is embarrassingly "stingy" and a feast with roast pig should be held, a substantial buffet may provide the compromise. What is significant is the attitude behind the compromise—whether both partners are willing to respect each other's needs and feelings and compromise so both find satisfaction, or whether one partner merely assents for expediency, but clings to grudges and resentments.

The creative adjustment takes place when both partners give up certain individual, cultural behaviors and evolve a new behavioral pattern. Or this may be a merging of cultural influences—his, hers, and those absorbed from travel, friends, and intellectual and emotional experiences—so that a totally new way of living gradually ensues. The creative adjustment to solve a specific behavior problem is a conscious procedure. It is sometimes chosen because too much conflict or competition exists between the two cultures and the partners cannot negotiate. Trying a new way will bypass the conflict.

Though it may include conscious decisions to solve specific problems, the evolution of a new, total life-style is ultimately the adventure in living of a flexible, emotionally-intellectually receptive couple. Perhaps this should not be called an "adjustment," but rather a "creation."

INTERCULTURAL UNIONS: THE POSITIVE VIEW

Creative, or culture-blending, marriages illustrate a point not to be neglected: The intercultural union is often a successful, mentally healthy one. If this chapter has concerned itself unduly with the problems and failures of interracial/inter-ethnic/intercultural marriages, it is because these unhappy unions are the ones that come to clinical attention. We need not look far to turn our attention to intercultural couples who lead satisfying lives together. In Hawaii, where this is written, we meet them in the next office, down the hall, at professional meetings, at dinner parties, P.T.A., and neighborhood gatherings. We have known many of them long enough to surmise with fair accuracy that they are as reasonably happy as any married couple; that they have made whatever adjustments needed to be made to each other's cultural values; and that, for some, the merging of two cultural backgrounds has made life a great deal more interesting. Admittedly, in the Hawaiian setting, where races and ethnic groups meet with less animosity than in many other places and where cultural intermarriage has occurred for generations, these couples have the advantage of living in a climate of social acceptance. When these marriages are in trouble, the problem often comes from interpersonal, rather than intercultural, factors.

REFERENCES

Calkins, F.: *My Samoan Chief.* New York: Doubleday and Company, 1962.

Caudill, W. and Weinstein, H.: Maternal care and infant behavior in Japan and America. *Psychiatry,* 32:12–43, 1969.

Caudill, W. and Schooler, C.: Child behavior and child-rearing in Japan and in the United States. *J. Nerv. Ment. Dis.,* 157:323–337, 1973.

Comer, J. P. and Poussaint, A. F.: *Black Child Care.* New York: Simon and Schuster, 1975.

Fish, J. E. and Larr, C. J.: A decade of change in drawings of black children. *American Journal of Psychiatry,* 129:421–426, 1972.

Landis, J. and Landis, M.: *Building a Successful Marriage.* 6th ed. Englewood Cliffs, New Jersey: Prentice-Hall, 1973.

Piskacek, V. and Golub, M.: Children of interracial marriages. *Interracial Marriages: Expectation and Realities.* I. Stuart and L. E. Abt (Eds.), New York: Grossman Publishers, 1973.

Stevenson, H. and Stewart, E.: A developmental study of racial awareness in young children. *Child Dev.,* 29:399–409, 1958.

PART IV

Culture and Clinical Practice

CHAPTER 14

Communication and Cultural Inquiry

Unless a patient is unconscious (or the hapless future victim of all-computer diagnosing!), most medical evaluations have a certain transactional quality; there is little in radiology, but a great deal in internal medicine. Question compels answer; answer prompts clinician's question—sometimes silent, sometimes stated. The patient reacts to the physician; the physician responds to the patient's reaction with added inquiry. But in the psychiatric evaluation, the transactional quality, controlled and duly noted, is a significant part of the assessment, for the psychiatric diagnosis is fundamentally impressionistic. Thus, it is particularly subject to variables. These arise both from the patient and from the psychiatrist.

Each patient brings to the interview his or her own ability to perceive and present his or her problem. Each voluntary patient has particular reasons for asking for help. One may want his or her way of life changed; another may want it confirmed. Each has an individual orientation to medical psychiatric care. The psychiatrist may be approached with trust or suspicion, as an equal or as an authority figure, as an opponent in a battle of wits, or as a possible object of seduction. Each patient has an individual concept of himself or herself in the sick role. These variables have been shaped by the patient's personal and social-cultural background.

Psychiatrists, trained though they are to recognize their own biases, are nevertheless influenced by individual sensitivities and personality factors, by professional orientation to the patient's problems, and by personal and social-cultural background.

The communication, in fact the total doctor-patient relation, may be adversely affected when cultures are dissimilar and when the psychiatrist is unable to overcome cultural barriers by experience, knowledge of the patient's culture, and heightened awareness of the possibility of misinterpreting what the patient says and misjudging what he or she has done.

EVALUATOR-CLIENT RELATIONS

Though they are not always recognized, the patient's culture sends subtle clues to the evaluator. If the patient is from a background where authority is felt as a strong, imposed (but, we hope, respected) power, the psychiatrist should take a more directive role in conducting the interview. If the patient's background is one in which authority functions in a more democratic way, the psychiatrist should establish the feeling of interchange, rather than direction given and received. He must avoid any suggestion that the patient is being ordered around, no matter how politely.

In certain cultures, the male-female dominant-subordinate role is very significant. In this case, the sex of evaluator and patient becomes an influential factor in the therapeutic process. A man from a male-dominant society might feel very uncomfortable with a female therapist. A woman who is used to having a subordinate position with men may misinterpret the equal relationship extended by her male therapist.

People in some cultures have strong convictions that private, personal or family matters should not be discussed outside the family. The psychiatrist is, at first, an "outsider." With such patients, it takes more than usual time and tact, and a certain warmth, before any pertinent information will be revealed. Patient and therapist must establish a feeling of trust and caring.

Demonstrating some knowledge and respect for the patient's culture will help establish the therapist as more the "insider" and less the inquisitive person from "outside." The situation is not limited to patients from some exotic land. As one East Coast psychiatric social worker reports from her rural Middle-West experience, "I didn't get anywhere until I spent most of an hour exchanging recipes!"

COMMUNICATION PATTERNS

The Japanese patient nods his head and keeps saying *hai* (yes). The Hawaiian youth never looks you full in the face. The Samoan misses an appointment. Does the Japanese really agree with you? Is the Hawaiian youngster evasive? Does the missed appointment mean resistance on the part of the Samoan?

Not necessarily. The patient's communication pattern, verbal and nonverbal, may be of his culture. The *hai* and the nod very probably show only polite participation in the conversation. The Hawaiian may avoid your eyes because he was brought up by a grandmother who taught that eye contact is extremely rude and has an aggressive meaning (and an open stare is an invitation to fight). The Samoan's missed appointment may mean no more than a cultural-social casualness toward fixed dates and arrangements. Many cultures combine a dislike for committing oneself to any definite appointment with an equal distaste for saying a flat "No." "I will be there" can really mean "I will be there if nothing interferes and I feel like it—but I don't think I will feel like it." The Chinese client who says, "My mother is always kind," when the mother has been dead for some time, is not necessarily suffering from unrealized, incomplete grief. The Chinese language has no past tense verb form; habitual use of the present tense in English is fairly common, even among American-born and educated Chinese.

The language of gestures and expression is also subject to cultural shaping. People of Oriental background tend to smile or laugh when they are embarrassed, anxious, or sad. And, indeed, in the United States, the patient who enters the office smiling may merely be demonstrating long practice in the art of salesmanship or acting as hostess in society. In one culture, to stick out the tongue is an insult; in another, it merely expresses surprise.

SICK ROLE, ILLNESS BEHAVIOR, AND THE PRESENTATION OF COMPLAINTS

By the time a person voluntarily sees a psychiatrist or enters a physician's office, he probably has already taken on the social-cultural role of a sick person. He is considered as being ill and wanting to get well. He needs the care of others. He is expected to be freed from ordinary social responsibilities. He is oriented to seek technically competent help so he may get well (Parsons, 1951). If he suffers from what his culture considers a negative sickness, one that bears a stigma, then he himself may be considered responsible for his illness (Twaddle, 1972). Historically, many cultures have a social and/or moral stigma attached to leprosy, venereal disease, and mental illness.

Cross-cultural variations of the sick role have not been systematically studied. However, fragmented evidence indicates that ethnic differences exist. For example, Twaddle (1972) compared different ethnic groups and found that Jews tended to seek medical care and cooperated with medical treatment, and Protestants were least likely to seek medical care.

Reaction to pain also may be culturally influenced. Italian Catholics and Jews have been found to respond emotionally to pain, while Irish Catholics and Protestants met pain more stoically (Zborowski, 1952; Wolff and Langley, 1968).

Culture—and let us remember that this includes education and socioeconomic class—influences the way a client presents his or her problem. It may shape the complaint based on projection: "I cannot hold my husband because I am under a curse." It may translate the patient's anxieties into somatic ills. Further questioning may bring an account of externally attributed cause and effect. "I urinated in the woods without asking permission, and the spirits punished me with this skin rash," may still be heard among Chamarros on Guam.

When Zola studied medical patients in 1966, he found cultural differences in reporting symptoms. Italians gave detailed descriptions and included disruptions in interpersonal relationships in their complaints; the Irish gave short accounts and denied any connection of symptoms with interpersonal relationships.

Every society has its own attitudes toward, and ways of dealing with, emotions. Some groups feel comfortable talking openly about their feelings; others don't. When social attitudes inhibit free discussion of emotions and anxieties, the patient with psychological problems will be more likely to insist he has a somatic condition. The frequent presentation of somatic complaints from a psychiatric patient may reflect not only a personal tendency to hypochondriasis, but also a culture's influence on this trait. Patients from cultures which consider sex a very private matter will discuss sexual matters with great reservation. The psychiatrist must explore the topic with great delicacy. In certain societies, ancestors are a very important, or even sacred, part of the family and discussed in virtual secrecy. Certain cultural beliefs hold that naming a dreaded doom or misfortune may make it happen. Present taboos —or just the shadowy, half-understood memories of old taboos—do exist. In dynamically oriented psychiatric practice, we constantly observe and handle resistance that stems from the psychology of the individual, but perhaps the concept of resistance should be expanded to include "culture-related resistance."

OBTAINING CULTURAL INFORMATION

Learning about a patient's culture may be part of the ordinary clinical interview, or it may require a special interview. Family, friends of the same culture, cultural experts, written material—all these are information sources.

No matter how the information is gained, the evaluator's ultimate emphasis should be on the patient's and his immediate family's views of their life-style and value system. These most directly affect the patient's mind and behavior.

Although the dimension of culture always exists in everyone's life, its existence is realized in various ways and degrees. In fact, some persons fail to recognize the cultural dimension of their lives. Another group may be aware of different life-styles, but deny completely the influence of cultural factors in their own lives. In contrast, another group may over-identify ethnic-culture factors and even overuse them as an excuse or defense for individual problems.

Few psychiatrists can gain comprehensive anthropological knowledge of a particular patient's cultural background. The search for information must narrow its focus. We suggest concentrating on areas discussed below.

Essential Life-cycle Knowledge

One way to get significant information is to ask about the customs and attitudes attached to the basic life-cycle: how birth is handled in a given culture, how a child is reared, what is emphasized on becoming an adult, how a mate is selected, how the marital system operates, how the old are provided for, and the rites of death and grief.

For example, a child psychiatrist in Indonesia may need to know that the people of Bali customarily tease their children, but the people of Java do not. The Balinese mother may tease her child into a temper tantrum, then pay no attention. This repeated teasing and general disregard of a child's bid for attention have been considered a part of the pattern leading to adult detachment and a certain flatness of response to stimuli (Chaney, 1956). Though the Balinese and Javanese cultures are remarkably similar in other respects, teasing is simply not a part of Javanese child-rearing (Geertz, 1959).

Brief Social Information

The social organization, political situation, economic status, language communication system, and religion of a patient all merit investigation. For example, elderly Indochinese refugees often suffer from "survivor guilt" ("I escaped, but the others did not"), from particular death fears ("What will become of my body? What if it is cremated? If I am not buried in a proper place, my children and grandchildren will suffer"), and from a longing for their traditional social-educational-religious center, the Buddhist temple.

Political upheaval, changed economic status and social organization, language and religion are all linked with these anxieties, fears, nostalgic desires, and sadness.

Mental Health-related Information

Also needed are answers to such basic questions as: What is the concept of mental illness in the client's culture? What is the attitude and reaction to mental problems?

Acculturation may bring about interesting shifts in how mental illness is viewed and how family members recognize it. Kitano (1970) provides a fascinating example in his study of Japanese schizophrenics and family members living in Los Angeles, Tokyo, Hawaii, and Okinawa. Traditionally, the Japanese belief is that mental illness is a hereditary "taint" that carries great stigma. Family backgrounds of prospective brides and grooms are often researched carefully to be sure no mental disorders have existed. Yet, in Kitano's study, family members of schizophrenics viewed initial symptoms as malingering, laziness, or lack of motivation. They tolerated disturbed behavior until disruption to work and family life became conspicuous or intolerable. They said the patient's condition came from economic and environmental hardships or some negative experience, thus lessening or denying the cultural emphasis that mental illness is inherited and shameful.

Inquiring into Group-shared Behavior

There is a need for the evaluator to know what is the customary behavior in the patient's culture in order to distinguish differences between individual and group behavior.

It is pertinent to know how a culture or group reacts to certain behavior and, in turn, how this shapes the individual's behavior. For example, how does an unmarried Hawaiian girl react when she finds she is pregnant? Does she hide her condition as long as possible? Secretly arrange for an abortion? Not if she is close to the traditions of her culture. Instead, she has the baby with no shame and decides whether to keep it or have it adopted, for in the Hawaiian tradition, the concept of illegitimacy did not even exist. All babies were welcome, and many babies were given to friends or relatives in the adoption system called *hanai.* Similar extended family parenting occurs in black cultures.

It may be helpful to ask the patient, "How would your family, friends, or people of your village or neighborhood behave in a given circumstance? How would they see your behavior?''

Problem-related Specific Information

Cultural information related to the patient's problem should be sought. For example, if the patient's distress is centered around a psychosexual problem, then it is relevant to know sexual mores and attitudes in his own culture: How are boys and girls reared, and what are the differences in bringing up a boy or a girl? What kind of sex-related rule or taboo is practiced, such as segregating a girl after menarche and before marriage? How is premarital sexual maturity observed or ritualized? What are dating practices? Is virginity emphasized? Is child-bearing important? With this cultural understanding, we can better understand the sexual problem.

LEILA: A CULTURE-INFLUENCED CASE HISTORY

The importance of obtaining cultural information as a part of the psychiatric assessment is illustrated by the following case.

Leila, age 22, married and the mother of one child, came to the clinic because of anxiety and depression. During the initial interview, a fact emerged which seemed especially pertinent: Leila and her husband had moved out of her mother's house, leaving their baby behind.

What have we here? An irresponsible young couple and an unloved, unwanted child? Not necessarily so, for Leila does not live in Des Moines or London or Sydney. She lives on Majuro, capital of the many atolls and islands that make up the Marshall Islands. To her non-Marshallese therapist, she presented a problem and a challenge. Treating her demanded more than professional acumen and intuition; it was also necessary to inquire into Leila's culture in order to understand Leila's behavior.

The cultural inquiry began with Leila's case history, condensed and considerably disguised here:

Leila is the eldest of six (four sisters, one brother). Throughout her childhood, she had no household tasks or responsibilities, though her sisters did. Home life was happy, and she believes her mother ''favored'' her. When she was 17, she acquired a ''boyfriend.'' We'll call him Joe. Soon, the young man moved in with her, in her mother's household. After about a year, Leila had a baby girl. When the infant was about three weeks old, Leila's mother took over her care. The mother's explanation was that Leila, sleeping with the baby, might turn over and accidentally smother her. (This does not explain why the grandmother also assumed the baby's daytime care.) According to Leila, her mother "didn't think I knew how to take care of a baby." When Leila was 20, the young couple formed a permanent union. This was marked by a family feast. Within a few weeks, they moved out to a home Joe had found. They left the baby with Leila's mother.

Leila's initial history stimulated cultural, as well as clinical, questions and speculations. Did Leila grow up exceptionally childlike, "spoiled" and overly dependent on her mother? Or were all eldest daughters excused from work and responsibility? What is the culture's concept of a favored child? Did the young couple flout social conventions or follow custom by living together? What were the feelings and possible prejudices when a child then resulted? Did interpersonal conflicts or cultural stresses cause the young people to leave? Had a young husband finally accepted head-of-his-household responsibility—or did all young couples so leave after their union became permanent? Did Leila "abandon" her child—or are babies customarily left with a grandparent?

And, more generally, when cultural factors were involved, to what degree did they stem from Marshallese customs? To what degree did they represent acculturation (or conflicts)? It should be remembered that the Marshall Islands have known Spanish, German, Japanese, and more recently, American influences. The jet age has now touched these atolls, and Majuro especially is sometimes called a "melting pot."

Cultural ways had indeed been followed when Leila and Joe moved in with her mother. Their status was that of *koba bagik. Koba* (together) *bagik* (only) means, less literally, "temporarily together." The term connotes a union in which sexual intercourse is expected and allowed, and the young man is treated as a son-in-law. Only a sense of commitment and permanency is lacking. Though many Marshallese insist that, traditionally, the couple live with the wife's mother, in practice young couples today may move in with either in-law. Availability of housing and personal compatibilities may dictate the choice. However, living with in-laws is still prevalent, though some couples move immediately into their own homes.

When Leila and Joe marked their intention of permanency with a family feast, they changed their status to that of *koba.* Today, this change of status may or may not be accompanied by a legal or religious wedding ceremony. No shame or guilt seemed involved in the birth of a baby before this permanent commitment. The Western-Christian concept of illegitimacy had not infringed on the *koba bagik* tradition.

American influence was evident in the couple's departure to their own home, for the decision was really Joe's, and Joe had been exposed to American ways for years. He had worked for a time on Kwajalein. There he had earned and saved enough money to buy his own home. There he had observed the American single-family home and absorbed some of the American feeling that a young man should be independent and master of his own household.

For Leila, the departure was fraught with both cultural and personal stresses. She was torn between wanting to stay with and depend on her mother, and wanting to be with her husband and be a more adult wife in charge of her home. Her mother, upset and frequently in tears, represented both cultural tradition and maternal possessiveness. She could strengthen and disguise her longing to keep her daughter at home with the preachment, "this is the custom." Her silver cord was well reinforced with the sinews of tradition. In the relationship of mother to daughter were personal elements that went beyond, or even distorted, cultural factors. This was evident in the favoritism shown to Leila. Consider the concept of the favored child as it exists in the Marshall Islands:

In the Marshallese tradition, the eldest child, whether male or female, is the "special" child. Though the eldest male sibling is usually destined to be the future family head, the eldest girl is also an eventual leader and authority figure. In considering Leila "special," her mother did indeed follow cultural ways, but, in excusing Leila from all tasks and responsibilities, she strayed from tradition, for the position of "eldest" carried with it obligations; the eldest sister not only was expected to work diligently, but was also responsible for her younger siblings. In the mother's favoring of Leila, personal feelings seem to have outweighed cultural factors. Even after Leila was established in her own home, her mother came to clean and cook for her, or sent the younger sisters. To her mother, Leila is still seen as being above mundane tasks or unable to do them. To what degree she is still seen as a "little girl" must be explored.

A possible conflict of cultures merits attention in the next element of this case: Leila's leaving her child with her mother. On the surface, this is clearly in accordance with tradition. The Marshallese custom was for any relative, but usually a grandmother, to keep the child. The practice is called *kokajiriri* (to take the child). This was done by mutual agreement—but the mutuality may be an idealized concept, since tradition also decreed that when a relative asked for a child, the child's mother could not say "No." In the past, the Marshallese mother may have escaped conflict by never really expecting to keep the child she bore. Today, especially in Majuro, American influence may have attached new stresses to the old custom. For example, the grandmother, attuned to tradition, may ask for the child; the mother, exposed to American ways and younger-generation views, may want to refuse; older relatives may pressure the mother to conform; young or Americanized ones may counsel rebellion and refusal.

In Leila's particular case, the personal aspect of ambivalence to responsibility must be investigated. There is the need to learn how most young mothers in the Marshallese culture feel about their babies and the role of motherhood. There is a need to learn how Leila, the favored girl-child, feels about her baby. Did she, relieved of all baby care (except breast-feeding), ever feel bonded in motherhood to her child?

And, whatever the answer, there is also the need for the therapist to separate himself from any personal conviction that, barring abuse, neglect, or impossible home conditions, a child really should be with his mother. In the Marshall Islands, this may not be so.

The many threads of personal and cultural factors that make up Leila's case cannot be neatly tied up here. She is still in therapy. Her case is presented here because it illustrates so well many of the questions that need to be answered when a psychiatrist evaluates a client from a completely different background.

REFERENCES

Chaney, M. V.: Child-rearing in Bali and its effects on adult personality. Mimeo. Interdepartmental Seminar 330, 1956.

Geertz, H.: The vocabulary of emotion: A study of Javanese socialization process. *Psychiatry,* 22:293–298, 1959.

Kitano, H. L.: Mental illness in four cultures (Los Angeles, Hawaii, Tokyo, Okinawa). *J. Soc. Psychol.,* 80:121–134, 1970.

Parsons, T.: *The Social System.* Glencoe: Free Press, 1951.

Twaddle, A. C.: The concepts of the sick role and illness behavior. *Advances in Psychosomatic Medicine,* 8:162–179, 1972.

Wolff, B. B. and Langley, S.: Cultural factors and the responses to pain: A review. *American Anthropologist,* 70:494–501, 1968.

Zborowski, M.: Cultural components in response to pain. *Journal of Social Issues,* 8:16–30, 1952.

Zola, I. K.: Culture and symptoms: An analysis of patients' presenting complaints. *Am. Sociol. Rev.,* 3:615–630, 1966.

CHAPTER 15

Assessment and Diagnostic Evaluation

Culture-free absolutes in psychiatric diagnosis are few. Organic brain syndromes and severe manifestations, such as psychotic delirium and psychotic hallucinations, are pathological by definition. The definitions hold good across cultures (Rinder, 1964). There is little transcultural disagreement in defining disorders which are more or less biological. There, the list of absolutes just about stops. Mental disturbances that are more or less psychologically based, and must be understood as functional, do not fit neatly into any transcultural consensus. Drinking, homosexual disorders, and personality problems all are necessarily judged both from accumulated psychiatric knowledge and in the light of the culture in which they manifest themselves.

CONCEPTS OF NORMALCY OR PATHOLOGY

What is pathological behavior in one culture is normal and even beneficial in another. The judgmental standard—that of society and psychiatry—is based to some extent on what we might call the "criterion of result." This rests on the premise that man strives to reach a certain goal by behaving in an organized manner. When this behavior is dysfunctional or disorganized; when it does not help him reach his goal or, in fact, defeats his purpose or harms him; when it disrupts the group or harms others, we call this behavior and the mental condition associated with it pathological. When this behavior does not limit function, disturb, harm, or even benefits, we call it normal. The possession state in folk religious practice contrasted with that in hysterical patients is one example. Both are states of altered consciousness with a change in personality which is said to result when a spiritual entity takes possession. However, the ritual possession takes place as learned, institutionalized behavior that answers a particular social need. It can be induced and terminated by a priest or shaman (Wittkower, 1970). It is controlled. It serves a purpose. It is neither abnormal nor pathological. However, hysterical possession is a reaction to stress or frustration, is without constructive goal, and is out-of-control behavior. This possession is pathological.

Criteria of Departure and Degree

We might also define pathology by using the "criteria of departure and degree." If a mental state or behavior departs, quantitatively or qualitatively, from society's norm, and this departure takes a disapproved, negative form, it can be called pathological.

Grief reaction, for one example, may be so judged. Under ordinary circumstances, an individual usually grieves over the death of a loved person with the intensity and duration customary to his society. He does his "grief work" pretty much in accordance with the norm. But if his grief is extraordinarily devastating and intense, or if it extends long after the customary period, we call his grief reaction pathological. The range of reaction may be subject to physiological and psychological factors (the long-expected death may bring less and shortened grieving; the person heavily sedated after a death may suffer a delayed or incomplete grief process). Yet the psychiatrist is aware of these factors. The broad definition of normal grief remains useful. When cultural factors unfamiliar to the therapist are involved, the judgment of what is normal and what is not is more subject to variables. For example, in some cultures, hallucinating the dead (seeing them and talking to them) for about a month is considered a normal part of grief. In others it would be abnormal. In still others, hallucinating the dead continues as a normal grief reaction for much longer (Pukui et al., 1979).

Odd or Negative Behaviors

Any behavior may be viewed as pathological, not just because it is a departure from the normal range, but because it is extremely "odd," "peculiar," or "eccentric." ("Extremely" is the consideration; mild eccentricities are often part of the interesting personality.) Running naked down Fifth Avenue in New York, wearing evening clothes at high noon on Miami Beach—these behaviors are definitely odd and eccentric. Screaming during a symphony concert is extremely peculiar; screaming during a rock concert may be normal.

A society may also view certain kinds of mental conditions or behavior as "sick," "queer," "wrong," or "abnormal." In various lay terms, the group is applying the label "pathological." There are many reasons for this negative verdict. For example, if a society has little tolerance for a certain behavior, it tends to label this behavior as abnormal. Contemporary Americans emphasize verbal communication; being a "good conversationalist," being "easy to talk to," the ability to "open up" are socially approved. Thus, less tolerance is given the person who is quiet and uncommunicative. He is apt to be labeled secretive, unfriendly, or passive. Mexican-Americans, especially, believe that a man should be assertive and aggressive. He must demonstrate the quality of "machismo." The culture has trouble accepting the man who is passive and retiring.

Finally, a society may view a behavior as abnormal or not, depending on how prevalent the behavior is. A society with widespread and long-established drinking or drug use tends not to see such phenomena as substance "abusing" behavior. In contrast, if a particular behavior is not prevalent, then it is possibly seen as "queer" and suspect behavior. Since a society applies criteria subjectively, the concept of pathology defined in this way may change at different times, may vary in different circumstances, and may not be shared by other groups (or by the psychiatrist). One society may view masturbation as "sick" behavior; another may consider it natural, normal, and inconsequential. If a behavior is seen as abnormal within the culture, but is seen as normal by an outsider, it is called autopathological. The reverse, a behavior that is seen as abnormal by an outsider, but as normal within the culture, is called heteropathological.

CLINICAL PERCEPTION OF PSYCHOPATHOLOGY

Psychiatry has developed a system of orientation, method, and terminology to evaluate and describe a patient's mental condition. However, this standardized system brings serious problems in transcultural use. For example, Tseng et al. (in preparation, a) showed a series of videotapes of American patients who exhibited various mental symptoms to evaluators of two cultural groups, psychiatrists in Hawaii and psychiatrists in Tokyo. Though the two groups agreed on many basic observations, they rated symptoms differently in several areas. They differed, not so much in distinguishing different emotional conditions as in regarding the expression of emotion as "labile" or not. The Japanese tended to rate the American patients as emotionally labile, while American raters did not. This suggests that American and Japanese cultures differ in the way emotions are expressed, and that this cultural difference influenced the evaluators' perception and interpretation of demonstrated affect.

In this same study, Japanese and American medical students also evaluated the videotaped patients. Both groups of students differed much more than the psychiatrists in rating degrees of anxiety, idiosyncratic speech, blocking, and delusions. The Japanese found these conditions more prevalent and pronounced than the Americans did. Japanese students also differed markedly on judging disconnected speech, rating it at both high (severe) and low (not present or slight) extremes of the scale. It is interesting that less difference in rating this was found between the American and Japanese psychiatrists. Clinical experience seemed to have overcome, to some extent, both language and cultural barriers. However, in general, assessments that concern speech and thought content and process (delusional thinking, bizarre ideation, blocking, for example) need to be based on information about the culturally normal way of thinking.

The setting in which patients are studied may also influence the assessment of psychopathology in an ethnic group. Katz et al. (1969) have illustrated this. They studied descriptions of Japanese-American and Caucasian-American acute schizophrenics before hospital admission and during their hospital stay. Before hospitalization, the Japanese patients were described as more socially obstreperous, nervous, and hyperactive than were the Caucasians. With both groups in the hospital, the picture changed. The Caucasian-Americans were rated as more excited and exhibiting more paranoid projection, belligerence, and disturbance in the motor or postural area than the Japanese. This is probably due to the fact that Japanese tend to behave more freely in private situations such as a home setting, and to act more cautiously in a public setting. The study suggested that patients' behavior in the usual community surroundings may be different in the institutional setting, and this difference may vary in different ethnic groups. It stressed the necessity of sampling behavior broadly and in a variety of settings in cross-cultural research.

Westermeyer (1975) emphasized much the same point. He pointed out that American Indian families tolerate pathological behavior quite well when it is bizarre and eccentric, but are less tolerant of violent-aggressive behavior. Therefore, the psychotic patients referred to mental health facilities tend to be violent and aggressive; the ones whose behavior is merely strange are kept at home. The psychiatrist can easily gain the false impression that the American Indian is prone to violence and aggression.

Cultural background influenced evaluations of childhood behavior in another study by Tseng et al. (in preparation, b). American psychiatrists in Hawaii and Japanese psychiatrists in Tokyo evaluated parent-child interactions in videotapes of families of different ethnic background: American (Caucasian), Japanese, Korean, and Hawaiian. The American and Japanese psychiatrists did not show much difference in their evaluation of a third ethnic group, such as Hawaiian or Korean; they showed greatest difference in evaluating Caucasian-American and Japanese families.

The major difference came from the evaluators' concepts of parental authority. Specifically, the Japanese evaluated the Caucasian child's antagonistic, rebellious actions towards her parents as not being negative. This is based on the fundamental Japanese assumption that a child simply is not permitted to display negative behavior. Therefore it didn't happen, even though they saw it with their own eyes. The Americans saw the child's behavior as negative. The Americans viewed the father as passive and therefore inadequate; the Japanese (accustomed to men's passive uninvolvement with domestic and parental concerns) did not. The two groups of evaluators did not disagree in assessing all areas of behavior—only in those in which their cultural values were most disparate.

PSYCHOLOGICAL TESTING

Whether or not psychological measurements—developed in Western society—are valid across cultures is a question that has been considered for some time. Some feel that, while non-projective instruments are suspect, projective tests are more or less culture-free. But is this true? Consider some pros and cons.

Rorschach Responses

Jilek and Aall-Jilek (1964) obtained Rorschach protocols and case histories on patients of the Wapogoro (Bantu) group, indigenous Africans of Tanganyika. They had these interpreted blindly by a psychologist in Montreal, and found a high correlation between case histories and the Rorschach interpretations. They suggest that projective tests can be used accurately in other than Western cultures.

However, Yang et al. (1962) held a contrasting opinion based on their study of the Rorschach responses of normal Chinese adults. In the "normal detail" response, the Chinese tended to give only about two-thirds of the detail that Beck, in 1950, described as usual for Americans. The authors linked this with the characteristic Chinese tendency of habitual inhibition, and suggested there is a need to establish a modified baseline of Rorschach D-response for evaluating Chinese. Johnson and Sikes (1965) studied Rorschach responses of three cultural groups: black, Mexican-American, and Anglo psychiatric patients. Prevailing diagnoses were anxiety and depression. Evaluation of the tests show marked differences in measures of hostility and overall patterns of handling hostility. The black patients saw themselves as vulnerable, as victims with impending violence all around them. The Mexican-Americans presented a picture of persons more secure, but still rather defensively on guard. They showed relatively greater "potential hostility" but little "victim hostility." The Anglos showed greatest internal tension and a kind of middle-of-the-road rating in their handling of hostility.

MMPI Translations Challenged

Although the MMPI is the most frequently used non-projective psychological testing instrument, its cross-national applicability is subject to challenge. Glatt (1969) studied French, Spanish, and German translations of the MMPI. He noted that it is difficult to give items in the F scale (the scale which measures, among other factors, the desire to appear "bad") the same connotation in other languages that they have in English. Responses in the three other languages are then scored as abnormal when those in English are not. He also found that Scale 5, which primarily measures masculinity-femininity, presents translation difficulties, probably because it is not sufficiently sensitive to sex-role differences in different cultures. For example, the English sentence, "I used to like hopscotch," refers to a game played more often by girls in North America. Translated into the French *"J'aimais jouer à saute-moutons,"* it refers to leapfrog, a game more often played by boys. Therefore, female subjects may get different scores when using the French version than when using the English.

Gynther (1972) reviewed the literature and disclosed distinctive differences between MMPIs of blacks and whites. He concluded that differences in MMPI performance of blacks and whites reflect differences in values, perceptions, and expectations that result from growing up in different cultures; that the most striking value exhibited by blacks is distrust of white society; and that there is no satisfactory evidence that blacks' MMPI performances indicated they are less well adjusted than whites.

It seems evident that when psychological testing is used across cultures, it should be administered with extreme care and interpreted with a certain degree of doubt. The possibility of an ethno-cultural bias in test results is very much present.

MENTAL STATUS EXAMINATION

Among the many questions psychiatrists ask to determine a patient's mental status are some that are virtually free from culture-caused misunderstanding. The simple inquiries to ascertain memory loss or orientation to place and time are usually culture-free. Mathematical exercises are usually valid across cultures, if the patient's schooling is known.

However, other questions may be meaningless or misleading because of cultural differences between evaluator and patient. For example, one way used in evaluating the thinking process is to ask the meaning of proverbs or proverbial sayings. Even though certain proverbs seem almost universal, they may be subject to misunderstandings of geography and culture. "A rolling stone gathers no moss" probably carries the same meaning almost anywhere —except where moss has never been seen or described. However, if the psychiatrist of German background asks his Samoan patient what is meant by saying "An angel flew through the room," the patient may have no idea that this refers to a sudden, uncomfortable silence that falls on a group. The therapist from America's Ozark region may consider the grasp-the-opportunity meaning of "When the pig is offered, hold up the poke" obvious, but unless the East Coast patient knows that "poke" means "sack" or "bag," the proverb means nothing. It is prudent to assume that the folk-saying of one country may be unknown in another. A better approach is to ask the patient what the proverbs of his culture are and what they mean, and then check his explanations with his family or friends of the same background. Ideally, family members or friends should be fairly close to the patient's age, for the meaning attached to proverbs is not static. To an old Jewish grandmother, the Yiddish saying, "Poor and gay wins the day" may mean that high spirits and a glad heart can compensate for poverty. To her grandson, even though he'd heard the saying for years, the message may seem to be about homosexual activist movements.

Questions about what we consider common knowledge are a useful way to check a patient's general information and judgment. These questions may be culture-specific. Asking the Midwesterner what the typhoon season is might be foolish. Asking how one drives on an icy pavement might baffle the patient who has never left Guam. No psychiatrist would make such blatant mistakes; the exaggerated examples are presented only to emphasize the point that the patient's background of culture, education, and class may all influence his responses to "common knowledge" questions. It is more relevant to ask an immigrant from rural Truk to name his village chief than to list the last five U.S. presidents; it is more to the point to ask the stockbroker to define the bull and bear terms of the stock market than to name the best selling fiction of the year.

When the patient comes from a different background, the therapist is wise to check his questions before he asks them. Will the terms used be understood? Does the content come within the patient's geographical-cultural-educational background of knowledge and experience?

DIAGNOSTIC CLASSIFICATION

Psychiatry has developed its own classifications for clinical use. Unfortunately, the same diagnostic term does not always carry the same meaning in all parts of the world. Variations in professional disciplines, political situations, and medical-historical backgrounds too often shade the meanings of the words. Different classification systems exist. The International Classification of Disease (ICD), developed by the World Health Organization, is more widely used in Europe; the Diagnostic and Statistical Manual of Mental Disorders (DSM) of the American Psychiatric Association is used more in North and South America.

The well-known USA-UK study of diagnostic patterns (Cooper et al., 1969) illustrates very well varying definitions and usages of terms. The study indicated that psychiatrists of the two nations tended to observe and describe the patient's psychopathology similarly, but they made different clinical diagnoses. What the USA psychiatrists termed more as schizophrenic disorders, the UK psychiatrists were more apt to call affective disorders. The concepts of schizophrenia and affective disorders obviously differed somewhat. The USA psychiatrists tended to define schizophrenia broadly and loosely; the UK psychiatrists, within more circumscribed limits.

In many countries, the term "hypochondriasis" is frequently used, and even "neurasthenia" appears in diagnoses. This is particularly noted in some Oriental countries where cultural traits build a preoccupation with somatic symptoms and thus shape patients' ills. Within these countries, both diagnostic labels remain applicable and useful, while they are being discarded in Western countries as imprecise.

The concept of borderline states is often used in the United States, but is rarely employed in Oriental countries. This may be a matter of professional patterns, or it may mean that the United States actually has many more marginally relating, confused, pre-psychotic patients. Whether this difference will also exist in another quarter-century is also open to question, for diagnosis, like culture, is subject to change. The recent shift in diagnosing homosexual disorders was greatly influenced by changing cultural attitudes in the West.

Many psychiatric conditions described in relation to particular ethno-cultural groups do not fit the contemporary psychiatric classification systems. The "Puerto Rican Syndrome," with its bizarre seizures and hyperkinesis, *amok* marked by a massive homicidal outburst, the "startle reaction" called *latah,* and Arctic hysteria are examples. The present classification systems may need expansion and revision to make them cross-culturally applicable.

DYNAMIC DIAGNOSTIC FORMULATION

As a part of the clinical diagnostic work-up, we use available information as a base for seeking explanations of why certain phenomena occurred so we may then ascertain the underlying causes of the patient's problems and how he or she reacts to and handles them. In this exercise of dynamic formulation, we rely on clinical knowledge. For example, if a patient has obsessive-compulsive problems, we give special consideration to personality formation related to anal characteristics, and we explore difficulty in managing and controlling aggressive drives. If the case is hysterical, we may focus on difficulty in solving the triangular relationship and problems of repression. But beyond this professional knowledge, our way of thinking and our interpretations of the patient's pathology are influenced more or less by our life experiences and our personal and cultural background.

If patient and therapist are from different backgrounds, the chances of diagnostic errors increase. Some, as we have noted, lie in tests and terms. Others come from ignorance of the patient's culture. Some lurk in the psychiatrist's own life experiences and cultural views. For example, if the patient evidences conflict with a sibling, and the evaluator comes from a cultural background (such as American) which emphasizes individual equality, he may particularly explore possible interference with the independence of the siblings, in addition to the possible existence of parental favoritism. If the evaluator's culture has emphasized sibling rank and hierarchy (as in some traditional Oriental countries and among upper-class English), he may look for differences in privileges given the elder and younger sibling and explore parental favoritism as a cause of conflict. If the evaluator comes from a society of frequent extramarital relationships, he may want to know if the siblings have the same father or not. (Indeed, in such societies the very nature of the parental relationship—or wondering about it—may contribute to the conflict.) In each example, the speculative direction of diagnostic formulation has come somewhat from the evaluator's own personal storehouse of experiences and attitudes.

Acquiring information about the patient's culture lessens the possibility of making inappropriate diagnostic formulations. If one's own city (or practice) has a good proportion of some other cultural group, this is not too difficult. Gaining an awareness of other cultures in general is also helpful. Exposure to Culture A and Culture B somehow increases sensitivity to both differences and similarities in Culture C.

This does not mean that the psychiatrist disregards or forgets his or her own cultural heritage—quite the contrary. With knowledge and thoughtful consideration of his or her own social environment, value system, and ethnic heritage, he/she can conduct the transcultural diagnostic evaluation with greater objectivity. Awareness of one's own culture sharpens the ability to discern the cultural mores and attitudes (and departures from them) of the patient. This is perhaps analogous to—or an extension of—the premise of psychoanalysis: The analyst is analyzed to become a better analyst.

REFERENCES

Beck, S. J. *Rorschach's Test: Vol. 1 Basic Processes.* New York: Grune and Stratton, 1950.

Cooper, J. E., Kendall, R. E., Gurland, B. J., Sartorius, N., and Farkas, T.: Cross-national study of diagnosis of the mental disorders: Some results from the first comparative investigation. *American Journal of Psychiatry,* 125:21–29, 1969 supp.

Glatt, K.: An evaluation of the French, Spanish, and German translations of the MMPI. *Acta Psychologica,* 29:65–84, 1969.

Gynther, M. D.: White norms and black MMPTs: A prescription for discrimination? *Psychological Bulletin,* 78:386–402,1972.

Jilek, W. F. and Aall-Jilek, L. M.: A blind interpretation of Rorschachs on the Wapogoro of Tanganyika. *Transcultural Psychiatric Research Review,* 1:139–142, 1964.

Johnson, D. L. and Sikes, M. P.: Rorschach and TAT responses of Negro, Mexican-American, and Anglo psychiatric patients. *Journal of Projective Techniques and Personality Assessment,* 29:183–188, 1965.

Katz, M. M., Sanborn, K. O., and Gudeman, H.: Characterizing differences in psychopathology among ethnic groups: A preliminary report on Hawaii-Japanese and mainland American schizophrenics. In: *Mental Health Research in Asia and the Pacific.* W. Caudill and T. Y. Lin (Eds.), Honolulu, Hawaii: East-West Center Press, Honolulu, 1969.

Pukui, M, K., Haertig, E. W., and Lee, C. A.: *Nana I Ke Kumu (Look to the Source),* Vol. 2. Queen Lili'uokalani Children's Center, Honolulu, 1979.

Rinder, I. D.: New directions and an old problem: The definition of normality. *Psychiatry,* 27: 107–115, 1964.

Tseng, W. S., Ogino, K., McDermott, J. F., Jr., Kinzie, J. D., and Ebata, K.: Cross-cultural Study of Mental Status Examination in USA and Japan. (In preparation, a).

Tseng, W. S., Ogino, K., McDermott, J. F., Jr., and Ebata, K.: Cross-cultural study of parent-child behavior assessment in USA and Japan. (In preparation, b).

Westermeyer, J.: Personal communication, 1975.

Wittkower, E. D.: Trance and possession states. *International Journal of Social Psychiatry*, 16: 153–160, 1970.

Yang, K. S., Su, C. H., Hsu, H. H., and Huang, C. H.: Rorschach responses of normal Chinese adults: I. The normal details. *ACTA Psychologica Taiwanica*, 4:78–103, 1962.

CHAPTER 16

A Cultural Differential Diagnosis of Cases

It is unfortunate that no instrument exists to allow the psychiatrist to assess just how much the client's culture has affected his/her behavior, caused or compounded his/her problems, or colors the chances for successful therapy. Like human emotions, cultural elements cannot be spun in a centrifuge or viewed through a microscope. Necessarily, they are identified and their importance assessed by yet another human—the therapist. For this identification and evaluation, the therapist depends on personal sensitivities, broad exposure to and continued learning about cultures, and the reported experiences of colleagues. In this chapter, we present reports of a few such experiences. These case examples are culturally significant for various reasons. They may be classified as: 1) cases in which the problem and coping mechanisms are imbedded in cultural elements (though they may not be typical of the culture); 2) cases related to culture-adjustment attempts; 3) cases in which culture is used as an excuse or as a disguise for intrapsychic problems. Specific psychiatric disorders formed by or existing only in certain cultures are discussed in a separate chapter.

PSYCHIATRIC CASES IMBEDDED IN CULTURAL ELEMENTS

In these examples, the cases are prominently influenced by what we might call "culture within a culture." Culture in its broad sense of country, race, or ethnicity makes possible, or reinforces, a certain pattern of living within neighborhood, occupational, or family group, which in turn formulates the problem and the attempts to cope with it.

Case One

Zelda, a 25-year-old California housewife and mother of two sons, was brought to the hospital crying, screaming, and talking almost incoherently. When she quieted a little, she repeatedly complained that a neighbor woman was ''making passes'' at her husband. Her history revealed a stormy marital life and an adolescence marked by family trauma.

The patient is the youngest of two girls and one boy. Her father was an alcoholic and ran around with a number of women Zelda believed were prostitutes. These she resented very much. When Zelda was 16, her father shot himself, not in his own, but in Zelda's bedroom. After Zelda had somewhat recovered from this (she recalls screaming and vomiting), she became very labile and suggestible. While she was in this state, a young building contractor persuaded her to marry him.

This marriage lasted four years. One son was born. After three years, the husband began having an affair with the married woman living next door. Zelda then had an affair with the woman's husband. Both couples then divorced, switched partners, and remarried.

Zelda's second marriage went well for a while, and she had her second son. Shortly after the birth, she had a hysterectomy which left her disturbed and depressed. Her husband began drinking heavily. Zelda then began drinking to excess to ''show him what he looks like when he's drunk.'' As her depression deepened, she began to believe that her neighbor, once her husband's wife, was ''making passes'' at her husband.

The case—it sounds like a soap opera—is obviously one of psychological predominance—one with underlying hysterical problems, strong ambivalent feelings toward the father, and basic insecurity as a woman. However, the actions in the case could have taken place only in certain cultures—in the United States, for example, or perhaps in permissive Amsterdam or certain Scandinavian countries. The next-door-neighbor affairs, the switching of marital partners, the retaliation of the woman in drinking as well as sexual matters, could not have taken place in, for example, traditional Muslim cultures where women's role is socially circumscribed, and probably not in Ireland with its strongly imbedded sexual guilts and inhibitions. Though these behaviors and coping attempts happened (as in this case) in the United States, they are not representative of all married couples in the United States. The behavior is unique to certain cultures, but not typical of them. Zelda's intrapsychic problems were worsened by the coping attempts learned from the patterns of living of her group.

Case Two

This case came to clinical attention after a couple attempted joint suicide. Both were rescued. These notes concern the young man in the case. He was a young physician, the son of a successful physician who was head of his own private hospital. We will call the son Dr. N. Dr. N was expected to succeed his father, eventually taking over his place in the hospital and upholding the family position in society. About a year before the suicide attempt, he had joined the staff of his father's hospital. There he met a nurse, a young widow with one child. The two fell deeply in love. When their attachment became apparent, it met strong opposition from Dr. N's parents. In their view—and that of their social-cultural group—marriage for this badly-matched pair was impossible! In the first place, any emotional involvement between doctor and nurse was taboo by family, hospital, and social class rules. Worse yet, the young nurse had been married. Even though her husband had died (in a traffic accident), and no quarrels or divorce had ever marred the union, still the young woman was not a virgin. She had also borne a child—tangible evidence of a previous alliance. A wife should not have had another man's child! The weight of parental, social, and cultural disapproval and thwarted love could not be borne; to die together seemed the only solution.

The case occurred in Japan more than 30 years ago. Almost every culture has its star-crossed lovers, yet this particular unhappy romance seems uniquely Japanese—not so much in parental opposition to the marriage as in the young couple's acceptance of it, their inability to rebel, and their attempted suicide as the traditional finale to love frustrated. The right of parents to arrange marriages, the rigidities of social and professional class structures, and the time-honored practice of suicide—these had long permeated Japanese culture and formulated Japanese attitudes. Many of the underlying attitudes that shaped the case of Dr. N still exist and color the lives and emotions of many Japanese. *Joshi,* the love suicide pact, is still fairly common.

The case of Zelda and that of Dr. N are an interesting contrast in living patterns: one of sexual and social permissiveness; one of rigid restrictions. It is difficult to imagine Zelda living in the Japan of post-war years or to visualize Dr. N as an American in California or Kansas. But if they had, would their emotional problems have been different because of coping patterns allowed or prohibited by their culture? Undoubtedly.

Case Three

"Johnny" was brought to a clinic at his kindergarten teacher's insistence. Here was a five-year-old with little experience in discipline and no knowledge of how to play with other children. Johnny refused to share toys, turned a deaf ear to the teacher's instructions, was one minute a crybaby, the next a young bully. Here, in short, was a bright, intelligent, exasperating despot of school and playground. What made Johnny like this?

Johnny was the only son of an only son of an only son. Johnny was the only person who would carry on the family name. The very fact he existed was, in family opinion, almost miraculous, for Johnny's mother had previously produced three daughters. After the last girl was born, pressure was strong for John (the father) to divorce his wife and remarry. Relatives believed the woman determined an infant's sex; a new wife, they said, may give you a son. Then—the miracle!—John's wife gave birth to a boy. Family members soon concentrated on guarding and cherishing the precious male. Johnny was not allowed to play with neighbor children. "He might be hurt," said his mother. His sisters had to give him even their favorite toys. What Johnny wanted, Johnny got. He was comforted the moment he cried, indulged in every whim. In this circle of overprotection and overindulgence, the grandmother was a key figure. She literally carried him everywhere on her back. Even when Johnny started kindergarten, the grandmother carried him the two blocks to school and later carried him back home. Johnny did not even know how to cross a street. He had no idea of give-and-take, and no social skills of childhood.

In the case of Johnny, a family pattern of thought and behavior stemmed from a cultural tradition, for "Johnny" is an American fictitious name. This was an affluent, newly immigrant Chinese family living in a large U.S. city. In therapy it was necessary to look beyond the father and mother and their relationships, beyond the psychological implications of an overprotective maternal figure. Some of the roots of this problem lay in generations of cultural belief in the value of sons ("It is better to raise geese than daughters," goes an old Chinese proverb) and the importance of carrying on the family name. Here, it was necessary to help two generations, Johnny's parents and the doting, ever-present grandmother, to change their value systems so they could change their behavior. In this case, a family system, a microcosm of culture, was ruining Johnny's life (and adversely affecting his three sisters) because it was formed and reinforced by the larger culture of Chinese tradition.

PSYCHIATRIC CASES RELATED TO CULTURE-ADJUSTMENT ATTEMPTS

Case One

Ahmed came to the United States to do graduate study. He is from an upper-class family in a Middle-Eastern country. Ahmed's initial adjustment was excellent. He adapted to living in a dormitory, accepted, if not enjoyed, American cafeteria food, coped successfully with an early bout of homesickness, and was in good academic standing. Yet, quite suddenly he suffered a severe psychotic break. When he came to clinical attention, he was very paranoid. The background of his break is as follows:

Ahmed came from a country that is extremely conservative in sexual matters. Marriages, at least in his social class, are still usually arranged. Women are either virginal, "nice" women, or prostitutes. Ahmed, therefore, came to his university campus with no experience in dating, no understanding of boy-meets-girl relationships, social or sexual. However, in a quiet, unexpressed, almost secret way, Ahmed became very fond of a pretty university secretary. For nearly a year he was content with talking to her in her office. He began to depend on her for help in language problems, advice in academic matters, answers to questions about American customs. Ahmed began to feel he was in love with her. During all these months of office chats, Ahmed had observed other students dating. Finally, gathering his courage, he asked the secretary to dinner, and she accepted. Ahmed prepared for the date in great excitement, dressing carefully and virtually rehearsing the evening. After dinner, the young lady told Ahmed she had just become engaged and invited him to the announcement party.

Ahmed reacted with shock, anger, and sadness. According to his value system, a woman promised to another man would never have accepted his dinner invitation. The secretary, he thought, was a bad, promiscuous woman—but she was also a lovely, desirable woman he now had lost!

Almost from that evening, Ahmed decided to change his conservative, sexually retiring behavior. He began to date constantly and indiscriminately, even picking up girls on the street. He formed or attempted immediate sexual involvements. ("If Americans are free and easy, then I'll be free and easy.") After a few weeks, Ahmed became depressed and began to feel people were laughing at him, saying he was "no good," "promiscuous," "a terrible person." A suicide attempt followed.

Clinically, Ahmed was a case of paranoid psychosis with deep depression. Culturally, he was caught in a state of bewilderment; he had attempted to shift his own regulatory—his own value—system and failed. He had tried to break his own rules with no clearly understood, cautiously tested rules to replace them. In a sense, he suffered from a self-created "culture shock."

Case Two

Whether the case of Kathryn C. quite belongs to this classification is open to question, for the trouble with Kathryn was that she needed to adjust to another culture, but really made no adjustment attempt. Instead, she tried to impose her cultural values where they clearly did not fit. Kathryn was treated briefly for mild, transient depression. Her depression resulted from the following experiences:

Kathryn, 33, divorced, previously director of nursing at a large U.S. hospital, was sent as a nurse-consultant to a hospital in Southeast Asia. The country is one of traditional values; the hospital is located in a fairly small community, not a tourist-filled city. Officially, Kathryn was sent there to upgrade nursing services. Privately, Kathryn felt she had another mission: She must raise the status of nurses and make them equal professional co-workers, rather than order-takers and "handmaidens" to physicians. Kathryn undertook her assignment with American gusto, feminist zeal, and a full-speed-ahead approach. She allowed no time for the getting-acquainted formalities of Asian custom. She scheduled meetings immediately, approaching nurses with blunt, "what are your problems?" questions. ("Why should I tell this stranger my problems?" undoubtedly was the unspoken response.) Her orientation was "let's get down to brass tacks"; that of her host country was one of reticence, subtlety, and indirection. As she confronted, both nurses and doctors retreated. She had been there only a short time when she discovered she was not being invited to hospital staff meetings or to social gatherings of nurses or physicians. Again, she took the aggressive approach and invited everyone to a party at her apartment. Very few came; everyone was embarrassed, for she had invited physicians and nurses to mingle as social equals! As effort after effort met resistance and failure, Kathryn's enthusiasm faded and depression followed. The whole point about Kathryn's case is that no adequate screening was done before she went on her assignment. Kathryn clearly lacked flexibility. She was neither sensitive to nor even interested in other cultural values. If an adequate psychological profile of Kathryn had been done previously, she would never have been sent on her frustrating assignment.

PSYCHIATRIC CASES IN WHICH CULTURE IS A DISGUISE FOR INTRAPSYCHIC PROBLEMS

Case One

Police brought Carol, kicking and screaming, to the hospital emergency room, from which she was referred for psychiatric evaluation. Carol was 36 and single. She had just been arrested for her violent, abusive actions during a minority group protest march. It was significant that, of perhaps 75 protesters, Carol was the only one arrested. It took only a little questioning to determine that Carol joined in the protests of any group she considered a minority, and that she always managed to be arrested. On one occasion, she had left the United States to "help the oppressed" in another country. Welcomed at first, she soon antagonized the others and was resented as a meddling American. With this group as well, Carol attracted official attention and was asked to leave the country. Carol was past the age of youthful, rebellion-against-authority protests; she had never been on a U.S. campus during the era of political activism. Why, then, was she so conspicuously in the forefront of minority movements?

Carol's personal history revealed financial affluence and emotional impoverishment. The only child of wealthy, socially prominent, politically conservative parents, Carol had really been reared by a black maid. Contacts with her busy parents were strangely formal visits, often on prearranged schedules. Occasional dinners with her parents were "dressed-up affairs to drill me on table manners." Clearly, the maid had been the only consistently nurturing, loving person in Carol's formative years. When she was 16, Carol was sent abroad for schooling. She reports no close or lasting friendships with her equally affluent Caucasian classmates, seeking companionship, her first year abroad, from a friendly waitress, and later from students who, she believed, were denigrated because of ethnic origin or religion. Her fleeting sexual encounters followed much the same pattern. Carol became active in protest movements when she returned to the U.S. from Europe when she was 22. (She was in Morocco when the 1965 march on Selma, Alabama, took place.)

Only a few interviews made it apparent that Carol's on-the-surface allegiance to minority causes was really an attempt to express, or even work out, a personal emotional problem. It was a projection of internal conflicts on an ethnicity-minority screen. Rebellion and anger against her own parents were displaced as protest against the dominant, "oppressing" group; affiliation with the kindly, nurturing black maid became an attempted allegiance to all groups who were of minority status, whether by color, ethnic ties, or economic circumstances. Yet, the internal conflicts refused resolution against this projected screen; the affiliation with minorities was fragile, if not basically false, for Carol did not become one with any minority. Nothing she told us suggests that her behavior was like, or even in harmony with, the values of the group. Always, Carol managed to separate herself from the group she apparently championed. Even before any public protest action, Carol had managed to alienate herself from most of the group's members; during public protests, Carol really arranged her arrest. She was never really one of a group united in a cause; rather, she was an individual sending out a message, "Pay attention to me! I am hurting!"

Trying to work out personal problems in group protest movements is fairly common with young persons. Carol's case, however, is one of long-standing problems of emotional deprivation that had for years sought solution under a cultural-affiliation disguise.

Case Two

Childhood memories with cultural overtones provided a smoke-screen for personal inadequacies in the case of Harold. Harold came in for counseling after his marriage failed. He was shy, hesitant of speech and manner, and appeared much younger than his 26 years. His feelings of inferiority were obvious; he had had few, if any, successes in school, jobs, or social life.

Born near the close of the Korean War, Harold grew up hearing his grandmother's constant admonition, "Don't waste good food. Think of the starving Koreans, the poor orphans who don't even have enough rice to eat." When he was 22, Harold joined the Army and was sent with the "peace-keeping" troops to Korea. There, the plight of orphaned children preoccupied him. With money inherited from the grandmother, Harold provided food and clothing and took on a kind of "big brother" role to several children. Then his efforts to help took on a more personal character. He became interested in a young Korean woman who was poor, undernourished, and ill. He arranged for her to be examined, and when tuberculosis was found, paid for continuing medical care. He visited her often. She responded with gratitude; he fell in love, and when she recovered, the two were married. After his discharge, they came to the United States. The young wife adjusted quickly, soon got a job, and became strong and self-reliant. As she became more and more confident, Harold became more retiring, hesitant, and ineffective. Before long, he lost his job and she became the sole wage-earner. He then left her.

Harold's case is clearly one of rescue fantasy. To feel strong, self-sufficient, even dominant, he needed to have someone weak and in need dependent on him. Sooner or later in his own culture Harold might have sought a girl who could make him feel like a protective, "take-charge" kind of man. Yet, until he went to Korea, he had not attempted to play out a rescuing, succoring role. His coping attempts had remained dormant until he found himself in a country which revived the admonition of childhood, "think of the starving Koreans."

CONCLUSION

We have sketched briefly seven case examples: Zelda, the partner-switching housewife; Dr. N, the star-crossed lover; "Johnny," the over-protected boy; Ahmed, the paranoid student; Kathryn, the feminist nurse-consultant; Carol of the group protests; and the shy, inadequate Harold. All have culture elements, but in markedly varying degrees of significance. Culture caused or precipitated the problem in some instances; in others, it was a fringe factor. During therapy, culture awareness, reeducation, or adjustment was involved in some cases; in others, it had no part.

Two cases required what we might call cultural re-education for life in a new environment. In the case of "Johnny," the parents and especially the tradition-bound grandmother needed to understand and accept certain values of the American way of life: that daughters as well as sons are highly esteemed; that daughters often bring honor to the family and make the family name remembered for generations. They were reminded that boys have a much better chance to grow up healthy and live long when they play vigorously with other children and learn to cross streets carefully; that boys have a much better chance to become successful, prosperous, and honored when they learn the give-and-take and the competitiveness of American culture through companionship and games with others. Some of these explanations, especially with the grandmother, were also expressed in the symbolic language of her upper-class and literary Mandarin tradition: "The flower which is sheltered from every breeze will wither in the first wind," she was reminded. "Johnny has not been allowed to feel the breeze."

With Ahmed, cultural discussions were designed to help him perceive American customs, especially in boy-meets-girl matters, so he could adapt to American ways without discarding his own principles.

The actions of Dr. N cannot be understood except in the light of his Japanese culture: one motivated by a fear of being shamed (and the doctor-nurse marriage would surely have shamed Dr. N's family); one imbued with strong family loyalties, respect for the head of the family, and that particular emotional need to be dependent, called *amae*. We cannot, then, label Dr. N an unusually dependent-passive-obedient son, as Western standards might define him. We need to reflect on the Japanese view of suicide as honorable and even poetically romantic. Yet the culture must also be viewed in its era. This was Japan only three years after the American occupation ended. Only a few Japanese were granted special permission to leave the country; Dr. N and the nurse could not travel to a less restrictive society. Also, young people were not yet expressing the independence of past values to the extent they do today. Cultural elements seem to have dictated most of this scenario. Yet the question persists: Did the young couple really have some hope of reconciling family and social tradition with the divergent needs of young love? Why, if they really intended to drown together, did they jump into a lake where there were fishermen to rescue them? It is possible that the suicide attempt was a help-seeking gesture framed in a cultural pattern. If so, it proved effective. Shocked at their near-loss, the parents feared their son would either make a second, successful suicide attempt, or when travel restrictions lifted, go abroad. Reluctantly, they allowed the young couple to marry, but with certain provisions. The young wife must give up her nursing career. Even with these conditions met, Dr. N's parents maintained a chilly, though courteous, attitude toward their new daughter-in-law for a number of years.

For both Carol and Harold, cultural factors were involved only in the beginning of therapy—as the patients' resistance and defense. Both needed to recognize their minority affiliation as the excuse-disguise it was before they could gain insight into their personal problems.

Kathryn needed to gain insight into her own driving achievement-oriented personality and, thus, to modify it. (Frustration in not achieving her goals had brought about her depression.) As she became aware of her own aggressive, impatient behavior, she was led to consider the behavior patterns and sensitivities of others. In therapeutic discussions she learned that there was another value system—one less achievement-oriented, more sensitive to traditional values, and less inclined to attempt or desire change overnight.

Different as they are, these seven cases serve to illustrate a basic point: The element of culture must be recognized so that its significance can be assessed; the psychiatrist must be aware of cultural implications so that he can dismiss them as inconsequential or incorporate them into the therapeutic plan.

CHAPTER 17

Various Folk Therapeutic Practices

Faced with problems of mind, emotions, and body, distressed by fears and anxieties, perplexed by indecision, humans have always sought ways to cope with psychic and physical unease. Their search, in many times and many cultures, has led them to develop folk psychotherapies. Varied though they may be in details, these fall into broad categories of supernaturally-oriented, naturally-oriented, physically-medically-oriented, and sociopsychologically-oriented psychotherapy. The order in which we have listed these categories very probably represents a historical progression down to the present, as indicated by anthropological information and the history of medicine and psychiatry (Tseng and McDermott, 1975). However, forms of healing practices in varied orientations may coexist and function simultaneously in any contemporary society.

SUPERNATURALLY-ORIENTED HEALING PRACTICES

Practice and practitioner go by many names: *mudang* in Korea; *babalawo* in Yoruba; *miko* or *rebai* in Japan; *dang-ki* in Taiwan; *hodja* in Turkey; *haka* in Hawaii's past; *hungman* in Haiti; *fu-i* in Manchuria; *yuta* in Okinawa. All have a common characteristic: They base their healing systems on belief in the supernatural. Their troubled clients also have something in common—similar problems. Possession by a spirit, soul loss, sorcery, a violated taboo—these are thought to cause physical ills and emotional disturbances. Consequently, their healers turn to exorcism, ritual performance, sacrifices, and prayer to solve a problem or ease sickness. One such practice exemplifies this type of healing system. It is shamanism.

Shamanism

In shamanism, it is believed that the healer, the shaman, has special powers to communicate with gods. Through religious rituals, a shaman puts himself into a trance state in which he is "possessed" by a supernatural power. The shaman thus acts as a spirit medium. Through him, the client receives counsel from the supernatural.

The Shaman as a Healer

As Hippler (1976) points out, shamanism varies in cross-cultural aspects. In Asia alone, the shaman of Taiwan *(dang-ki)* is usually a man; in Korea, both men and women may be a *mudang;* the Japanese *miko* is more often, but not necessarily, a woman.

The personality of the shaman is by no means standardized. When Hippler reviewed the literature, he found that different investigators who take a cross-cultural look at shamans see them as varying from deviants to well-integrated personalities. One aspect that points to personality difference is how a person had his first "spirit possession" that identified him as a shaman. Sasaki (1969) studied 56 shamans in Japan. Of these, 40 achieved their first possession after a period of *shugyo* (self-training). The other 16 had spontaneously become possessed before they decided to become shamans. Five of these 16 had experienced possession without any other psychopathological syndrome; 11 had pathological possession syndromes associated with a need for psychiatric treatment.

In Taiwan, Tseng (1972) made a study of shamans. In his view, becoming a shaman always fulfills the individual's psychological needs and solves his own personal problems, such as feeling insecure or inferior. However, he noted that the successful shaman, one who could help his clients with their psychological problems, was always a perceptive, sensible, and mature person.

Healing Practice and Therapeutic Implication

The client who consults a shaman may present any one or more of a wide variety of problems. In Taiwan, for example, these may include physical and psychological illness, behavior problems, interpersonal conflicts, or any situation that calls for careful decision. Some clients want help for troubles they think are related to the mind and to gods; these, they believe, can be solved through supernatural powers (Li, 1976).

The therapeutic effect comes basically from the client's belief that the healer is a powerful person. A shaman's dramatic performance of supernatural possession enhances this. This powerful one whom the gods possess has another therapeutic tool: a positive answer, a definite interpretation of the cause of the problem. Thus, the known relieves fear of the unknown. The shaman is, in fact, following what Torrey (1971) called the "Principle of Rumplestiltskin." The principle operated in fairy-tale allegory in the Grimm Brothers' story of a tiny and evil man who threatened to take the Queen's child unless she could guess his name. For days the worried queen made wrong guesses. Finally—after a little detective work by a courtier—she called him correctly "Rumplestiltskin." The tiny man promptly "split in two" and vanished. Beneath the allegory, the message reads: The anxious client tries to put a name to his trouble, attempts to find out "what is wrong with me." When shaman—or therapist—provides a definite, acceptable explanation, the anxiety may not quite vanish, but it lessens. It can be dealt with.

Both symbolism and the supernatural may enter into the shaman's interpretation. The two may have merged in the following example. A middle-aged Chinese woman brought her husband to a shaman. The husband sat silent and passive; the wife did all the talking:

"My husband is no good," she complained. "In ten years of marriage, I have never seen him show good judgment or make a correct decision. He fails in business. He never acts like the master of the household. He never makes plans for the future."

All this was told in a hostile, condescending manner. The shaman induced his own trance state and then gave his verdict.

"Your household has been 'eviled' by a male tiger. Your tongue has gotten lost and a male tiger's tongue has replaced it in your mouth. Your husband can't hear a woman and a wife talking; he hears the tiger. He can't be master of a household where this tiger speaks."

It was an astute, "open-ended" interpretation. It could be accepted as a metaphor, as personal advice clothed in symbolism. Or, with clients who believed in animal spirit possession, the "tiger's tongue" could well describe the entry of a dominating, male tiger-spirit into the woman's body. With either, the message to a castrating woman seems clear.

Very often, a shaman finds a god or a devil or a ghost is the source of the trouble. The supernatural then may be used to symbolize a real and significant person in the client's life. One example: A young man had lost his natural mother when he was a baby. He had been reared as an only child by a

foster mother. After he married, he developed many psychophysiological problems. Apparently, he had difficulty handling the rival relationship between his bride and his foster mother. He consulted a shaman who, after an appropriate interval of trance, told him the troubles were caused because the spirit of the man's deceased mother was disturbed; her spirit was being neglected. The young man and his wife were then told they should propitiate the mother's spirit with periodic offerings of sacrificial food.

Behind this surface account lie subtleties of Chinese thought and behavior. One is a dread of open confrontation, especially in the close relationship of family. One is the ready use of symbolism. One is the cultural view that the filial relationship is more important than the marital; that deference to elders is a social and moral obligation. Thus the shaman could use the shadowy, non-threatening spirit of a never-known mother as a symbol of a jealous, neglected, foster mother and as the reminder of a young couple's duty ("pay more attention") to the living household matriarch. And in this extended household, the neglected matriarch would witness the repeated food offerings at the family altar and know that, in symbolism, she was being offered apologies and deference.

A shaman's therapeutic practice is not necessarily limited to a supernatural framework; it is free to shift into a psychological orientation. Harvey's (1976) case presentation of a Korean *mudang* illustrates this. The *mudang's* client, an obviously worried woman in middle life, related the following story: Her two sons were apparently headed for aimless, shiftless lives. However, her immediate worry almost overshadowed maternal concerns. Her husband, a successful merchant, was having a passionate love affair with a young girl. The client—just that morning—had tried to bribe the rival into giving up her husband. When she refused, the wife came to the *mudang* and asked for sorcery to make her husband lose interest in the girl. This the *mudang* refused to consider. She performed divination rituals (Korean shamans may do this) for the entire family, thus enlarging the dimensions of problem and therapy. Later, she gave highly practical, commonsense advice:

"Bribing the girl won't work . . . you'll lose double that way . . . she's a leech . . . will bleed your husband for at least ten years. Get your first son a wife . . . get your second son [who failed his college entrance exam] into a vocational school . . . your husband will [eventually] come crawling back."

Her advice included a strong warning not to intervene in her husband's affair. This would be "like fanning a burning fire."

Many other components of therapy are involved in shamanism. Opler (1936) mentions faith; Frank (1961) notes expectation; Murphy (1964) points out the beneficial public aspect of shamanism procedures. The client is surrounded by people he knows, people who want him to get well. He has group support. The very presence of the onlookers gives public recognition to the healing drama. Cultural beliefs about the causes and cures of sickness are revived or reinforced. Psychological interaction among shaman, client, and the group contributes to the therapeutic effect of the curative procedures.

Variations of Shamanism

Customarily, only the shaman goes into the trance or possession state. Yet there are exceptions. In the Zar cult of the Egyptian Nubians, both healer and client fall into some degree of trance. While both are in a dissociated state, dialogue—and, indeed, bargaining—take place. The Zar, the possessing spirit, then specifies what gifts he must be given to relieve the client's suffering (Kennedy, 1967; Prince, 1980). In one Japanese healing cult, only the client is possessed. In his dissociation, the client can perform a social role he cannot do in conscious life (Lebra, 1976). This hinges on the fact that the entire family is present. For example, a daughter-in-law can say, while possessed, "My god, or spirit, says you must be kinder to me." In conscious life, she would not dare to speak so frankly to an oppressive mother-in-law. The message from the god, or spirit, is acceptable when direct speech is not. Godly message and girl's anger may both come from suppressed hostilities; when the unconscious communicates via the supernatural, truth may be spoken.

Prince (1980) even reported healing ceremonies without a healer! These take place before the tomb of an Islamic saint in Lucknow, northern India. There the client becomes possessed and describes how the spirit is disturbing him and what measures must be taken to become free of the spirit. It is, says Prince, self-healing mechanism in operation.

Perhaps all healing practices that use trance or possession states have a common therapeutic denominator: The dissociated state is utilized to perceive and reveal underlying psychological problems which normally are difficult or impossible to disclose in the sociocultural context of ordinary, conscious life.

Mental Health Implications

A review of the literature shows that shamanism as a healing practice has been given both praise and adverse criticism. It has been seen as a harmful and/or an adequate mental health practice. The shaman has been called fake or sincere. Some investigators believe that shamanism, as well as other folk healing practices, can be used and integrated with modern, orthodox healing systems to extend their limited availability. Others dispute this. They emphasize that folk medical therapies may delay prompt and effective modern treatment (Kiev, 1964), or feel that folk practice may be "malpractice" (Prince, 1964).

By definition, a shaman is a spirit medium. Perhaps when he stays within that defined role, he heals as often as he harms. If the shaman is wise and experienced enough to know his "professional" limitations, and not so ambitious that he thinks he can solve all problems, he may avoid present or potential harm to his clients. We praise folk healing in terms of its cultural relevancy, but we do not really know how often, and to what degree, it is beneficial. When folk therapy is found to be genuinely helpful, we still need to know more about the processes that benefit the client. Case-oriented outcome and follow-up studies are needed to gain this knowledge.

Divination

Whether it is called *janka, ifao, chou-chien,* "pointing in the Bible"—or at least a dozen other names—it means divination or diviner. Each represents yet another human attempt to obtain divine instruction through esoteric means and, thereby, learn how to handle problem or perplexity. Each is based on the belief that there are certain principles and ways of life which supernatural power regulates. Divination—though some shamans use it—varies from shamanism in that there is no need to demonstrate the presence of god or spirit by quite dramatically becoming possessed.

Various Divination Practices

Exactly how divine instruction is sought varies. For example, among the Balahis in central India, the *janka* (healer-diviner) employs physical means. With his left hand, he feels his client's pulse; with his right, he pulls the fingers of the client's hand. With each pull, he mutters the name of some god or spirit. The patient's finger joints often crack during the pulling. By counting the "cracks," the *janka* discovers which supernatural force caused the disease. He also learns what offerings must be made so the patient can be cured (Fuchs, 1964).

In Western Africa, the Yoruba seek counsel in *ifa* divination. *Ifa* is rich in resources; the diviner can summon and question some 256 spirits. The spirits "speak" by placing in the diviner's heart several verses of a vast religious-medical poem called the *Odus*. Though the spirits are thought to decide which particular verses apply to the patient, the diviner tosses palm nuts as part of the decision-making. He then interprets the verses and prescribes what sacrifice is indicated (Prince, 1975).

Taiwan has an intricate Chinese system of divination plus folk counseling that takes place in a temple. In the temple is an old man—not a diviner-healer, but an important counselor-interpreter. The divination is called—for its ritual props—*chou-chien* ("drawing the bamboo stick"). Near the alter stands a bamboo pipe filled with small bamboo sticks called *chien*. Each stick bears a number. The client first worships the god and confides his problem. Then, at random, he picks out one of the sticks. The old man gives him a *chien* paper with the same number. On each paper is a poem and a fixed set of answers to important questions: questions about wealth, travel, sickness, social achievement, childbirth, or finding a mate. The poems are usually quite ordinary ones that describe nature, events, or ideas in symbolic terms.

When the client finds the poem difficult to read and understand—as many do—he consults the old man. Here enters the interpreter's personal judgment. He may give one of the answers on the *chien* paper, or he may inquire in detail about the client's situation and his problem, and so provide counseling (also often in words of symbolism).

To illustrate: A young man asked whether or not he should go abroad to study. Questioned by the interpreter, he explained that he was the eldest son. Because his parents were getting old and his only brother was still quite young, he worried about leaving his parents unattended. The interpreter read the following poem:

"A carp can swim against the stream. A big bird can fly across the ocean. If you climb over a mountain, you will find a village full of cherry blossoms."

This, he told the young man, was a good sign, one that encouraged him to leave. The young man, delighted but still anxious, asked, "But who is going to take care of my parents?"

The old man resorted to direct speech. "Your parents know well how to take care of themselves," he said. "Do not worry. Go abroad. Study. Be trained. Then come back without delay. There will be plenty of time for you to be a devoted and attentive son."

In another case, a young woman asked the interpreter whether she should marry.

"No," said the old man. "I shall read you this poem: 'The tree is still covered by snow; spring flowers have not blossomed yet. The moon is shadowed by the dark black cloud, waiting for the wind to blow away the veil.' This means you are not ready to choose a wedding mate."

Anxiously, the woman protested, "But we have been seeing each other . . . going out together for three years. We love each other very much."

The old man's rather stern manner softened. "Young lady, the poem told that the time has not yet come. It does not mean you have chosen the wrong man. Be patient. The god blesses the young couple who really love. The time for your marriage will not be too far in the future."

Obviously, these "old men" temper their interpretations to fit the client.

The rural South and the Ozark hill regions are rich in practices that relieve anxiety, as well as those that inspire anxiety. One method of finding counsel and comfort is to "point in the Bible," a ritual that goes back to England centuries ago. In this, no diviner or healer is needed. The troubled one prays, shuts his eyes, opens the "Good Book," and points a finger somewhere on the page. The Bible passage thus indicated and interpreted by the worried one provides the answer to the problem.

"I putten my faith in the Good Book and God done showed me the way," one old woman of the Ozarks reported.

Psychotherapeutic Implications

People who seek help through divination usually must make a crucial decision about an important matter. Divination may be useful because it always provides an answer or instructions. It ends the agony of indecision; it alleviates the anxiety of being uncertain. Unless physical harm results (as in not getting medical care), it does not matter whether the answer is correct or not. What does matter psychologically is that there is a definite answer. In reality, the client himself decides how to put suggestion into action, how to adjust counsel to his needs. Often he really provides his own answer, rejecting what does not agree with his own wishes. The Christian in Kentucky who "points in the Bible" often keeps on pointing until he reads a passage he can interpret and accept. The Japanese man in Tokyo who seeks out a particular form of divination called *kuji-biki* is allowed freedom of choice. The client selects a slip of "lucky paper" *(kuji)* from a small heap placed on the temple altar. Each slip contains cryptic advice or prediction. If the first bit of paper gives an unwanted message, the advice-seeker ties it to a tree in the temple yard—thus returning it to the god.

Mathematics may also be arranged in the direction of "positive thinking." A statistical analysis of Chinese *chien* poems showed that 50% indicated good fortune, 25% told of just average luck, and 25% meant bad luck (Hsu, 1976).

But what if the cards are literally stacked towards dire predictions? Studies of divination by cards in Peru showed that cards of ill-fortune appeared in high ratio. This, said the investigator, allowed the healer to tap the patient's particular personal conflicts and stresses which might be contributing to his physical or emotional discomforts (Dobkin, 1969).

Such leeway of interpretation, favorable mathematical odds, and, very often, wise counseling all suggest that many divination systems are quite carefully designed to fulfill a special therapeutic purpose.

Religious Faith Healing

Though religion, with its influence on mind and emotions, forms a separate chapter, the more specific aspect of religion linked to healing must be noted here. Faith healing exists in possibly every spot on earth; its rites take many forms. Yet all such healing rests on the patient's—or should we say petitioner's—belief. The sick person believes there is a supernatural power; he believes that, through prayer and the very power of his faith, his sickness can be cured.

In the Western world, most such healing is within the framework of Christianity. Yet there are many different ways of thought and ritual. As Hufford (1977) reminds us, these range from the practices of Christian Science to the fundamentalist stance of such healers as Oral Roberts, to the often ecstatic participation of recent (1970s) charismatic congregations, to the Roman Catholic rite of Anointing of the Sick. (This is a fairly new ritual, entirely different from the long-established Last Rites for the Dying.)

Therapeutic Implications

Because both the healing philosophies and practices of religious denominations—and how individuals interpret them—vary, the specific therapeutic implications for individuals also vary. Hufford (1977) analyzed it thus: When the healing system states that if one meets the requirements (strong faith, fervent prayer), he will be healed, then all the responsibility falls on the patient. If he is not healed, the patient not only remains ill, but also suffers an additional psychological burden. He has been given evidence that he is unworthy, that he lacks spiritual grace.

On the other hand, if the healing system holds that if one does his best to carry out the will of God then what follows is God's will, the patient may benefit. The hope for supernatural aid can increase a sense of security and well-being. Even if no healing (or spontaneous remission) occurs, the matter has been placed in the hands of a higher power. Illness and suffering can be accepted as part of a supernatural plan.

NATURALLY-ORIENTED HEALING PRACTICES

Underlying these practices is the belief that basic principles of nature rule everything, including human life and behavior, that natural phenomena determine the nature of human problems. It is healing based on the concept of macrocosm and microcosm: What happens in the universe influences what happens to the individual. The reasoning goes somewhat like this: If the big world (or the geographical portion I know) becomes cold, then my mood becomes cold, grey, and melancholy. If my part of the big world becomes hot, my temper becomes heated. Thus, to discern cause and cure of what has brought me trouble, my larger world—perhaps the entire universe—must be studied. To do this, I may need to seek an expert. The expert sought is very often an astrologist, a fortune-teller, or one who is learned in physiognomy.

Astrology and Fortune-telling

Astrology narrows the field of microcosm-macrocosm. In one version, the basic assumption is that the life of each individual corresponds with a star. One's life, behavior, and fate are related to the location and movement of his or her particular star. Predictions are made and problems explained within this person-to-star framework.

Other types of problem-solving or healing fortune-telling take in added territory; the natural factors that relate to and determine human events may include a person's birth time, name, location of his house, and geographical features of his home surroundings. In this orientation, problems are explained as the result of an imbalance or disharmony with underlying natural principles that govern the universe. The object is to help the client find out how to live compatibly with nature, and adjust to the environment more harmoniously and with a greater degree of stability.

Among fortune-tellers are those who counsel and, in the emotional and psychological sense, do some measure of healing. There are also those who merely predict or give set "yes or no" answers to questions. Our discussion deals only with those we call counselor or healer. These are the fortune-tellers who ask questions, observe, and talk with their clients. The best of these may observe a young girl's immaturity, find out she is "in love with love," and advise or predict no marriage for three years. Prediction, advice, or explanation for the young girl's present restlessness may be couched in terms of stars or name or physical surroundings; the counsel itself comes from wisdom, observation, intuition, and common sense.

The psychotherapeutic implications of these practices are quite similar to some in shamanism. The cause of the problem is always explained, and ways to deal with it are always given. This in itself is therapeutic, no matter what the explanation is. Very often the explanation is so abstract or metaphysical that the client cannot understand it. However, just knowing that a reason and a coping procedure exist brings some satisfaction.

Two cases, both from Asian cultures, illustrate this point. In the first, an aged woman was badly worried after her grandson, daughter-in-law, and husband became sick, one after another. She consulted a fortune-teller who visited the woman's home. After a careful examination of the house, he declared it had a structural defect. The window on the south side was not big enough to let the summer wind blow in! The woman eagerly followed instructions to enlarge the window. She now had hope that the ill fortunes within the house would improve.

Why did enlarging a window bring hope? Partly because of the troubled woman's faith in the knowledge and authority of her counselor. The fortune-teller in some Asian and Pacific cultures was—and often still is—a kind of site surveyor. He decides where a house should be located for safety, sunshine, and ventilation. Partly because the woman's anxiety lessened with some positive, decisive action. (And if any family member had died, she would have been satisfied and comforted by knowing she had done all she could to help them live.)

The companion question: Why did the fortune-teller give this advice, rather than prescribing prayers or rituals? One reason is probably because he practiced, quite literally, a nature-oriented therapy. People in many Asian countries live and sleep in crowded conditions, or even in one small room. The room may have "smelled of sickness." The sick ones may, in fact, have been in need of fresh air. It is not always necessary to understand the spread of contagion in Western medical terms.

In the other case, a middle-aged Chinese merchant, plagued by doubts of his business ability, went to a fortune-teller. "My business fails more each year," said the merchant, "even though I work harder each year."

The fortune-teller inquired about the time of the man's birth, about the deaths of his parents, and exactly where they were buried. He then pointed out that the parents' tomb was on the north side of a hill, and that this was in conflict with the rules of nature. This, he declared, was causing the failure of his business. The remedy was to relocate the tomb.

In Western thought, the remedy makes no sense at all. In its Chinese setting, it is rich in meanings—symbolic, realistic, philosophical, and ethical. Symbolically, and in nature, North is cold, shadowed, dreary; the northern side of a hill is a cheerless, inappropriate burial site for honored parents. Practically, the north side may have soggy or shifting soil, or be swept by cruel winds; this is no place for the day-long ritual visits family members pay to family tombs. Ethically, the son had done wrong. He had not given due and loving consideration to his parents' resting place. He had not been a good son.

Being a "good son" in the Chinese tradition of family continuity extends merit in three directions. Fulfilling obligations and paying honor to parents or ancestors (alive or dead) brings prosperity, success, health, and happiness to the son. It also confers these blessings on descendants. Ancestors, honored and at peace, send beneficent influences downward, even to grand- and great-grandchildren, yet unborn. Ancestors, neglected or dishonored, can put into operation negative or harmful influences.

A "good son" is also a generally "good person." Being a "good person" brings the most tangible of benefits—success. The benefits of virtue become horizontal and outward, as well as vertical and family-centered. Perhaps the practical joins the ethical-philosophical at this point, for the merchant who feels confident of his own success is more apt to deal with his customers with friendly and cheerful ease. And in town or village life where gossip spreads, the merchant who has clearly demonstrated he is a good son will become known as a good and ethical merchant. In East or West, customers bring their business to the man (or the firm) they trust.

Physiognomy

Physiognomy assumes that the structure of the body, as a part of nature, determines man's behavior and life events. The physiognomist attempts to read, from the client's face, skull, or palm, signs that relate to his or her problem. For example, a man's well built, high-bridged nose is interpreted as a sign of strong will and masculinity; a thin lip with a wide mouth is a symbol of a talkative woman who may not be able to manage a household.

The physiognomist who reads such body signs may be only applying a kind of memorized formula. Or he may be following his own previous observations of body characteristics and mental acumen or behavior. Or he may be projecting his own fears, fantasies, or failures onto his client. "Your head is flat, so you cannot marry," the afraid-to-marry or impotent physiognomist may say. "Your nose turns to one side; your life will change in middle-age," may be the projection of the physiognomist trying to deny his own loss of youthful vigor.

Basically, the system of physiognomy shifts the focus of concern from the natural or supernatural world to the client himself; it views problems as originating from certain physical predispositions in the individual. Within this concept, the purpose is to let clients know more about themselves and their body-mind predispositions, so that they can live and function with their weaknesses as well as assets.

PHYSICALLY-MEDICALLY-ORIENTED HEALING PRACTICES

The premise in these practices is that the function of mind is based on the physiological condition of the body, and that mental dysfunction is a disease. Therefore, physical medical treatment, with the emphasis on supplementing deficiencies, recuperation, and compensation, is considered the way to heal it. Because a psychological effect occurs in such treatment, such practice may be seen broadly as a kind of psychotherapeutic intervention.

Animal Magnetism (originally called Mesmerism)

Though mesmerism has long meant suggestion or hypnotism, it was originally thought to be a physically-based therapy. But let us go back into history, to 18th century Vienna. It was there that Franz Anton Mesmer developed both theory and practice of "animal magnetism." Mesmer believed that planets influence physiological and psychological phenomena and that this influence flows through a special, universal, magnetic fluid. Insufficient fluid in a person caused illness; some humans with vast stores of "animal magnetism" could restore mental-physical balance; so could metal magnets.

One treatment description tells that a tank full of fluid and metallic powder (iron filings) stood in the center of the room. Patients stood around the tank and held a metal rod extending from it, thus letting the magnetic power be discharged. The therapist, in a long, purple robe, stretched out his arms to touch his clients so that special fluid from him could be liberated, and thus heal (Mora, 1975).

Later, physicians speculated that the patients had been in a trance state and that those who responded favorably had suffered from hysterical problems. In the 19th century, an English physician, James Braid, confirmed this and coined the words "hypnosis" and "hypnotism" (*Encyclopedia Brittanica,* 1975).

However, Mesmer's own belief in the physically-based therapy of "animal magnetism" has lived on to the present day. Today, people wear "magnetic belts" for health, vigor, and sexual potency, or copper bracelets to cure or ward off arthritis. In Japan, a few years ago, thousands bought devices to produce static electricity and cause it to circulate within the body, thereby improving health. Belt, bracelet, and gadget—like Mesmer's magnets and fluid—are all equally inert; yet the anxious will always think them potent. They are an expression of man's wish to link himself with a larger, more powerful force, and so acquire some measure of strength. Seeking cure and courage from a supernatural power has been replaced by (or added to) seeking them from what is "magnetic," "electric," or "scientific."

Autogenic Training

As hypnotism became an accepted therapy, autohypnotism or autogenic therapy followed. This sophisticated psychophysiologic form of psychotherapy was founded about 40 years ago by J. H. Schultz, psychiatrist and neurologist in Berlin. In the last three decades, it has become widely known in Europe. The method stemmed from research on sleep and hypnosis that found autohypnotic exercise had a remarkable recuperative effect on psychiatric patients, particularly those with psychosomatic disorders. The patient learns autohypnotic exercises and does them daily at home. This is said to be helpful in the treatment of psychophysiological disorders, as well as behavior disorders (Luthe, 1963).

Rest Therapy

This is based on the premise that the patient is suffering from an asthenic condition of the nervous system that requires rest and recuperation. Rest therapy—it was called the Rest Cure—was founded in the West by S. Weir Mitchell at about the turn of the last century. Dr. Mitchell, a prominent Philadelphia neurologist, advocated the use of complete bed rest, isolation, a rich diet, daily massage, and electro-stimulation for six to eight weeks. This was recommended for neurasthenia and hysteria.

From a psychological point of view, rest therapy allows a client to detach himself from his usual daily duties, burdens, and stresses. It lets him retreat and reexamine his life. After this mandatory rest and social deprivation, many patients return to normal activity with a new appreciation of life and its complexities.

SOCIOPSYCHOLOGICALLY-ORIENTED HEALING PRACTICES

Fundamental to this is the concept that mental problems are related to the client's behavior and psychological condition and his social environment. Problems are considered the result of internal psychic conflict and/or external maladjustment. The essential core of treatment is to modify the client's concepts, attitudes, or behavior, or to improve his relationship with others. Most of the modern Western psychotherapies belong to this system. For example, in analytic therapy, resolving conflict is considered the core of the therapy, while in behavior therapy, relearning and correcting errors are the essence of the practice. In most therapies originating in the East, such as meditation therapy, the aim is to obtain tranquility of the mind, while in Zen training, self-enlightenment and change of one's philosophical attitude are the ultimate goal of treatment. In order to focus on the cultural aspect of such healing practices, two therapies founded in Japan will be illustrated.

Morita Therapy (Personal Experience Therapy)

A Japanese psychiatrist, Shoma Morita, established this therapy in about 1920. Philosophically, he was influenced by Zen Buddhism. Clinically, he agreed with the prevalent concept of the period that neurasthenia resulted from exhaustion or enfeeblement of the central nervous system and that rest was therefore called for. But to Mitchell's use of rest and isolation, he added guidance, rehabilitation, and work therapy. Morita's method was later modified.

For the first four to ten days, the patient is asked to lie in bed 24 hours a day. Only meals and trips to the bathroom interrupt this bed rest. All activity, even conversation, reading, and smoking, is prohibited. After this initial isolation, the patient craves activity. In graduated treatment stages, he is allowed to leave his room and do some light physical work, such as yard or household tasks. Gradually, he is permitted to do some occupational work (folding paper boxes, for example) and to join recreational and social activities.

Beginning with the second phase of rehabilitation, the patient keeps a diary which is read and commented on by the therapist. Initially, the diary is always full of descriptions of the patient's suffering and many complaints. Comments of the therapist are apt to be along these lines: "It is natural to suffer." "Do not think you are the only person with such problems." "Learn to like your symptoms." The diary is continued as the patient progresses from isolation to conversation, to periods outdoors, to manual work, and, finally, to outside excursions and social life. With the ending of the initial total isolation, the patient is given access to the outdoors. He is given encouragement to appreciate his natural surroundings of flowers, trees, and animals so that, as he opens a mental-emotional channel toward nature, he also "opens up" to his genuine self (Kondo, 1953).

The entire process operates on the premise that what is learned through this experience is more deeply acknowledged and felt than any lessons gained through intellectual understanding. Specifically, the patient learns that his mental-physical-emotional nature is not "wrong," that his symptoms are natural phenomena which he, personally, has interpreted as being pathologic; therefore, he should learn to live with himself, his total nature, and his symptoms. The neurotic patient, with his attention completely absorbed in his egocentric demands, remembers that happiness, contentment, and inspiration also exist in life (Kondo, 1953).

Morita therapy is said to be particularly useful for patients who are preoccupied with hypochondriacal complaints, and those so overly concerned with difficulty in interpersonal interaction that they are afraid to relate to others (so-called "anthrophobia"). It is also supposed to help those obsessed with trying to "make the impossible possible," and those troubled by feelings of inferiority and incapacity. All the above are common neurotic problems among Japanese patients (Ikeda, 1971).

It is apparent that Morita therapy puts to use a basic philosophy of Zen Buddhism: *arugamama,* literally, "as it is," or more loosely, "accept things as they are." There is no attempt to change objective reality; instead the patient is directed toward changing inner attitudes to unchangeable realities (Iwai and Reynolds, 1970). If Morita therapy is successful for him, he learns to accept "things as they are."

Naikan Therapy (Introspective Therapy)

Though Morita and Naikan methods begin at the same starting point—isolation—their destinations are in opposite directions, and their therapeutic pathways soon diverge. Morita's primary goal is to live with oneself; that of Naikan is to live with others. Yet the Naikan method seeks to achieve interpersonal and social harmony through introspection. The very term *naikan* literally means ''inside looking.''

This introspective therapy takes its philosophical base from Jodo-Shin, the most popular of Japan's Buddhist sects (Murase, 1976). It was developed by a layman, Inobu Yoshimoto. The method is as follows: The patient sits alone from early morning until almost bedtime for a week. He occupies a corner of a room, shut off by a screen. Here he meditates. But this is not meditation (as in other moments of Japanese tranquility) on the arrangement of flowers or the design on a scroll. This is directed, guided introspection. The therapist makes frequent, brief visits only to give structured directions in self-observation and self-reflection. The patient is asked to recollect and examine memories of the care and kindness he has received from a particular person – usually a very close family member – at a particular period in his life. He is also asked to examine what he has done in return. This remembrance of a parent, for example, may then be extended to take in several other family members or significant persons. After a week of therapy, the patient is asked to continue this reflective process by himself.

Two cases – sketched in broadest outline – provide examples: The first concerns a housewife, depressed because of the caretaking burdens she carried in her large household. She was directed to meditate on the attention and affection given her by that most important person, her mother-in-law. She recalled that when she was hospitalized, her mother-in-law visited her daily, bringing quantities of expensive fruit, and, in spite of a heart condition, walking up five flights to her room. And what did the daughter-in-law do in return? She remembered with guilt that when the mother-in-law had been sick, she had visited her only once, carrying a small gift.

The other case dealt with a young man who had been arrested for the first time for stealing. He was initially reluctant about following the instructions for self-introspection. Later, he began to recall the first time he had stolen in childhood. Resenting the attention his mother paid a younger brother, he stole money from her. He also remembered incidents in his mother's life: She had always walked instead of taking the bus, to stretch the family income; she had trudged from market to market to find the lowest-priced food. Guilt was dwelt on: While his mother saved with such effort, he had stolen from her. The "reward" he had given a good mother was becoming a thief.

As Murase explains, Naikan therapy utilizes an important element of Japanese culture: To harm someone close, especially parental figures, is a severe violation of social ethics; acknowledging this produces strong guilt feelings. Basically, the Naikan method functions on guilt realization. It is not followed by guilt removal. The Naikan therapist is neither religion's father-confessor nor psychiatry's respected authority-figure whose continuing acceptance brings self-absolution. The Naikan therapist remains the deliberately uninvolved instructor.

To comprehend this therapy, we need to consider the type of guilt that is utilized; we need to consider the role of guilt in Japanese life. The guilt, when the Naikan method succeeds, is not amorphous and diffused neurotic guilt. It is specific, authentic guilt. Such guilt is a useful, accepted quality in the family, social, and business life of Japan. To say "I am sorry. I did wrong," is admirable. Even the dignified businessman whose error has cost his firm expresses his contrition with unashamed tears. He expects, and receives, forgiveness. Apology and pardon are the preliminaries that lead to restored self-esteem and mutual trust, harmony, and affection. As Murase emphasizes, guilt has its positive, healthy side. Recollecting the experiences that brought guilt leads to integration of one's personality; one accepts both one's virtues and one's faults.

In the two case illustrations, both patients realized that, in spite of their wrong and selfish actions, others continued to love them. Therefore, they must be worthy of love. Or, more in the context of *Jodo-Shin* Buddhism, wrongdoing is part of man. Thus, one cannot escape from guilt; one must live with it.

Naikan therapy seems exclusively for the Japanese—but not all Japanese. It is said to be most successful with delinquents, criminals, and drug addicts. It is not advised for patients with endogenous psychosis or compulsive, severely self-punishing neurotics. If the therapy is to be effective, patients must already have a consciousness of guilt and readiness to change. The guilt can then become motivation for change.

SUMMARY

In spite of the vast differences in the many types of folk and modern psychotherapies, scholars have pointed out the universal elements in all kinds of healing practices. The mobilization of hope (Frank, 1961), faith in the therapist (Opler, 1936), active participation of the client and his family (Carstairs, 1964), provision of an authoritative figure (Lederer, 1959) and the warm personal quality of the therapist (Torrey, 1970) are some of the factors cited as necessary. From the operational point of view, the analysis and identification of the cause of the problem, no matter what the explanation, are always helpful to the client who is suffering from doubt and uncertainty about it. The prescription for change itself, again regardless of what is suggested, is always helpful to the client who needs guidance and support to cope with his or her problems. In spite of the common therapeutic elements, various forms of psychotherapy do differ in their referential systems, style of operation, goals, and details of method or ritual.

How people attempt to heal their bodies and spirits has always been influenced by the time and place in which they live and the beliefs that their culture evolves and embraces.

REFERENCES

Carstairs, G. M.: Healing ceremonies in primitive societies. *The Listener,* 72:195–197, 1964.

Dobkin, M.: Fortune's malice: Divination, psychotherapy and folk medicine in Peru. *Journal of American Folklore,* 324:132–141, 1969.

Encyclopedia Brittanica, p. 995, 1975.

Frank, J. D.: *Persuasion and Healing: A Comparative Study of Psychotherapy* New York: Schocken Books, 1961.

Fuchs, S.: Magic healing techniques among the Balahis in Central India. In: *Magic, Faith, and Healing.* A. Kiev and J. D. Frank (Eds.), New York: The Free Press, 1964.

Harvey, Y. K.: The Korean mudang as a household therapist. In: *Culture-Bound Syndromes, Ethnopsychiatry and Alternate Therapies.* W. P. Lebra (Ed.), Honolulu, Hawaii: The University Press of Hawaii, 1976.

Hippler, A. E.: Shamans, curers, and personality: Suggestions toward a theoretical model. In:

Culture-Bound Syndromes, Ethnopsychiatry and Alternate Therapies. W. P. Lebra (Ed.), Honolulu, Hawaii: University Press of Hawaii, 1976.

Hsu, J.: Counseling in the Chinese temple: A psychological study of divination by chien drawing. In: *Culture-Bound Syndromes, Ethnopsychiatry and Alternate Therapies.* W. P. Lebra (Ed.), Honolulu, Hawaii: University Press of Hawaii, 1976.

Hufford, D.: Christian religious healing. *Journal of Operational Psychiatry,* 8:22–27, 1977.

Ikeda, K.: Morita's theory of neurosis and its application in Japanese psychotherapy. In: *Modern Perspectives in World Psychiatry.* J. Howells (Ed.), New York: Brunner/Mazel Publishers, 1971.

Iwai, H. and Reynolds, D. K.: Morita psychotherapy: The views from the West. *American Journal of Psychiatry,* 126:1031–1036, 1970.

Kennedy, J. C.: Nubian zar ceremonies as psychotherapy. *Human Organization,* 26:185–194, 1967.

Kiev, A.: Implications for the future. In: *Magic, Faith and Healing.* A. Kiev and J. D. Frank (Eds.), New York: The Free Press, 1964.

Kondo, A.: Morita therapy: A Japanese therapy for neurosis. *American Journal of Psychoanalysis,* 13:31–37, 1953.

Lebra, T. S.: Taking the role of supernatural "other": Spirit possession in a Japanese healing cult. In: *Culture-Bound Syndromes, Ethnopsychiatry and Alternate Therapies.* W. P. Lebra (Ed.), Honolulu, Hawaii: University Press of Hawaii, 1976.

Lederer, W.: Primitive psychotherapy. *Psychiatry,* 22:255–265, 1959.

Li, Y-Y.: Shamanism in Taiwan: An anthropological inquiry. In: *Culture-Bound Syndromes, Ethnopsychiatry and Alternate Therapies.* W. P. Lebra (Ed.), Honolulu, Hawaii: The University Press of Hawaii, 1976.

Luthe, W.: Autogenic training: Method, research and application in medicine. *Am. J. Psychother.,* 17:174–195, 1963.

Mora, G.: History and theoretical trends in psychiatry. In: *Comprehensive Textbook of Psychiatry-II Vol. 1.* A. M. Freedman, H. I. Kaplan, and B. J. Sadock (Eds.), Baltimore: Williams & Wilkins, 1975.

Murase, T.: Naikan therapy. In: *Culture-Bound Syndromes, Ethnopsychiatry and Alternate Therapies.* W. P. Lebra (Ed.), Honolulu, Hawaii: The University Press of Hawaii, 1976.

Murphy, J. M.: Psychotherapeutic Aspects of Shamanism on St. Lawrence Island, Alaska. In: *Magic, Faith, and Healing.* A. Kiev and J. D. Frank (Eds.), New York: The Free Press, 1964.

Opler, M. E.: Some points of comparison and contrast between the treatment of function disorders by Apache shamans and modern psychiatric practice. *Am. J. Psychiatry,* 92, 1371–1387, 1936.

Prince, R.: Indigenous Yoruba psychiatry. In: *Magic, Faith, and Healing.* A. Kiev and J. D. Frank (Eds.), New York: The Free Press, 1964.

Prince, R.: Symbols and psychotherapy: The example of Yoruba sacrificial ritual. *J. Am. Acad. Psychoanal.,* 3:321–338, 1975.

Prince, R.: Variations in psychotherapeutic procedures. In: *Handbook of Cross-Cultural Psychology, Volume V.* H. C. Triandis and J. Draguns (Eds.), Boston: Allyn and Bacon, 1980.

Sasaki, Y.: Psychiatric study of the shaman in Japan. In: *Mental Health Research in Asia and the Pacific.* W. Caudill and T. Y. Lin (Eds.), Honolulu: East-West Center Press, 1969.

Torrey, E. F.: Indigenous psychotherapy: Theories and techniques. *Curr. Psychiatr. Ther.,* 10:118–129, 1970.

Torrey, E. F.: *The Mind Game: Witchdoctors and Psychiatrists.* New York: Emerson Hall, 1971.

Tseng, W. S. Psychiatric study of shamanism in Taiwan. *Arch. Gen. Psychiatry,* 26:561–565, 1972.

Tseng, W. W. and McDermott, J. F., Jr.: Psychotherapy: Historical roots, universal elements, and cultural variations. *Am. J. Psychiatry,* 132:378–384, 1975.

CHAPTER 18

Culture-relevant Therapy

When the therapist and the patient have different cultural backgrounds, an interaction of cultural components is involved in addition to the usual elements which make up the process of therapy. It is necessary for the therapist to be culturally oriented if relevant therapy is to be carried out and meaningful treatment results achieved.

GENERAL CONSIDERATIONS

Orientation and Expectation of Therapy

We have emphasized how the psychiatrist may perceive (or misperceive) the patient of a different culture, and how this affects the therapeutic process. Now let us exercise our imaginations and try to see how *patients* view both therapist and therapy of a culture not their own. These men and women often have their own preconceptions of practitioner and process; a few have no idea of who or what a psychiatrist is.

Consider the very real case of the patient who, innocent of medicine's specialities and terminology, nevertheless knew exactly the kind of help she needed. This patient, a woman from Samoa, was referred by her family doctor, who told her she was "going to see a psychiatrist." On her first visit, she soon asked the question that puzzled her.

"Doctor, I know," she said, "I know baby doctor, bone doctor, but I never know psychia—what do you call it?—yeah, psychiatrist. What kind doctor are you?"

The psychiatrist, knowing that the Samoan culture is characterized by physical expression and human relationship rather than abstract thinking and intellectual discussion, answered, "I am a heart doctor. I help people with worry in the heart."

The patient was then sure she was seeing the "right kind of doctor," for, as she explained, "my heart has lots of worry."

Consider next the admittedly imaginary man from Iowa who, finding himself depressed and troubled in an isolated South East Asian village, seeks help from a shaman. He comes to the appointment prepared to relate his symptoms, family history, and even last night's dream. Imagine his shock when the healer wants no information except his age and date of birth. Now, in imagination, let us transport one of the shaman's clients to the consulting room of a behavior therapist in Des Moines. Try to share this man's feelings when he finds that he is not going to be "healed" by someone else's efforts and powers; instead he must "work on" his problems himself, and even be given rewards and punishments in the process.

Varying preconceptions of just what a therapist is and what he or she does exist even within what, at first thought, we call the "same culture." For example, within the same United States city, one patient may expect therapy to consist of "lying down on a couch and talking about sex." Another may expect all problems to be resolved when the psychiatrist suddenly reveals a traumatic occurrence that happened back in childhood. One patient may look forward to "intellectual discussions," and another confidently expect hypnosis to effect an instant "cure." Education, popular magazines, movies, and television dramas all influence the patient's ideas of what psychotherapy is going to be like. They also influence preexisting ideas of the therapist. One patient may expect a replica of Freud, complete with beard and European accent, and be shocked to see instead a small and Asian woman. One may fervently hope to see a fellow black and instead greet a white man. Color of skin and ethnic origin may be an initial barrier to successful therapy. So are less obvious preconceptions and expectations. One patient may expect a priest-healer; another, a firm but kind father-figure; and yet another, a dispenser of pills and potions. All these anticipations and preconceived images, judgments, and prejudices exist even when patient and therapist are of the same culture; they need especially careful attention when the cultural backgrounds are different. The practitioner must encourage and answer the questions the client may be too timid or respectful to ask. He may want to know what therapy means. Why must he see a therapist? Why must he talk about his life instead of merely telling his symptoms? A clear explanation of the kind of therapeutic process planned must be provided as soon as possible.

Therapeutic Rules and Contracts

Though it is always good practice to establish a therapeutic contract at the beginning of treatment, a great deal more explanation may be needed in intercultural situations. In some medical systems, patients often see many therapists simultaneously with no commitment to any particular one. A patient from this system may take it for granted that he can stop seeing the therapist at any time or continue seeking other healers and remedies. In some cultures, prearranged appointments are shunned and little value is placed on being prompt; these patients may see little reason for keeping their appointments and arriving on time.

Confidentiality is crucial in analytically oriented therapy. However, this may not apply to a culture in which the concept of sharing is almost absolute and the idea of mental privacy nearly absent. Parents who emphasize family communication may reject the idea that their child can talk in confidence to the psychiatrist.

Greek psychoanalyst Leonidas Samouilidis (1978) notes some cultural factors that operated among his Greek patients. He found that most Greeks regarded a psychiatrist as a neurologist, that they approached therapy with great shame, resisted long-term therapy, came for help after family members made the appointment for them, and that usually the whole family came to the office for the first appointment. Samouilidis writes that, " . . . my experience and intuition tell me, most of the time, to invite everybody in and then start the identification procedures." His Greek patients, he found, "favor a family approach to the problem, without necessarily perceiving the problem as being a family one."

Cultural Impact on Transference

When the therapist and the patient come from different racial or ethnic backgrounds, both culture-related transference and countertransference may take place. Each one's previous knowledge of, and attitude toward, the other's culture—very often based on stereotypes—can affect the therapeutic situation. Each may extend previous experiences, and the feelings these experiences produced, to the other (Hsu and Tseng, 1972). The most obvious examples come when white therapist treats black patient, or vice versa.

The black may feel the therapist is a kind of master he must please, or a symbol of all he wants to be, or an object of mistrust and hatred. For the therapist, the black patient may stir old feelings of guilt over white oppression or long-buried vestiges of racial prejudice. The black patient may withhold disclosure of his true feelings; the therapist may err by losing objectivity and neutrality. He may perceive the patient's problems as stemming almost completely from being black in a white society and overlook personal pathology. The patient's transference may swing to the extremes of positive and negative or may, if we may coin a phrase, be a "false transference." The psychiatrist's brief identifications with his patient may be blocked; instead, he may tend to work out some of his own racial guilts on the patient. These hazards lurk particularly when the black patient is strongly allied to black culture; distortions in client-therapist perceptions of each other lessen when the black patient lives comfortably with the values and life-styles of whites and when the socioeconomic class of both are similar.

Griffith (1977) studied client-therapist matches in three groups: white therapist-black client, black therapist-black client, and black therapist-white client. He characterized relationships, in general, as being one of trust-mistrust between white therapist and black client; one of identity for black therapist-black client; and one of status contradiction for black therapist-white client. Underlying the white therapist-black client relationship is the black man's distrust of whites and the therapist's need to replace this with trust. In the black therapist-black client relationship, the therapist's own acceptance or denial of his blackness is at issue. If he rejects his own blackness, then this rejection extends to his client. If he over-identifies with blacks and feels too close a bond with his black client, he may become too involved with racial issues in his client's difficulties. It is vital that the black therapist resolve his own feelings about being black and about his own status with the dominant whites. For the black therapist-white client, status contradiction enters the relationship. For the white client, Griffith writes, the black therapist may have low status because he is black and, at the same time, hold high status because of his profession.

In either black-white combination, difference of color must not be ignored. The issue of race should be discussed openly in the early stages of therapy; the "taboo" against discussing racial facts and feelings is removed and therapy has a far better chance of proceeding against a basis of reality. To pretend "we are all alike" is false and harmful.

Assessment of Value Systems

Among the therapist-client interactions that take place is, very often, an exchange of value systems. The therapist ascertains his patient's value system and thereby understands him more fully. The client is introduced to the therapist's value system as another way to cope with problems. On the therapist falls the responsibility of assessing both value systems, for incompatability of values can impede the therapeutic process. This is particularly true when cultures meet. For example, the concepts of marriage and attitudes toward divorce and illegitimacy vary greatly in different cultures. Relationships with authority, beliefs and customs of hierarchy in family or group, the obligations of friendship, are not necessarily the same around the world. The expression and control of aggression and sexual drives and the desire for property and possessions differ among societies. The therapist from a culture in which divorce is taboo may fail to explore divorce as a solution for marital problems, even though his client's culture freely permits it. The therapist whose culture advocates early independence from parents may err in encouraging this for the client whose culture considers moving away from the parental home a serious, if not irreparable, break in relationships. There must be a fundamental congruence in value systems.

The Matter of Culture Empathy

Though a great deal of cultural information can be gained by questioning the client, formal study, and reading, none of this quite results in cultural empathy. Really to know, understand, and share a client's feelings in his or her life situation is a different and more difficult matter. A client may explain his custom in which all cousins are considered siblings and father and uncle are addressed by the same term. Yet the feeling of family life in this setting is impossible to grasp without some actual exposure to this extended family. Very often, we must be content with cultural knowledge rather than experience. Yet in many cases we can arrange the kind of contacts that build cultural empathy. One way is to visit the patient's home or neighborhood. Most large cities have ethnic communities. Visit these quietly and alone. Join the residents in their religious ceremonies and folk festivals. Eat in the restaurants where families gather. To have an old Japanese lady explain that each year the souls of deceased relatives return to visit merely lets you know her belief; to watch elderly Japanese during the *okuri* (sending off) ceremony which returns the souls to paradise lets you know—perhaps even share—her feelings about this link with now and eternity, living and dead. The Spanish-Catholic patient can outline her cultural-religious convictions and you know what she thinks. Walk along with a Spanish-Catholic procession honoring the Madonna and you sense the depth of Spanish religious emotion. Find a Greek festival, or a cafe where the people dance, and you better understand the Greek exuberance—the surge of joy called *kefi.* In a subtle, unspoken communication, such cultural exposure minimizes the distance between therapist and client.

The Goal of Therapy

The goal of psychotherapy, most of us agree, is to relieve symptoms and help the patient become a healthier, more mature person who is better able to deal with life and the problems it presents. The goal seems to apply to all cultures. The cultural variations enter into the concepts of "healthy" and "mature." Mental and even physical health may be defined by culture. Maturity, in Western thought, includes living up to potential qualities and abilities; it carries with it a certain requirement for independence. In other societies, maturity may entail graceful compliance: merging with the group, rather than establishing individuality. "Successful living," "being well-adjusted," "self-actualization"—these may have far different meanings for the therapist and for the client who comes from another culture. The client's definitions and desires should be sought and explored so both therapist and client can reach mutually understood and agreed-on therapeutic goals.

TECHNIQUE AND STRATEGIES

Flexibility in Therapeutic Approach

In intercultural therapy, unusual flexibility is usually required. The psychiartist must not let himself be locked rigidly into any one therapeutic system. He should feel free to give a physical examination as a part of the therapy if the client considers this an important part of treatment; to act as a social worker in financial, occupational, or housing matters, if that will help the client; to give medication as a part of treatment, if the client is oriented to this. The rituals and comforts of religion may be called on, though the therapist must not let himself be trapped into the role of priest or minister. Language should be in accord with the client's cultural background. If an old Chinese woman complains that her "liver fire is elevated," the therapist would do well to inquire what made this "liver fire" flare up (what happened to make her nervous and agitated). Among many American subcultures today, guilts and griefs often surface in dreams or culturally normal visions in which a deceased person appears. In one case, a troubled woman reported that her husband's spirit kept appearing in visions without speaking. In therapy, the approach was not of negating the spirit, but of exploring "what the spirit is trying to tell you." In this way, the patient was led to introspection and a realization of guilt, previous ambivalent relations in her marriage, and subsequent blocked grief work. At one point when time was ripe, she was encouraged to follow cultural tradition and ask the spirit to "go to your rest now and leave me alone" (Pukui et al., 1979).

Most cultures have their own remedial measures: ways, often ritual, of handling grief, separation from the dead, relieving anxiety, and restoring harmony within family or group. Sometimes these can be employed as a kind of parallel to more orthodox psychotherapy. Careful judgment is needed that they do not become delaying tactics or substitutes for working on underlying psychological issues or solving realistic interpersonal problems.

Utilization of Cultural Assets

Even though it is customary to utilize the client's personal strengths and assets as aids to recovery, an important dimension may be overlooked if the therapist is not aware of additional sources of support that exist in the client's cultural system. In fact, even personal strengths—the ability to endure stress, tolerate loneliness, to accept separation from family members—these differ to some extent among societies. So does the support from groups. In some cultures, support comes from the nuclear family; in others, from the extended family; in yet others (Belau, for example), from a system of siblings or mate's siblings. In one culture, women may form a kind of supportive circle around an ill or troubled woman; in another, the relationship may be competitive. One religion may offer a social support system; another may concentrate only on spiritual matters. The loyalties and obligations of friends or between employer and employee, the closeness or fragility of interpersonal relations, are all influenced by culture, both in its ethnic sense and in the definition of urban *vs.* village or rural living. These culture-system strengths merit careful consideration.

Exploration of Available Coping Avenues

Very often a patient will believe he has only one or two ways to cope with a problem. These are usually dictated by his culture and class. The upper-class youth in Japan and Taiwan who fails his college exams may see suicide or army service as his only "solutions." In this case, the therapist may outline for him other avenues to satisfactory living that exist in other cultures or in the changing trends of his own setting: that people without college degrees often work in less prestigious (in an Asian sense) occupations, save their money and establish their own businesses; that the poets, philosophers, novelists, and civic leaders of many countries are often also craftsmen or farmers. The goal is to help the client broaden his knowledge of coping mechanisms within his own culture and also, in the larger context, of other cultures with other values.

Working on Individual and Cultural Levels

The therapist with a client from another culture has an opportunity to work on problems on the cultural, as well as individual, level. For example, a Hmong tribesman and his wife, immigrants to the United States, were referred for counseling after a social worker feared he was abusing his wife. The wife worked as a waitress. Her husband had hit and slapped her for smiling at male customers. He had gone to the restaurant several times to watch her, and created a scene each time he saw her smiling.

On the personal, individual level, counseling could have explored the man's own self-image and hurt pride (he had no job), the suspicion and jealousy engendered by low self-esteem, his loneliness while his wife was away at work and the fertile ground this provided for imagining flirtation or unfaithfulness. Discussion might have considered the wife's possible dissatisfactions with her husband; her desire for attention, change, and excitement, social or sexual; her attraction to other men. (It was quite obvious that smiling at strangers was not a spontaneous and natural behavior for her.) However, in this case, the cultural approach was indicated, for the objection to a smiling wife was, in fact, rooted in Hmong social belief. Virtuous wives, in Hmong society, did not smile at other men. For this Hmong wife, smiling was a part of keeping her badly-needed job. Her employer had ordered her to smile; he had reprimanded her for not "acting friendly" to the customers. Accordingly, a kind of cultural education took place. America's habit of smiling without any special meaning was discussed. The husband was asked to note that Americans even put little signs with smiling faces on their desks and on restaurant and office walls. Waitresses who smiled at their customers were just being polite, American style; waitresses who did not smile were considered unpleasant or "grumpy." They got smaller tips and sometimes lost their jobs. In short, smiling in the couple's old environment and smiling in their new setting meant quite different things.

More personal feelings, of course, exist within their cultural guise. Therapy on the cultural level and that which addresses individual psychological factors may both be used. Often difficulties may first be worked out on the cultural level, and therapy may then proceed to the personal. Or, therapy may remain focused on cultural dimensions when the personal factor is too painful to be faced, when insight into underlying feelings is not yet desirable.

SPECIAL ISSUES IN THERAPY

Selection of Therapeutic Modalities

Psychotherapy has evolved into various modalities. Based on structure, it may be individual, group, or family therapy. Based on theory, the therapeutic approach may be analytic, behavioral, or existential. Therapy, group or individual, may take any of the various forms of what we call folk healing. The psychiatrist who treats a patient from a different culture considers the choice of therapeutic modalities, not only from the viewpoint of the patient's pathology, but also from his/her cultural background.

A great deal of careful thought must be given to the choice of individual or group therapy for clients whose lives are closely intermeshed with their families. Just because Indian or Japanese or Chinese cultures are characterized by the extended family does not mean family therapy is ideal for the Indian or Japanese or Chinese patient. Other elements, individual and cultural, require attention. For example, our experience with Oriental patients has indicated that family members have been available and apparently agreeable to family therapy. However, they tend to show resistance in viewing a problem as family-related. In addition, therapy is apt to be impeded if the therapist encourages a child to oppose the parents. In Oriental families, parental authority is not to be challenged and parents are not to be criticized by children, especially when non-family members are present. If the therapist can establish himself as a trusted friend rather than an "outsider," family therapy may be indicated.

All the usual considerations in balancing individual versus group therapy exist when a patient is from another culture. Yet, in addition to weighing the patient's individual problems and personality, certain cultural factors may affect the decision (as, indeed, they affect the patient's nature). Does the culture value openness or privacy? Are emotions restrained or expressed freely before others? Are certain topics culturally taboo? Can men admit weaknesses, or only women? What are the culture's views on complaining? On confrontation?

When a therapist speaks the language of a number of patients, and their problems are not too deeply personal, group therapy may be a practical or necessary choice. Two examples from the literature indicate that same-language group therapy may be especially indicated when the clients' problems are essentially those of adjustment to a new country. In one instance, group therapy held with Spanish-speaking women in California resulted in beneficial changes, as self-isolation gave way to group identity and mutual support (Hynes and Werbin, 1977). Dunkas and Nikelly (1975) describe open-ended group therapy with recent immigrants from Greece. Men and women were in separate groups. The Greek language was used. None of the group members had had emotional problems in their homeland; these had developed with efforts to adjust to a new country. The group became, symbolically, the Greek family, providing support and cohesiveness and, initially, a "father" in the person of the psychiatrist. Later, members felt themselves more definitely independent individuals. The authors suggest that group therapy is a unique, indicated solution when cultural adjustment stresses themselves bring about psychological difficulties.

Ethnic Variations of Psychopharmacological Response

Whether, and in what degree, patients of different ethnic/racial background respond differently to psychiatric drugs is an interesting question that needs further study. Reports based on clinical impressions suggest that such variations in response do exist (Collard, 1962; Itil, 1975; Blackwell, 1977). The literature indicates that in Oriental countries smaller doses of antipsychotic or antidepressant drugs have essentially the same effect as larger dosages in Western countries. Of course, this may be due to differences in the degree of pathology in the patients or circumstances of hospital settings, or it may merely reflect varying professional habits of medication not necessarily related to the actual pharmacological effect. Also often reported is the impression that the Oriental patient shows side effects, such as extrapyramidal signs, sooner and with greater severity than Occidentals. Whether this occurs because of a difference in psychological sensitivity to somatic symptoms or because of an actual biological difference is a question worthy of investigation.

CONCLUSION

Basic Principles Provide a Cross-cultural Guideline

The therapist faced with a patient from a different, perhaps unfamiliar, culture must consider so many factors of race, ethnicity, and often contrasting value systems that exhaustion and confusion may result. A few checks on one's own practice and thinking may be in order, as, for example: If I am incorporating the patient's cultural customs in therapy, am I doing this because they have real therapeutic value or because I find them fascinating? When I ask the patient for cultural information, do I make it sufficiently clear that my purpose is to use this knowledge to help him, not to educate me? Do I sufficiently demonstrate that my interest is in the patient's problems, not in the patient as a kind of "cultural specimen" to be studied? Am I allowing my interest in this culture to make my Japanese or Icelandic or German patient more essentially Japanese or Icelandic or German than he really is? Do my sympathies toward a minority group cause me to see a minority patient as a social victim and neglect the psychological aspects of the patient's condition?

Sometimes conscientious cultural psychiatrists may acquire so much sociocultural information about clients that they suffer mental indigestion. A sense of how to approach the case is obscured. In this situation, it is wise to put this unassimilated, seemingly directionless, mass of facts and impressions aside for the moment and review the basic principles of psychiatric evaluation and intervention. In these are certain universal precepts that can clarify thinking and provide guidance in formulating treatment plans, for in any culture the troubled are more apt to be treated successfully when their psychiatrist/healer/priest/shaman has an empathetic understanding of the client's problems; when he/she provides hope, takes a firm and positive approach that the problem will be solved and anxieties and stresses eased, and utilizes the strengths and assets that the client and the group possess. These guidelines to healing cross the boundaries of culture.

REFERENCES

Blackwell, B.: Culture, morbidity, and the effects of drugs. *Clin. Pharmacol. Ther.,* 19:79–86, 1977.

Collard, J.: Drug responses in different ethnic groups. *Journal of Neuropsychiatry,* 3 (suppl. 1): 114–121, 1962.

Dunkas, N. and Nikelly, A. G.: Group psychotherapy with Greek immigrants. *Int. J. Group Psychother.* 75:402–409, 1975.

Griffith, M. S.: The influence of race on the psychotherapeutic relationship. *Psychiatry,* 40: 27–40, 1977.

Hsu, J. and Tseng, W-S.: Intercultural psychotherapy. *Arch. Gen. Psychiatry,* 27:700–705, 1972.

Hynes, K. and Werbin, J.: Group psychotherapy for Spanish speaking women. *Psychiatric Annals,* 7:52–63, 1977.

Itil, T. M. (Ed.): *Transcultural Neuropsychopharmocology.* Istanbul, Turkey: BOZAK Publishing, 1975.

Pukui, M. K., Haertig, E. W., and Lee, C. A.: *Nana I Ke Kumu (Look to the Source)* Vol. II. The Queen Lili'oukalani Children's Center, Honolulu, 1979.

Samouilidis, L.: Psychoanalytic vicissitudes in working with Greek patients. *American Journal of Psychoanalysis,* 38:223–233, 1978.

PART V

Directions for the Future

CHAPTER 19

Research, Training, and Therapy

Among the truths which have become clichés is the advice that to foresee the future, we need first to look backward over the past. The truism applies as we chart a proposed course of cultural psychiatry in years to come.

Our backward look surveys a specialty that in less than a century has advanced far from its beginning of sporadic research into culture-related, often "exotic" conditions. Its purposes have been defined; its message stated: Culture-related conditions are investigated, not because they are curious, unique, and interesting; they are investigated with the clinical usefulness of data gathered and insights gained always a goal. Cultural psychiatry can now list its quite specific purposes as follows (Wittkower and Prince, 1974; Favazza and Oman, 1978):

- To study how culture interrelates with personality development, behavior patterns, and adaptive styles so that we may know better how it influences mind and behavior.
- To explore culture-related stresses and problems and the coping mechanisms the culture provides for them.
- To investigate cultural influences on psychopathology, in terms of symptom formation, manifestation of pathology, clinical picture, and the frequency of certain mental illnesses, and to study culture-related specific psychiatric conditions.
- To understand the cultural dimensions of illness behavior: how patients perceive, conceptualize, and present their problems; how they seek help;

what kind of healing systems are available and utilized within each cultural setting.
- To sharpen our awareness of the impact of culture on the practice of psychiatry, in evaluation, diagnosis, and treatment.
- To examine cultural influence on theory in psychiatry; to evaluate the universal applicability and culture-specificity of the theory and principles of psychiatry.
- To improve cross-cultural research methods.
- To work with other health scientists and with social scientists and political and community groups in efforts to change damaging patterns of life into healthful ones.

With these purposes as guideposts, cultural psychiatry in the future will necessarily travel what we might call a three-lane highway: one in which research, therapy, and training progress along parallel routes that lead to the destination marked An Applicable Body of Knowledge. Let us examine each of these routes.

RESEARCH: A BASIC REQUIREMENT

In the past, a large number of research studies have been primarily either macroscopic or microscopic. They have concentrated either on the broad, cross-cultural, epidemiological investigation of a disorder or on in-depth case studies of a certain condition in a certain place. Both types of research have provided interesting, often needed, information. Yet they lack connective links. The need is for integration of information on a continuing basis (Brodsky, 1970). The intensively followed individual cases can then be seen against the broad epidemiological framework; the cultural uniqueness or universality of a condition then becomes clear. A constant correlation of studies is, in our opinion, a future model for research (Wittkower and Rin, 1965).

The same need for continuously integrated work applies to researchers in cultural psychiatry and their colleagues in the social sciences. In the researching of mental disorders and culture, the psychiatrist needs to know human behavior from the cultural as well as clinical point of view; the anthropologist needs to incorporate clinical information in his reports. An immediate way to attain this integration is for psychiatrist and anthropologist to work as a team (Pattison, 1967). A long-range approach may be the creation of a new specialist, the researcher with a fund of knowledge in both fields. Special training would develop what we might call the psychiatrist-anthropologist or anthropologist-psychiatrist.

The two-viewpoint approach also must be used in another sense—the knowledge and interpretation of the "insider within the tribe" need to be utilized. For example, the anthropologist or psychiatrist—or, ideally the two-discipline team—from the United States that goes to study a condition in Indonesia should be joined by their Indonesian counterparts. With this method, a balanced, less biased, more truly objective study can be made. Nuances of meaning that might escape the "outsider" are brought out and understood. Conversely, when only the "insider" views his or her own group, he or she may miss a vital point that the investigator from outside, with vision unobscured by familiarity, can see. It is also important that researchers know, as objectively as possible, their own culture. The investigator from France who studies aging or neurotic disorders in Micronesian society also needs to know about aging and neurotic phenomena and cultural attitudes to them in France. With this knowledge he can then consider, for example, what elements in Micronesia's approach to aging might or might not be applicable to France, itself a narrow reference system.

Comparison in itself sharpens observation. However, this comparison should go far beyond that of "your country vs. mine" or Culture A vs. Culture B. Multiple and diverse culture samples should be studied if we are to perceive the differences in cultural factors and avoid making false generalizations. This diversity must come from more than differing cultures; within each culture studied should be included different levels of social and occupational class, taken from urban and rural environments.

We are admittedly thinking in large and ambitious terms, foreseeing what amounts to a global picture of how culture affects man's behavior and mental health. The comprehensive approach we visualize can never be done by a few researchers working in virtual independence. The future we foresee is one of large-scale collaboration in which a number of psychiatrists and anthropologists from various places work together on the same general condition or problem. This extensive collaboration will necessitate the careful choice of subject matter most pertinent to the most lives. Human concerns more than academic interest should be considered. A common problem, rather than a rare and obscure condition, must be the topic chosen. One way to determine areas to be investigated is to survey psychiatric conditions vertically through time and horizontally across cultures.

Areas of Interest for Investigation

A study of the clinical observations of any long-established psychiatrist gives us a kind of telescopic look at mental disorders from years past on down to the present. We can extend this horizontally; we can, in effect, take the cinemascopic view by studying the observations of many psychiatrists from many cultures. Both views show similar phenomena.

Downward through time and across cultures, we see changes in manifest psychopathology (Klaf and Hamilton, 1961; Murphy, 1973; Shinfuku et al., 1975). Certain types of disorders have gradually undergone alteration. In the area of major disorders, the frank psychosis is seen less often. Psychotics are less disturbed than in the past (Grinker, 1973). For example, in the group of disorders in schizophrenia, the catatonic and hebephrenic subtypes have become less common (Hare, 1974; Sakurai et al., 1965). Instead, the paranoid subtype occurs more often. This shift is noted as countries develop; more primitive societies have more of the "primitive" subtypes in which the disturbance takes the form of confusion or psychomotor expression (German, 1972); the body exhibits the ills of the mind, as in the stupor or waxy flexibility of catatonia and the directionless activity and grimacing of hebephrenia. In paranoia, the disorder is manifested in a more sophisticated and intellectual way.

The manifestations seem to progress from body to mind as societies become more civilized and complex. In some countries where the psychoses have become less disturbed, an increase in borderline states is noted. We might at least speculate that these borderline states are a kind of minor schizophrenia and that a transition of the frank and bodily expressed psychoses to the more intellectualized manifestations of paranoia to the marginal schizophrenia or borderline state somewhat parallels the progress of a society's development. However, as the disorder becomes less frank and less disturbed, it may take a somewhat longer course.

In the minor disorders, many classic neurotic conditions, such as phobic or obsessive-compulsive disorders, are being replaced by anxiety, depressive disorders, simple adjustment reactions, or somatoform disorders. In many countries, the classic conversion hysteria is disappearing or taking the more subtle form of psychosomatic disorders (Chodoff, 1954; Grinker, 1973). The hysterical trance is often being replaced by the chemically induced trance. Even many of the so-called psychosomatic or somatoform disorders, in which emotional conflicts are expressed by the body, are gradually changing to more psychic expression as depression or anxiety.

There are two possible explanations for these changes in minor disorders. One may be that people have become more "psychiatrically sophisticated" and more verbally expressive (Hare, 1974). Insight has been gained into mind-emotion-body interaction; emotions are talked about more freely. The other may be changes in the life-style itself. In a culture with a great deal of elaborate ritual and a great many restrictions and regulations of behavior, the patient needs to express his disorder in elaborate, even ritualized, ways. In a culture free of this emphasis on ritual and rules, he can express his condition in a simple, less complicated manner.

Whatever the causes, the shifting symptomatology of past decades carries a clear message to cultural psychiatry: The nature and manifestations of mental disorders, like time itself, do not stand still. We must not stagnate in the past or become transfixed by localized or exotic phenomena. Certain mental illnesses should be disregarded as choices for cultural psychiatry research. Schizophrenia is a paramount example. This was rightly studied intensively in the past because it was—and still is—a major disorder with global occurrence. We now realize that though subtype manifestation is culture-related, the basic disorder is primarily identified with biological factors. Yet we continue to study and study it in its classic forms.

We believe that future emphasis should be on minor psychiatric disorders. These are psychological in nature and thus more closely related to culture and social conditions. In addition, accurate social-cultural information is easier to obtain from the neurotic patient than from the psychotic. The rewards—practical as well as intellectual—are more attainable when research efforts are concentrated on the minor conditions. On the practical side, correlating symptoms of these disorders with social-cultural factors may help us identify trends and perhaps even predict future mental conditions. To the extent that this succeeds, some prevention may be possible. Certainly many present-day minor psychiatric disorders—neuroses, personality disorders, adjustment reaction, neurotic depression—demand attention. Questions of today and tomorrow require answers: The diagnosis of depression is increasing in developed countries; is this a necessary accompaniment of civilization? How is biological depression related to psychosocial factors and how do they interrelate? What social-cultural factors contribute to depression? Or, more specifically, to depression in childhood? Depression in the aged? Do certain cultural elements further or prevent sexual disorders? Why do some countries have serious and widespread drug or alcohol abuse, and others have these problems rarely or not at all? In what cultures is violence more recently prevalent? Seldom known? Do some cultures demonstrate ways to control violence?

About one to two decades ago, many cross-cultural studies of child-rearing were done by social scientists (Whiting and Whiting, 1975). However, child-rearing patterns were never linked with adjustment or maladjustment or with clinical problems in child psychiatry. There is a need to focus on the cultural patterns in child-rearing that lead to personality differences and contribute to what is often called national behavior or national character. There is a need to research clinical differences in psychopathology as related to cultural variations. Childhood depression and adolescent behavior problems are obviously related to social-cultural factors, yet these have never been adequately studied cross-culturally. To ascertain which elements in which cultures most contribute to these conditions might provide some guidelines for prevention.

In addition, future cross-cultural research might well investigate such childhood conditions as autism or minimal brain dysfunctions (MBD). Although these are generally considered to be biological or genetically determined, controversy exists over possible links between culture and diagnosis. For example, MBD in the United States is said to exist in 3% of the normal child population and 30–40% of the clinical child population, while in England less than 1% of the clinic population is diagnosed as having the condition. If MBD is truly biological, why should incidence show this great variation even within Western countries? Could it be that the condition blends in and is thus less conspicuous and identifiable in one culture—but stands out and is readily identified in another? Or do criteria vary?

A rich field for cross-cultural research has to do with language. Already some studies indicate that the type of written language used contributes markedly to reading disabilities (Makita, 1968). Extension of such research on a cross-cultural level with cultural and child psychiatrists, educators, linguists, and psychologists working together might eventually prevent or lessen dyslexia. It is an exciting prospect, for this impairment in basic communication often starts its own chain reaction of other learning difficulties and unrealized mental potentials.

CULTURE AND THERAPY

Though anthropology first called attention to the various traditional ways man has tried to heal himself, folk therapy quickly became a favorite subject for psychiatric investigation. Shamans, healing cults, and ceremonial practices have all been studied. In the beginning, efforts were devoted to describing ritual, looking for similarities with orthodox psychotherapy, and, to a lesser extent, ascertaining whether or not the folk healing helped its troubled client. When the therapy seemed beneficial, the reasons for its success remained speculative: because the ritual provided hope or gave a definite answer or was supportive; because the client responded positively to the personality of the healer. Sometimes the judgment was unduly favorable and the folk therapy was considered ideal within its culture. Too often neglected was the other side of the picture—cases in which therapy did not work or was harmful, not only because it delayed other medical/psychiatric treatment but because it was misleading, instigated guilt, or increased anxiety. If cultural psychiatry is to benefit from future studies of traditional healing, rose-colored glasses must not be worn; evaluations must include long-term follow-up of clients who were not helped, as well as those who were.

With adequate follow-up, we may have answers to more specific questions: If the treatment was successful, why did it work? Suggestion? Personality? Because of a one-to-one therapeutic relationship—or because the therapy mobilized family or community support? If it worked for one client and not another, what accounted for the different results?

Part of the study of various therapies will be to determine their cultural suitability and the reasons for this. The varied styles and techniques of orthodox therapies need to be included: These studies should not be limited to the folk rituals of primitive societies. The progression of time and the changes within a culture need attention, for these affect the nature of therapy and its acceptance and effectiveness. A few examples: Morita therapy in Japan is less effective than formerly. Is this because the Japanese people are changing? Why is family therapy now so popular in the United States? Does this reflect efforts of families to remain intact in culture marked by divorces? Why did Western encounter groups surge and diminish?

Determining the reasons why a therapy is suitable to one culture may help determine its suitability in another culture (Kelman, 1960; Meadow, 1964; Redlich, 1958). If psychoanalysis was favored by the Jewish population because Jewish people look for and discuss reasons and deeper meanings behind surface actions (Meadow and Vetter, 1959), was psychoanalysis not accepted in Japan because the Japanese are "private," shame-oriented people who resist revealing hidden facets of their nature (Doi, 1964)? Can family therapy be successfully adapted for the family with absent father and dominant mother? To what extent therapies can borrow each other's theories and techniques across cultures is a prime concern of cultural psychiatry. The question has already been addressed to a considerable extent, but more investigation and a vastly increased exchange of clinically gained knowledge are needed in the future.

CULTURAL PSYCHIATRY TRAINING

If this culture-conscious, clinically-oriented knowledge is to be exchanged on a broad, presumably global, basis, a particular kind of competency will be called for. The psychiatrist will need to be aware and informed about cultures; the anthropologist will need an understanding of clinical psychiatry. This dual knowledge will be arrived at through special training. We visualize this training as operating on several different levels:

- A program to create a new discipline: that of the anthropologist-psychiatrist or psychiatrist-anthropologist.
- Advanced training in cultural psychiatry for practicing clinical psychiatrists and psychiatric residents. Inclusion of a course in cultural psychiatry in the general psychiatry curriculum, just as psychopharmacology and family therapy are included (Foulks, 1980).
- Provisions for training psychiatrists from another culture (Chen, 1978; Mittel, 1970; Sata, 1977; Wong, 1978). For example, the Indonesian psychiatrist might study in England or the United States; the British or American psychiatrist might take some training in China.

Each of these programs would have a somewhat different purpose. Education for the new psychiatry-anthropology discipline would concentrate on preparing leaders in broad research efforts, rather than clinicians. We envision these colleagues as planners, coordinators, and consultants. The advanced training for clinical psychiatrists and psychiatric residents will probably also supply its share of leading researchers, but this is not the primary intent of the program. The goal is to enable these clinicians to acquire certain knowledge and skills. This training would be twofold. Didactic seminars and classroom lectures will be needed so a body of knowledge can be acquired. Clinical practice with patients from unfamiliar backgrounds must be included so applied skills can be gained (Bradshaw, 1978). A culture-sensitive supervisor is vitally important, for clinical work under such supervision enables the psychiatrist to become aware of his own cultural biases, his own cultural impact on the patient, and his own scotoma to significant cultural elements in the patient's problem.

After didactic instruction and supervised clinical work, the psychiatrist should have some firsthand experience living in another culture. This does not necessitate a trip to a foreign country. Most large cities have a variety of racial/ethnic enclaves. Cultural experience can be had by living for a while within the black, Chicano, Chinese, Vietnamese, Greek, or Italian sections of a metropolitan center. Living among and preferably working with another culture is an effective way to become very much aware of one's own cultural habits and ways of thinking.

In sum, a successul training program will enable psychiatrists to:

- Increase their sensitivity to cultural factors in their own as well as the patient's life.
- Obtain cultural information from patients of different backgrounds.
- Become aware of the value system of a patient from a different culture.

- Differentiate between what is culture-related and what is not in the patient's attitudes, behavior, and choice and manifestation of symptoms.
- Maintain openness and flexibility to modifying the therapeutic approach so it is suitable to the patient's culture.

The ultimate objective is to benefit the patient of another culture. The culturally trained clinician is not expected to solve the problems of another country. The expectation is that he will apply what he knows of other cultures and his own to understand better the patient whose culturally tinged problem and culturally influenced personality might otherwise be incorrectly perceived and whose therapy might otherwise be misdirected.

Yet other benefits can be expected. These are long-range and less directly client-centered. They will come from contributions culturally experienced and sensitive therapists make toward improving mental health in the future. We believe that, just as psychiatrist-anthropologist teams will play a part in planning future healthier ways of life for large societies, so the practicing cultural psychiatrist can equally help his or her community to draw a blueprint for tomorrow. This belief rests on the premise that neither tomorrow's mental health nor tomorrow's culture is wholly at the mercy of implacable fate. With this belief we explore the possibilities of culture planning.

CULTURE CHANGE AND CULTURE PLANNING

If culture were static, there would be no way to alter it and its effect on mental conditions. If culture were static, our premise that healthier ways of life can be planned would be untenable. However, behaviors, ideas, and attitudes do change. Entire cultures have arisen, flourished, and become extinct. That altered patterns of living can alter mental conditions is evident. We believe that intelligent humans can, to some extent, direct change, that they can, to some extent, direct their future style of living and social environment. We believe that cultural psychiatrists can contribute to planning tomorrow's culture so it will follow the pathways of mental health more than pathology.

In many countries, conscious planning of segments of the future environment is already being done. Marine biologists, nutritionists and agriculturalists investigate oceans and land-based aquaculture for tomorrow's protein supply. City planners project ways to fill needs for housing, schools, transportation and recreation. Population experts advise (and in China, decide) future family size. In many cities, seminars, public meetings, and university courses address themselves to such topics as, Our Community Fifty Years From Now.

Not all these meetings, investigations, discussions, and projections are productive, but they are welcome evidence that men and women are giving serious thought to shaping their future world instead of just "letting it happen." They demonstrate that the concept of future planning on more than an individual or family basis is well accepted in many parts of the world. Yet this concept is generally interpreted as planning physical environment and ways to fill physical needs. Seldom included is the concept of planning a way of life favorable to mental health. We suggest that cultural psychiatrists can first of all stimulate decision-makers and planners of community or country to keep this concept in mind, and to consider the impact their projects may have on the people's mental well-being.

We live today in an era of rapid change. Some of this originates with the direct decision of an authoritative body; some results from the innovations of science and industry; some—particularly changes in social and sexual attitudes and behaviors—are speeded up by modern communication and entertainment media. Mass communication and transportation not only cause new ways of thought and behavior to spread more rapidly, but also make it easier for the astute observer to discern trends more quickly. This in itself may make it possible to correct pathological trends before they become entrenched. For example, established statistic-gathering and mass communication in the United States has made the rise in childhood suicides quickly evident.

Change is often predictable. When a government decides to bring an isolated tribe into the mainstream of civilization, when civic officials decree that slum dwellers leave their neighborhood and move into high-rise housing, when lawmakers dictate the rules for or against abortion—change is inevitable. The planned and deliberate decision that will result in change is particularly in need of the contributions of psychiatry, for questions of great importance to mental health must be answered: Should the change be made? If so, at what rate should it take effect? What will be the adverse effects of change and can they be ameliorated? How can people be prepared for a new environment? Are there ways to help them retain old values, customs and comforts as they are moved into the new neighborhood, or as the new way of life invades their territory? What will be the effects of government-decreed or -allowed abortions? Do readily available abortions decrease respect for human life, increase promiscuity, or even in a sense brutalize humankind? Or will forbidden abortion bring about more guilt, shame and death for women, more unwanted children who grow up in strife-ridden homes or become wards of the state? Should cultural psychiatrists—and their colleagues in pediatrics, child psychiatry, public health, and social work—inform and advise their lawmakers on this specific issue?

Every community—that important segment of the larger culture—faces problems that inevitably will be subject to some official action. Some of these are as localized as a school board decision; many parallel national or international concerns—the education of children, rising crime and violence, pornography, alcohol and drug abuse, the problems of aging, the assimilation of refugees, the unrest of military veterans. Though these problems are existing and often longstanding, how they are handled in the present surely plays a part in shaping mental health tomorrow. Cultural psychiatry alone cannot solve these problems, but as a body and as individuals psychiatrists can make a contribution so these situations will be carefully studied and ultimately eased or controlled, if not remedied. What is called for is to participate: to join with other disciplines and groups so that representatives of medicine, social sciences, and government address the problem together. What is needed is for cultural psychiatry to share the answers it knows and seek to answers to what it does not know.

As individuals, cultural psychiatrists can contribute the knowledge gained from their pertinent clinical experience and training. For example, the psychiatrist who, as part of cultural training, lived in a French, Indian, Italian, or Samoan community or treated French, Indian, Italian, or Samoan patients can provide valuable guidance on the problems of such ethnic groups. The child psychiatrist should be enlisted in accumulating knowledge on child-rearing, education, and family structure. If the decision will affect Vietnamese refugee families, for example, then the child psychiatrist and the expert on Vietnamese family patterns are needed members of the planning body.

As a body, cultural psychiatry can seek the answers that individual clinical experience cannot supply, and can correlate and interpret the clinical experience and the research findings of many individuals, so that general principles can be discerned and theories proved or disproved. The conclusions thus made may lead to finding causes and remedies for society's problems and forestall their future perpetration. A good starting place is the cross-cultural study of family structure, child-rearing, and the educational-social environment that surrounds children, for how children learn to channel their aggression, whether they grow up able to love and care for others, whether they respect or oppose reasonable authority, the examples they witness, the role models they follow and the heroes they worship—all these help mold the nature of their adult society.

Eventually and on the broadest scale, cultural psychiatry may throw light on the cultural factors involved in misunderstandings and conflicts between nations. We believe that knowledge of the feelings, attitudes and motivations of nations will help diplomats and national leaders to better understand the other country's needs or demands—the rules of behavior can be agreed upon. Without this mutual knowledge, two countries will act as if they are in a card game, one believing the game is bridge, and the other believing it is poker. A clash over the rules and moves is inevitable. We believe that cultural psychiatry can fill a vital role as interpreter of cultural values.

In conclusion, we believe that as individuals and as a body, cultural psychiatrists will move forward from mending mental ills and disorders that are often culture-formed to research that ascertains culture-related causes of mental illness to taking part in planning future cultures that will foster mental health. This progress will take place on many levels—that of community, country, and the international scene.

Whether what we have outlined will remain a hopeful belief or optimistic prediction or whether it becomes reality depends a great deal on the participation of cultural psychiatrists with other disciplines, other organizations, and community and country leaders. This participation has not yet really begun. Too often the voice of the clinician is not heard beyond the walls of the office; the knowledge of academician or researcher issues only indirectly from classroom or professional journal. If we are to solve present problems and prevent future ones—and therefore help to shape our future culture—the knowledge and guidance of the cultural psychiatrist must extend beyond professional circles. We must move from the Ivory Tower and take up residence in a House By the Side of the Road.

REFERENCES

Bradshaw, W. H., Jr.: Training psychiatrists for working with blacks in basic residency programs. *Am. J. Psychiatry,* 135:1520–1524, 1978.

Brodsky, C. M.: Macrocosm and microcosm: The interface of anthropology and clinical psychiatry. *Comprehensive Psychiatry,* 11:482–491, 1970.

Chen, R. M.: The education and training of Asian foreign medical graduates in the United States. *Am. J. Psychiatry,* 135:451–453, 1978.

Chodoff, P.: A re-examination of some aspects of conversion hysteria. *Psychiatry,* 17:75–81, 1954.

Doi, L. T.: Psychoanalytic therapy and "Western man": A Japanese view. *Int. J. Soc. Psychiatry,* Special Edition, No. 1, 1964.

Favazza, A. R. and Oman, M.: Overview: Foundations of cultural psychiatry. *Am. J. Psychiatry,* 135:293–303, 1978.

Foulks, E. F.: The concept of culture in psychiatric residency education. *Am. J. Psychiatry,* 137: 811–816, 1980.

German, G. A.: Aspects of clinical psychiatry in Sub-Saharan Africa. *Br. J. Psychiatry,* 121: 461–479, 1972.

Grinker, R. R.: Changing styles in psychoses and borderline states. In: Changing Styles in Psychiatric Syndromes: A Symposium. *Am. J. Psychiatry,* 130:151–152, 1973.

Hare, E. H.: The changing content of psychiatric illness. *J. Psychosom. Res.,* 18:283–289, 1974.

Kelman, H.: Existentialism: A phenomenon of the West. *Int. J. Soc. Psychiatry,* 5:299–302, 1960.
Klaf, F. S. and Hamilton, J. G.: Schizophrenia—A hundred years ago and today. *Journal of Mental Science,* 107:819–827, 1961.
Makita, K.: The rarity of reading disability in Japanese children. *Am. J. Orthopsychiatry,* 38: 599–614, 1968.
Meadow, A.: Client-centered therapy and the American ethos. *Int. J. Soc. Psychiatry,* 10:246–259, 1964.
Meadow, A. and Vetter, H. J.: Freudian theory and the Judaic value system. *Int. J. Soc. Psychiatry,* 5:197–207, 1959.
Mittel, N. S.: Training psychiatrists from developing nations. *Am. J. Psychiatry,* 126:1143–1149, 1970.
Murphy, H. B. M.: History and the evolution of syndromes: The striking case of latah and amok. In: *Psychopathology: Contributions from the Social, Behavioral, and Biological Sciences.* M. Hammer (Ed.), New York: John Wiley & Sons, 1973.
Pattison, E. M.: Psychiatry and anthropology: Three models for a working relationship. *Social Psychiatry,* 2:174–179, 1967.
Redlich, F. C.: Social aspects of psychotherapy. *Am. J. Psychiatry,* 114:800–804, 1958.
Sakurai, T., Shirafuji, Y., Nishizono, M., Hasuzawa, T., Kusuhara, T., Yoshinaga, G., and Hirohashi, S.: Changing clinical picture of schizophrenia. *Transcultural Psychiatric Research Review,* 2:97–98, 1965.
Sata, L. S. (Ed.): *Culturally Relevant Training for Asian American Psychiatrists.* Report of a Symposium held at the Battelle Institute, Seattle, Washington, March 30–April 1, 1977. Washington, D.C.: American Psychiatric Association.
Shinfuku, N., Karasawa, A., Yamada, O., Tuasaki, S., Kanai, A., and Kawashima, K. Changing clinical pictures of depression. *Transcultural Psychiatric Research Review,* 12:144–145, 1975.
Whiting, B. B. and Whiting, J. W. M.: *Children of Six Cultures: A Psycho-Cultural Analysis.* Cambridge, Ma: Harvard University Press, 1975.
Wittkower, E. D. and Prince, R.: A review of transcultural psychiatry. In: *American Handbook of Psychiatry, Second Edition.* S. Arieti (Ed.), New York: Basic Books, 1974.
Wittkower, E. D. and Rin, H.: Recent developments in transcultural psychiatry. In: *Transcultural Psychiatry.* A. V. S. DeReuck and R. Porter (Eds.), Boston: Little, Brown, 1965.
Wong, N.: Psychiatric education and training of Asian and Asian-American psychiatrists. *Am. J. Psychiatry,* 135:1525–1529, 1978.

Name Index

Subject Index